T0197051

PEACE IN THE MIDST OF HELL

A Practical And Spiritual Guide To Going Through The Fire (The Book of Life)

JAWARA D. KING

authorHOUSE®

AuthorHouse™
1663 Liberty Drive
Bloomington, IN 47403
www.authorhouse.com
Phone: 1-800-839-8640

Published by AuthorHouse 5/22/2012

ISBN: 978-1-4772-0561-7 (e)
ISBN: 978-1-4772-0560-0 (hc)
ISBN: 978-1-4772-0559-4 (sc)

Library of Congress Control Number: 2012908692

Table of Contents

Part 1: Control Your Mind

- The Academy of the Universe

- Unlimited Creative Power

- Magical Thinking

- The Great Creative Process

- The Art of Mental Imagery and Psycho-Pictography

- The Creative Power of Your Subconscious Mind

- The Magnetic Power of Thought

Jawara D. King

The Academy of the Universe

Program your subconscious mind for success while preparing for the worst. Common sense prepares for disaster and always executes proper preparation. Preparation for the worst is not fear, which is why Dionysius of Greece said, "Forethought is better than repentance." Knowing that you've done all that can be done makes it easier to not worry about what might happen. You properly program your subconscious mind when you live by the maxim "Expect the best, but prepare for the worst." During the creation process, expect the unexpected.

Success is the result of the force created through the agreement between will power and imagination. When they are pulling in different directions, imagination always wins. Imagination and willpower are to work together, but if they are in conflict with each other, what you're trying to manifest will be hindered as a result of these two forces pulling in opposite directions. Use your imagination to break any bad habits, and listen to what it's telling you.

Combine your determination with willpower to repeat affirmations to yourself over and over again for 60 to 90 days without missing a single day. Get your willpower and your imagination working together. Your conscious mind makes the decisions and uses willpower to take the first step. Your imagination reprograms your subconscious mind with whatever's imagined. Use your imagination to program into your subconscious mind what you really want until you become obsessed with the idea of it. Intense desire is the kind of desire necessary to make something happen. You achieve your desires taking it one day at a time. You can only take action one day at a time anyway, so think about what you can do TODAY to bring you closer to achieving your goal.

Eliminate bad habits by going one day without doing the bad habit. One day without doing something can turn into two or three days without the bad habit you want to get rid of. Days become weeks, weeks can become months, and then eventually

4

the bad habit is completely broken. The key is to start today. Use your mind to turn the negative into positive. Combine the force of willpower with your imagination to get them working together. Dismiss everything against your inner being and keep imagining your desired end. All you have to do is convince yourself of something and it will be on its way to you.

Imagination, which programs the subconscious mind, is much more powerful than the willpower of the conscious mind. Make decisions with specific deadlines to help avoid procrastination. By studying what others have done, you can learn from their failures or successes. Be positive in thought and action, and conquer all fear. Conquering one thing will help you in conquering other things. Most fear is completely unjustified. Fear can also be a motivator to you and beneficial. If fear is stronger than a negative desire and keeps you from it, the fear was beneficial. Psychological, groundless, and unjustified fear is the problem. Once you get rid of your fears, worries, and anxieties, the circumstances of your life will improve tremendously.

Some things won't change until you decide to do something about them. At the bottom some won't act until they can no longer tolerate themselves the way they are. Imagination, not willpower, is the key to success because what you see in your mind's eye is programmed into your subconscious mind. Properly using your imagination to concentrate on anything positive programs your subconscious mind with good pictures. Decisions are made with willpower, then imagination draws in the benefits. Success is the result of the irresistible force of imagination and willpower in agreement.

Resistance is bombarding a problem with willpower alone without using your imagination to visualize the attainment of your goal. The esoteric meaning of the phrase "Resist not evil," from the Sermon on the Mount in Matthew 5:39 means to relinquish willpower. Nonresistance is the opposite course of not fighting a problem with willpower. Problems will begin to dissolve and disappear as you use your imagination to visualize your desired end. To be successful, you must exalt mind over will by using your conscious mind to habitually think about all the advantages (good things) that will be yours when you achieve your goals.

The mighty powers of your subconscious mind can improve health tremendously, help serious problems, and relieve serious illnesses. Programming your subconscious mind positively will increase mental awareness, improve mental attitudes, and maintain good health. Cooperate with the Creative Principle by doing whatever you can to bring yourself closer to manifesting what you want. Control your mental state by not getting emotional, fanatic, or upset over every little thing that happens against your vision. Whatever you've chosen with your conscious mind programs your subconscious mind. Monitor your inner and outer conversations while refusing any recitation of troubles, fear, accusations, anxiety, and warnings. Fake it until you make it because once you 'convince yourself,' you'll no longer have to pretend. All that matters is what's going on in your mind.

Through perseverance, you'll achieve total success. A lack of perseverance prevents the attainment of your innermost desires. Perseverance is the most important personal character trait necessary to accomplish goals and succeed in life. Persevere by refusing to give up or acknowledge defeat in the midst of temporary setbacks. If you study the lives of great individuals, past and present, without exception, they all were down for the count over and over again. Most people will be cast down more than once, but it's the great ones that always bounce back. Perseverance turns failure into success, defeat into victory, and can take you from the bottom of the top. Persistence and determination are needed for total success because nothing else alone will achieve it. There are many unsuccessful men with education and talent, but without proper use of mind power, these men are gifted derelicts. The only man that can't be held down is a persistent one. Those who succeed never give up.

Meet all temporary failures and setbacks with perseverance. Stubbornness and perseverance aren't the same because the stubborn man never changes his methods, refuses to admit his errors, and condemns himself. When you're not getting the results you want, admit your mistakes and employ a new approach. Convince yourself that you can have what you want, and monitor your beliefs. A problem is only insoluble when you believe solutions aren't possible. Right thinking will eventually attract the right solution to you. You can reach your goals by being persistent and never giving up. Many have succeeded after failure as a result of never giving up, and the history books are full of examples.

Use daily affirmations to program what you want into your subconscious mind. What you desire will only be yours when you persevere. Persistence pays off when combined with the repetition of daily affirmations. The most successful people are those who never gave up. The power of repetition effectively programs your subconscious mind and allows it to reach the goals you've given it. The cumulative process of daily repetition wears down the resistance of conflicting ideas working to prevent the acceptance of the affirmed proposition. Repetition is required to program what you want deep into the subconscious mind. In the physical realm, repetition, through practice, is needed to perfect your abilities, skills, and talents.

Practitioners of physical practices should also practice continually in their minds. Important events should first be gone over in your mind before ever beginning. After writing your goal down, picture in your mind exactly what you want to do. As you picture the end result, your subconscious mind will take over and direct you to do whatever is necessary to achieve your goals. With sports and other activities in the physical realm, the content in one's mind is most important. Through the power of right thinking, an athlete can be successful with no actual practice whatsoever. Practice is necessary, however, the activities of the physical world are 90% mental, 8% physical, an 2% mechanical. Don't just concentrate on the physical, but practice in your mind also. Work on the picture in your mind first, then focus on physical action.

Setbacks, opposition, and hardships are a part of life.

Perseverance is necessary to get through pain, disappointment, and fatigue. You can't live a successful life without persistence and determination. James K. Van Fleet, author of 'Hidden Power: How To Unleash The Power Of Your Subconscious Mind,' published by Prentice Hall, said, "It is usually not possible to win total success without paying a high price of some sort, often in the form of opposition, hardship, and setbacks of some sort, often in the form of opposition, hardship, and setbacks of one kind or the other. Few are those who can cross the river of life without getting their feet wet. ...Perseverance means to hold out, to last to the end, to remain steadfast and loyal. Perseverance is the ability to put up with pain, pressure, fatigue, distress, and disappointment." It's obvious that perseverance is the key to success, without which, your innermost desires will go unattained.

Dr. Turi says, "The greatest secret of all is uncovering your own divinity and its relationship with the Universal Mind." You are a divine being, and what you program into your subconscious mind withdraws the answer from the Universal Mind. We are to use our minds to focus on our own ideas, regardless of our external reality. So, if your external reality isn't what you want, you are still to only think of what you want in your inner reality. Your mind is a creation tool that you are to use to create your own reality, consciously. Your ideas should be the mental focus of each day, not what someone else wants for you. Marjorie Blanchard said, "If you are not working on your ideas each day, you're working on someone else's." You use your mind to create your reality because no one else can jump in your mind and think your thoughts for you. In your life, your ideas are foremost.

Scientific studies link the mind to disease and one's physical health. Psychoneuroimmunology understands the interrelationship between mind, body, and the immune system. There's an undeniable connection between the mind and the body. Therefore, when working on a goal in your mind, take care of your body. Get a decent amount of sleep because loss of sleep effects the entire nervous system. Not getting the proper amount of sleep your body needs makes you susceptible to infectious and contagious conditions, emotional strain and stress, and negative suggestions from others. Rest and recuperation allow the mind to stay alert and sharp. Consciously reject negative input coming from the television, the religious community, and other people. Quiet meditation improves your spiritual, mental, and physical condition. Deep breathing exercises renew the body. Several minutes of rhythmic breathing eliminates waste products and brings in fresh oxygen and strength. Conscious breathing/breath awareness takes you out of mind and brings you into the present moment (because you can only be aware of each breath now).

Your life experience is based on the habitual thought activity of your conscious mind. Cast down any thought that you don't want to see come into your physical experience. Only read books about things that you don't mind coming into your life. Don't be critical of others because the anger and resentment is in you. Ulcers come from negative feelings 'in you' toward others. Take care of your own life challenges instead of taking inventory of someone else's defects. Don't read books about diseases you don't want in your life, though you can educate yourself and become well-informed on medical conditions. People who constantly read books about diseases and such almost always develop the symptoms of all the undesirable ailments discussed by the author. In order to improve your physical well-being, you must read positive books focusing on health instead of the disease you don't want. If an ailment manifests, don't discuss it with anyone. Constantly talking about any physical problems negatively programs your subconscious mind and will make you sicker.

Being optimistic about life connects you to the power of life itself. Proverbs 17:22 says, "A merry heart doeth good like medicine: but a broken spirit drieth the bones." The modern translation of the New English Bible has the last half of the verse saying "low spirits sap a man's strength." The verse tells us to be happy and focus on the things that make us happy. Looking on the bright side of an extremely undesirable life situation is good for your heart and overall body health. In the midst of an extremely undesirable life situation, always focus on any positive side of the situation. Try to keep your thoughts focused on the bright side of the worst of situations, which creates an atmosphere for healing. Sickness is created when you program your subconscious mind with thoughts of disease and fear. What you believe programs your subconscious mind. Choose not to believe anything negative said about you coming from others, even if from your Doctor! James K. Van Fleet, author of Hidden Power: How To Unleash The Power Of Your Subconscious Mind, published by Prentice Hall, says, "I have seen people receive a death sentence from the doctor, accept it, and go home to die. I have seen others receive the same death sentence, refuse to accept it, and outlive the doctor."

Placebos expose the power of one's subconscious mind. Medical patients have been given sugar pills and told the pills were medicine that will cure them. The Doctor's words caused the person's conscious mind to believe he or she was getting the healing medicine, thus programming the individual's subconscious mind with the idea of being cured. The end result is always wellness, once the person imagines the placebo as the real cure. Once the conscious mind believes ANYTHING to be true, it's transmitted to the subconscious mind. The subconscious mind accepts whatever the conscious mind has programmed into it, whether positive or negative, and acts accordingly. There are no limits in the realm of thought.

The images in your mind can produce disease. Most ailments are emotionally induced. Those who think and speak sickness almost always develop all the symptoms of the disease they're focusing on. Emotionally induced illnesses are caused from emotional problems and imagining illness. By controlling your emotions, you can prevent conditions of sickness or illness. When symptoms of illness arise or pain appears, we can't let our imagination run riot, which will create sickness and disease. Imagining yourself to be sick will eventually manifest sickness because your subconscious mind can't tell the difference between what's real and imagined.

Thinking about anything other than good health programs your subconscious mind with illness ideas. Universal Law says that you will always become what you think about.

Emotionally induced illnesses are caused by emotional stress and strain. Rheumatism and arthritis are caused by tension and stress. Even if arthritis is only caused by infection or injury alone, stress and tension will always make it worse. Mental stress depletes the body's energy. The anticipation of pain or anything not good, even if it never manifests, causes severe nervous strain, emotional stress, and emotionally induced disease. When the body is under tension, strain, or stress, physiological changes always occur. Avoiding emotional and mental tension, stress, and strain prevents rheumatoid arthritis and other health crises. When sick, emotional strain increases pain and exhausts the body's energy producing mechanism.

It's a known scientific fact that stress, tension, and strain affect one's health. Stressors cause complete exhaustion of the adrenal glands and the autonomic nervous system, leading to arthritis. The prolonged nervous stress of one's environment (a bad job, any disappointment, unhappy marriage, unpaid monthly bills, etc.) will degrade one's health. Our modern world is full of frustration, rage, depression, unhappiness, suppressed anger, and other emotional tensions, which is why sickness is on the rise. Some people live in a constant state of stress and tension from morning to night, causing blood sugar to flow out of the liver in response to the increased energy demands of the body. All these physiological changes in those who struggle with the troubles of our modern world prepare the body for fight or flight: a dilation of the bronchial tubes leading to the lungs, extra red blood cells are released from the spleen to carry extra oxygen to the muscles, an increase in the contractions of the heart, a blood shift from abdominal organs to organs essential to muscular activity and exertion, and an immediate cessation of digestive tract activity.

Your mental and emotional state ALWAYS affect your health and physical well-being. Control your mind and thoughts.

The anticipation of something that never comes can have a harmful physic affect. Mental phantoms are imaginary problems created by the mind that have no substance. A mental phantom is an illusory fear-based thought structure based on groundless fear. Allowing mental phantoms to dwell in your mind is creating a mental prison for yourself whose bars are made of thought forms. Mental phantoms don't exist and have no reality, but become real when you accept them. Once accepted, in your mind, they construct a house made of thoughts which is a dwelling place for destructive activity, which negatively programs the subconscious mind. Life is a battle in your mind, and each moment is a mental battle for your life. Those living in the Light use visualization therapy to ensure that the right mental picture is formed in the mind. Whatever you wage mental war against will eventually go away because the conscious mind sets the course of your life.

Being joyful or laughing in the midst of trouble, physical hurt, or mental pain troubles your trouble and begins the healing process. Emotional stress and mental strain cause palpitation of the heart, chronic indigestion, high blood pressure, and rheumatoid arthritis. You never get away with negative thinking, which works against the physical body. The most important decision of your life is resolving not to torture yourself anymore by wrong thinking. You literally can worry yourself sick by devoting all your energies toward the dark side of life. Under trying circumstances, try to be as happy as possible by doing whatever makes you happy. A simple change in attitude will give you better physical and mental health, guaranteed! In the midst of hell on earth, stay determined to be happy and joyful anyway. Miracles happen when you laugh and be happy in the middle of trying and unhappy life situations.

Many men have been told by Doctors to get their earthly affairs in order because a negative diagnosis said they would die soon. Some who've been given less than six months to live have refused to accept their doctor's verdict of death. Those who fully accept the doctor's six month death sentence die, while those who refuse to accept the bad news AND TAKE POSITIVE ACTION, create a possibility of healing. One man left the doctor, ignoring the bad news, and created his own cancer treatment program. His DAILY meditation regimen involved daily meditation periods and excessive amounts of Vitamin E and C. Some cancer patients in full control of their conscious minds, (not ruled by medical opinions), have healed themselves using mental pictography to visualize cancer cells being eaten by white blood cells. Using the visualization therapy technique, many have formed a mental picture of their illness/cancer/sickness and miraculously healed themselves.

Scientific studies can link the mind to disease or physical health. Cancer and many diseases are caused by negative emotions. Positive thoughts and constructive meditation can heal almost any health problem. The interrelationship between mind, body, and the immune system is undeniable, which is how many have healed themselves through the power of right thinking. One man treated his cancer with visualization therapy alone. His cancer didn't regress or grow larger, but eventually started appearing smaller on x-ray. The doctors noticed that over time, the cancer was shrinking and disappearing. Though the man was not completely cured of cancer, it became smaller, and he lived more than 6 years beyond the doctor's original 6 month verdict of death.

Severe stress impairs immune system function and increases the risk of multiple diseases. Depression and such hinder white blood cells from fighting off sickness/disease/illness in the body. Positive thinking, mental imagery, and visualization therapy increase thymosin, the body chemical which increases the potency of the white blood cells that fight against cancer cells. All health problems can be healed by eliminating tension, stress, and thinking contrary to what you really want. Emotional factors can cause and intensify asthmatic attacks and other ailments. Fear of any sort can start an asthmatic spasm. The art of daily meditation used consistently over time can lower high blood pressure and alleviate any health condition. Even though physical ailments can be either physical or mental, or both in cause, meditation therapy and a properly programmed subconscious mind can fight disease, no matter what it is.

Relaxing relieves stress and tension. A relaxed meditation session allows the body to produce its own internal natural beta blockers. High blood pressure and hypertension are medically treated by synthetic beta blocker drugs produced by pharmaceutical companies. You can improve your health naturally through relaxation and meditation. Program your subconscious mind to expect what you want through your daily affirmations. Create affirmations to combat any negative frame of mind and keep your subconscious mind well programmed. Once your subconscious mind is properly programmed, it will not do everything for you. You must cooperate with it by taking action and following instructions given from within.

How you think and speak programs your subconscious mind. If you habitually say that someone is "a pain in the ass," you're opening the door to rectal pain and discomfort in your life. If you constantly call someone "a pain in the neck," you may eventually become troubled with shooting pains in your neck. You can overcome any problem you've caused in your life (through your words) by reprogramming your subconscious mind and changing your attitude. You create your own problems by how and what you are thinking. Improper attitudes and negative thinking program your subconscious mind improperly and cause physical problems. You can only heal yourself when you stop negatively programming your subconscious mind.

Only those who refuse to accept defeat will be successful. A positive attitude alone will cause you to succeed when normally you would have failed completely. No matter how difficult your life situation is, you must accept it and manage it through right thinking. When you only think about what you want, you're programming your subconscious mind properly. Most people spend most of their time thinking about their problems, but their problems won't decrease until attention is taken away from them. You can forget your own problems by devoting your life to helping others. As you forget your problems, they will mysteriously begin to disappear. Keep your mind off of anything that troubles you.

All physical ailments and diseases can be healed or improved by using affirmative prayer to properly program your subconscious mind. The mighty powers of the subconscious mind can improve your health and manifest total healing, no matter what the illness is. The mind alone can create illness without apparent reason, which is why some conditions doctors can't solve. Negative programming can make you physically sick. For one who is suffering from an extremely undesirable health condition, a conscious explanation of what's really happening can solve his or her health problem. When the mind is the 100% cause of a health issue, there will be no apparent reason for it and doctors will have a hard time discovering what's wrong. Usually, conditions your doctor has been unable to solve, or when the doctor discovers nothing wrong when you know something is wrong, those are the ailments or diseases caused 100% by mind. Once you reprogram your subconscious mind properly, your health and entire life will be literally turned around.

Output always equals input. What you lose on the level of form, you gain on the level of essence. The law of gain and loss says that you can't gain without losing or lose without gaining. First give to others because how you treat others will determine how people will treat you. Life is a mirror, so your actions will always be reflected to you from another person. Divine Law says that it's impossible to give of yourself to another individual and get absolutely nothing in return. Though you should serve others, stay away from those who criticize your character defects, faults, and frailties. Don't prove yourself to others, rather, only allow those in your life who accept you just as you are. Tolerate with kindness those who you're forced to work with. Practice the Golden Rule with everyone, but know how to deal with people. An old saying (from an unknown person) goes, "Never explain what you say or do to anyone. Your friends don't need it and your enemies won't believe it."

Unlimited Creative Power

You think your life into existence (via your prolonged thoughts). All your power is in your thoughts. Anything you think about or mention, you draw into your life. Whatever you want in life, think and feel as if you already have it. The science of living is the fact that whatever you think and feel must come to you. The New Thought movement is about only thinking and speaking about what you want. The Law of Mind says that you draw to you whatever you habitually think about. Your mind is a magnet. You rule your own life when you tell your mind what to think, tell your feelings how to feel, and tell your body how to react. The great secret of the ages is that your thoughts and feelings create your life experience.

Use your words to intentionally declare what you want. Use your mind to think of something beyond your reality. Use your feelings and emotions to show you what direction you're going in. Feeling good means you're manifesting more good. Negative feelings and emotions mean that you're manifesting more negative circumstances that won't make you feel good. Your feeling nature is your God. Let your feelings be a preview of what's to come. When you don't 'feel good,' work on shifting your feelings to keep you on the 'feel good' frequency.

Live a life of belief and action, and have faith in the supernatural. Your power comes from your knowing and believing, based on the meanings in your mind. Normal reality is 'meanings already present,' as defined by 'the world mind.' The world thinks for those who don't consciously make up their own minds. Don't let others do your thinking for you. Your words have power and are creative. The subconscious mind (the listener) hears everything you say and brings into your life whatever it is impressed with. The subconscious, called 'the heart' by ancient philosophers and the Bible, is impressed by everything you feel and think. Say what you want until you feel it. Many people have been healed after they were tricked into believing a new reality (placebo). Live through a higher state of awareness by living life with an absence of judgment (judging what's possible or impossible, curable or incurable, based on the world mind).

Your thoughts send chemical impulses throughout the body. What you think, believe, and feel gives direction to each one of the 100 trillion cells in your body. Every cell is commanded and instructed based on what you believe about your body. Your cells accept your instructions without question. Thoughts have chemicals that represent them in the body. The hypothalamus transmutes thoughts into chemical signals, transmitted to every cell in the body. Your body is a reflection of your thoughts. By changing your thoughts, you can change any physical condition. Nothing is incurable unless you believe it to be so. You think your life into existence, so use your thoughts to create the life you want. Instead of believing in what the 5 physical senses present, choose to believe in the supernatural.

God is within, which is why every human being has an unlimited, infinite, and powerful force within. The powerful, infinite, and unlimited force within YOU is your subconscious mind. The key to conscious creation is realizing that a powerful subconscious mind exists and learning how to use it properly in life. To get whatever you want, you must contact and communicate with your subconscious mind. It is your hidden infinite and unlimited power. Once you program your subconscious through repetition, it starts working for you through its unlimited, inexhaustible, and infinite power. Your subconscious mind works 24 hours a day, never rests, and continues working for you even when you're sleeping. Your subconscious assists you by giving you fresh ideas, activating your imagination, and inspiring you with new thoughts.

Living a life of anger, frustration, and resentment will affect your health. Eliminating tension and stress relieves health problems, and a change in attitude heals emotionally induced illnesses. As you program your subconscious mind with goals you want to reach, you must deal with negative emotions. Most fears are psychological, not physical, so FEAR NOT. Failure in life is the result of not having goals in life. Everyone should have some goal down in writing and never discuss it with anyone. The power of your subconscious mind is the key to your success. Repetition and perseverance manifest successful achievement. On the road to success, don't concentrate on what you fear, and prepare for the worst. Preparation for the worst is wisdom, not fear.

Everyone has two minds: the conscious mind and the subconscious mind. Reason and logic are used by the conscious mind to make decisions and come to conclusions. The conscious mind is behind your decisions and choices in life. Everyone should learn how to use his or her subconscious mind properly, which leads to divine inspiration. The decisions and choices of your conscious mind will be influenced and directed by the information received from your subconscious mind when you program it properly. The purpose of your subconscious mind is to manifest the goals that your conscious mind has given it. This is the relationship of your dual mind. Your subconscious mind will not work for you if your conscious mind doesn't give it problems to solve or goals to reach. Your subconscious mind will not act or think on its own initiative or volition. Its actions, hidden power, and functions are directed by the conscious mind. The subconscious mind has the ability to solve unbelievably difficult tasks after the built-in conscious mind assigns and directs it to do so. You must use your conscious mind to tell your subconscious mind what to do and give it specific goals. Use your words to get what you want in life programmed into your subconscious mind by affirming the desired end a countless number of times over a 90-day period. Those who live miraculous lives know how to relax and let their subconscious minds do most of the work for them.

Moral judgments aren't made by your subconscious mind and are the responsibility of your conscious mind. Your subconscious mind only works on the goals you've set for it, regardless if they're immoral or moral, evil or good, wrong or right. The purpose and responsibility of one's subconscious mind is to manifest the objective and goals programmed into it by the conscious mind. Your subconscious mind works 24 hours a day to achieve the goals set by your conscious mind, even if they're illegal, evil, or immoral. Positive affirmations should be used daily to give your subconscious mind the proper goals to manifest. With the subconscious mind, output always equals input, so if you program it with failure, it will work to ensure that you fail. Those who program their subconscious minds for success will be successful. Success or failure is your choice because it doesn't matter to your subconscious mind what its goals are.

Screening what's presented to the subconscious mind is the sole responsibility of your conscious mind. The subconscious mind only works to achieve the objectives and goals it receives from your conscious mind. Your conscious mind sets the goals for your subconscious mind to achieve, so you must give it the proper goals to reach. Even illegal, evil, or immoral goals can be achieved through the subconscious mind because it doesn't judge what's presented to it as good or evil. While carrying out the responsibilities you've given it, your subconscious mind doesn't use logic, moral judgment, or reason to monitor its instructions. The job of your subconscious mind is to manifest the objectives and goals it receives from your conscious mind. Keeping one thought fixed firmly in your mind influences the subconscious mind. Real truth cannot be repeated too often; for repetition reaches and gives orders to the subconscious mind.

There is a relationship between the conscious and subconscious minds. Your conscious mind issues orders, and your subconscious mind can only follow orders. It obeys and carries out your instructions to the letter without question, whether positive or negative. To the subconscious mind, the conscious mind is its lord and master because it directs the subconscious mind to go to work. You can only contact your subconscious mind through your conscious mind, which gives your subconscious mind instructions. Your subconscious mind won't do anything for you if your conscious mind doesn't give it instructions and goals to achieve. Your conscious mind is supposed to tell your subconscious mind what you want in your life, then you are to believe that you receive what you've asked for. Your conscious mind must reject every suggestion or thought of failure and worry. Fear of failure, worry, and anxiety improperly program the subconscious mind to manifest those fears into reality. Fears come true for you, according to Job 3:25, which says, "For the thing which I greatly feared is come upon me, and that which I was afraid of is come unto me."

Your subconscious mind controls all involuntary muscles, while your conscious mind controls all voluntary muscles. The difference between man and other life forms is the functions of the conscious mind: logic, reason, and deduction to make decisions and reach conclusions. Decisions are made by your conscious mind, which uses the five senses to gain knowledge. You think, know, and act through your conscious mind's cognizance of the objective world. Education, observation, observation of one's environment, and experience are how the conscious mind learns. The subconscious mind controls cardiovascular activity, digestion, metabolism, breathing, and the rest of the involuntary nervous system. Life is about giving proper directions to the subconscious mind, which is your hidden power. All emotionally induced illnesses can be healed by a change in what you're programming into your subconscious mind. Program your subconscious mind with positive goals, positive success ideas, and positive thoughts, while rejecting all negative failure thoughts. Many people have healed themselves of incurable diseases/ailments by programming their subconscious minds with joyous and happy thoughts.

To live a supernatural life, the conscious mind must be put to rest so that the subconscious mind can function at the Alpha, not Beta level. When you turn things over to your subconscious mind, it will work to bring you answers. The power of your subconscious mind comes into play when the reasoning, logic, and deduction of your conscious mind can't reach a decision. Just because you can't solve a problem through thinking, or can't make up your mind, doesn't mean it's all over. The hidden power of your subconscious mind can defuse and deactivate previous failure ideas if you'll think and speak properly. Whatever you think of yourself as, you're programming into your subconscious mind. Most people allow the news, religious institutions, and others to program their subconscious minds with negative ideas. If you have a thought of yourself as a failure, your subconscious mind will work to make you a failure.

Taking things too seriously is counter productive. (You can become your ambition and desire by listening to and acting on guidance received from the subconscious mind. The inner state of your conscious and subconscious minds determine the outer conditions of your life.)

Practice self-evaluation to make sure you are programming your subconscious mind properly. Your own mind is the answer, not religion or help from someone else. Imagination is more powerful than will power. Most people believe that willpower will solve their personal problems, but imagination always wins in an imagination vs. willpower conflict. Anything done through perseverance and enthusiasm will withdrawal result-power from your subconscious mind. The more your conscious mind relaxes, the more of the hard work your subconscious mind will do for you. This is the true meaning of 'let go and let God.' Healing and obeying God's voice is actually operating on inner guidance from your subconscious mind. Trusting God is turning over your problems to your subconscious to solve for you. All power is within.

When life-challenges emerge, take the necessary action. Turn all your problems over to your subconscious mind by faithfully practicing the principles and techniques explained in my book 'Beneficial Instructions Before Leaving Earth.' When you relax and forget about your troubles and struggles, the right answer will come to you as a flash of inspiration or intuition. Your subconscious mind communicates with you during periods of complete relaxation. The conscious mind is to be used for fact-gathering, intensive thinking, and brainstorming, NOT negative thinking. The inventor Thomas A. Edison solved problems by casting them out of his conscious mind and turning them over to his subconscious mind. He would lie down and take a nap, then awake with the answer.

Your words program and direct your subconscious mind. Your words tell your subconscious mind what you want and let it know exactly what you expect from it. Don't tell your subconscious mind how to work for you or bring your goals to pass. Leave it up to your subconscious mind to figure out how to make something happen. It will bring you the answer to your problem, and when you receive it, act upon the instructions received. Your conscious mind thinks by using deductive and logic, while the subconscious mind feels the answers. Instructions and guidance from the subconscious mind come in the form of one feeling what needs to be done or feeling reassurance from a source outside of themselves. Your subconscious mind will compel you to do things a certain way, sometimes defying reason and logic. Even if something sounds ridiculous, follow your intuition or instructions, unless they are harmful to you or someone else.

Intuitive guidance comes from the subconscious mind. Your subconscious mind gives you creative inspiration or ideas when your conscious mind intensely thinks about something. When you think about an issue, have an overpowering obsession, sense a burning desire within, and contemplate all possible courses of action, you will withdraw power from your subconscious mind. There is a maxim based on universal law which says, "desire is the first law of gain." Desire is symbolic of power, so if you have the desire to manifest something, you have the power to achieve it. A burning desire is the key to getting problems solved and achieving anything worthwhile.

Worry and struggle in your conscious mind only delay your desired end result. What you see in your imagination is what you are creating. Follow your inspiration, and monitor all ideas in your mind. Refuse to accept defeat, pretend that it's impossible to fail, and act on ideas coming from the subconscious mind and success will be your end result. Help from your subconscious mind to solve life's problems comes from thinking or reflecting deeply upon a situation. You will receive guidance from within through daily silence and meditation. Problems will come your way, but the right answers will come to you when you relax your conscious mind. The answers you need will come when you clear your conscious mind of all negative thoughts, distractions, and worries. The conscious thinking mind must be cleared to be receptive to the subconscious mind's guidance. Meditation clears your conscious mind to allow the answer to your problem to come through your subconscious mind. Religious fundamentalists feel like answers come to them from a source outside of themselves, like a god of one of the three monotheisms, but it's really the power of their own subconscious mind revealing the perfect answers. God is within, and everything you need comes from within.

Magical Thinking

The power of right thinking is the key to a successful life. Magical thinking is directing your thoughts to only think in agreement with what you really want. You unleash the power of your subconscious mind based on the content of your conscious mind. Clear your mind of negative thoughts by not thinking about your problems. Trouble will eventually disappear when you think about something other than a problem. The less you think of a problem, the more it will fade away. No matter the origin or source, whatever you need to know to solve your problems will be transmitted to your conscious mind through your subconscious mind. When answers come, it's your job to do what needs to be done to complete the alchemy. To the conscious mind, directions received from the subconscious mind may seem ridiculous, but, they should be followed as long as they're not harmful to yourself or others. If you don't follow your inspiration and inner directions, you will fail to get the results you want.

Sometimes things can get so bad in life, from the perspective of worldly thinking, that you have nothing to lose and everything to gain. Repeating affirmations for 60 to 90 days without missing a single day is calling on the subconscious mind for help. The subconscious mind goes to work on your last thoughts before sleep, so sleeping on the problem can get results for you. Those who know this usually wake up during the night with a solution to a problem, then write down the ideas that came from their subconscious mind while they were asleep. Stop worrying about the troubles of this world and leave things up to your subconscious mind to take care of for you through the power of right thinking. When you turn the cares of this world over to the Power by not worrying, the Power within you continues to work on your behalf while you're sleeping, meditating, or engaged in other activities.

What you receive from your subconscious mind is intelligence more valuable than conclusions based on a long process of thinking by the conscious mind. You get what you expect. When your conscious mind is on the proper frequency to receive your answer, the Power within will help you solve your problems and find the solution. Use your conscious mind to visualize what you want, which brings forth answers from your subconscious mind. Think only about God (anything positive) to properly program your subconscious mind. Persistence in anything will always pay off if you don't give up.

The electrical energy produced by the brain is measurable by an electroencephalograph (EEG). Brain energy rhythms are measured in Beta, Alpha, Theta, or Delta waves. You go about your normal day in Beta. When you are falling asleep, daydreaming, or just waking up, you're in Alpha. While sleeping, you're in either Theta, Alpha, or Delta, with Delta being the deepest sleep. During anesthesia, the brain is in the Delta state. Most sleeping is done in Theta, with a mixture of Alpha. Alpha is the key because it's the state in which the subconscious mind transmits messages to the conscious mind. This exchange of information usually takes place during the night while asleep or in a meditative state during the day. Use meditation to get into the Alpha state. Sitting relaxed in silence with your eyes closed will bring you to the Alpha state. Don't pass on into Delta or Theta by falling asleep. You can sit down and relax, and immediately go into the Alpha state within a few minutes. Once in Alpha, you may see the answer clearly in your mind's eye. Through your conscious mind, your subconscious mind will lead you to the correct action. The better you learn to use your mind correctly, the more power your subconscious mind will release on your behalf.

Everything you say is heard by your subconscious mind, which makes it your personal and intimate friend. When you are alone, talk to it as if talking to someone else. Actually, whenever you speak, you're carrying on a conversation with your subconscious mind. It is not abnormal or strange to talk with yourself, which is actually only thinking out loud. Talk to your subconscious mind as if talking to another individual. Instruct and order it through your positive affirmations, while ignoring fears and doubts. Once programmed properly, your subconscious mind will use the power of mental pictures and imagination to help you achieve success. Your subconscious mind will devise the methods to make your fantasies come true.

A seed of thought is planted into your brain from the external world or from within. If the conscious mind allows it to germinate over time, the subconscious mind will water and fertilize it. This is why negative thoughts must be cast down before they take root. Proper use of the mind will unlock the door to abundant living for all mankind. Creative imagination will help you find solutions to personal problems and get whatever you want. Your subconscious mind cannot tell the difference between what's real and what's imagined. It responds to the information you program into it by the conscious mind. You must program your subconscious mind effectively because it not only reacts to what's true, but also to what's imagined. Emotional fantasies are stored in your subconscious mind as reality. By seeing yourself as who you want to be and believing what you want is possible, you are programming your subconscious mind to help you. Imagination programs the subconscious mind to bring fantasy into reality.

God created man, then man is to finish the act of creation. Out of all the creations in the universe, man is the only one permitted to finish the act of creation on his own. We are creators, and our thoughts influence the physical circumstances in our lives. Use your conscious mind to visualize everything you want and believe that you already have them. By believing that you can have what you want, you're programming your desires into your subconscious mind. Spiritual law says that you can have whatever you can visualize. Jesus frequently told people, "if thou canst believe, all things are possible ... as thou hast believed, so be it done unto you." Your subconscious mind will work to manifest whatever you program into it, provided that you believe it is possible. Either real or imagined, your subconscious mind doesn't distinguish. See yourself as already being who you want to be or having what you want because your subconscious mind will not work for you if you don't believe. Pretending that the work has already been done transmits a message to your subconscious mind based on successful feeling and thinking. Allow your mind to work for you, not against you.

Your habitual mental pictures program your subconscious mind. Be aware of the pictures you're creating in your mind's eye. If they're negative, recreate the scenes in a positive light to guard the subconscious mind from creating negativity. Extremely detailed pictures on your mental screen influence the subconscious mind. As you picture in your mind's eye exactly what you want to experience, your mental picture will eventually carry over into the physical world. Your imagination can help you out in life when you make up your own mental picture of your ideal scene. Visualizing and using mental pictures withdraw power from your subconscious mind. Your mental pictures help your subconscious mind assist you. As you picture to yourself mentally exactly what you want to achieve, the creative power of your subconscious mind will start working for you.

The subconscious mind is a goal-seeking mechanism, so it only goes to work after given an objective to attain or goal to strive for. Your subconscious mind only goes to work for you AFTER you clearly see in your conscious mind specifically what you want. Knowing exactly what you want releases your subconscious mind's creativity, which is more effective than the conscious mind and willpower alone. Most people attempt to achieve their goals through willpower and determination, but it's more effective to picture to yourself mentally exactly what you want. Relaxing and refusing to worry allows your subconscious mind to take over and work for you. One is never relieved of effort and hard work, so always take some sort of action toward your goal. Imagination and initiative must be combined because goals are achieved only when they work together.

Act, look like, and be who you want to be NOW. Anything can happen if you can convince yourself first. Once you're convinced, there's a 90% chance that your goal will be achieved. The other 10% comes from initiative, hard work, and action. Acting is a key component to manifestation. Use the mirror technique and talk to your reflection. Those who've watched their reflection in the mirror and kept repeating aloud what they wanted (healing) have seen actual physical changes in their bodies. Say things (affirmations) believing fully that they are true. Some spiritual travelers face their reflection each morning in the mirror and say worthwhile things to themselves. The mirror technique is a method to strengthen your belief and help you get everything you want out of life. Look into your eyes and believe what you tell yourself, which establishes a creative climate for your subconscious mind. The mirror technique is another way for you to play with your creative powers.

The subconscious mind will never work for you unless you create a need by giving it some sort of goal or objective to achieve. You have to program it through the activity in your conscious mind before it will go into action. Daily affirmations for 60 to

90 days give the subconscious mind incentive to place in your conscious mind new ideas and a better way of doing things. Pressure, emotion, a requirement, urgency, or a need influences the subconscious mind to come up with new ideas to solve your dilemma because you've given it a valid reason to do so. The creative climate necessary for the subconscious mind to work is created when you: know exactly what you want, are specific with your goals, and do everything you can to attain your objective. Once your subconscious mind reveals an answer to you, you must take immediate action. If you don't do what your subconscious mind tells you, it will stop working on your behalf. Why would it give you new ideas and thoughts if you refuse to follow up and develop what is already revealed? Action is the last step of the creation alchemy.

Your subconscious mind gives you inspiration, creative genius, and new ideas, but not the initiative to fulfill your imagination. Imagination without initiative is wishful thinking accomplishing nothing, leaving the subconscious mind with no objective to achieve. The power of commencing is knowing exactly what you want and combining imagination with initiative. The thinker must do something or else he or she accomplishes nothing. A person's subconscious mind is the origin of all great ideas and gives him or her better ways of doing things. None of the living masters have a monopoly on creativity. Anyone can be creative by giving his or her subconscious mind the proper thoughts. Your thoughts and deep-rooted desire get your subconscious mind working for you to achieve the results you want. Notice your desires, monitor your thoughts, and do what you enjoy doing. Take action when your subconscious mind shows you a new way of doing things. Creation is actually 2% imagination and 98% initiative! Take the first step and get the process going.

Negative thinking produces negative results. Positive results come from positive programming of your subconscious mind. If you don't control the thoughts in your conscious mind, negative ideas can be fed into your subconscious mind. Negative imaginations allowed to remain in your mind can work against you and keep your subconscious mind from working properly for you. This means that we must guard what we think, hear, say, and see (give our attention to). Most of the time it is OTHER PEOPLE who plant negative ideas into YOUR conscious mind (television programming, religious institutions, the educational system, etc.). Negative ideas planted by others into your conscious mind, which are allowed to remain, will be transferred to your subconscious mind. You can keep others from turning off your creativity by keeping most things a deep secret to yourself. When you tell others what you are doing, either they won't understand, criticize, ridicule, or introduce doubt to your vision. By telling people absolutely nothing about a proposed project, you won't scatter your forces. Asking a doubter for his or her opinion causes you to lose your connection to your subconscious mind if you allow him or her to destroy your confidence via criticism, doubt, or ridicule. Don't tell others anything at all about what you're working on until it's complete. People shouldn't know what you've been doing until your project is complete.

Life is all about programming your subconscious mind with the proper material. You get exactly what you've programmed into your subconscious mind. Wrong kinds of thoughts destroy your life. Spiritual law says that the output of your subconscious mind always equals its input. Good results cannot come from bad thoughts and actions, and bad results aren't caused by good thoughts and actions. The output of your subconscious mind can only equal its input, which is why we must direct our thoughts. To become successful in whatever you do, you must program your subconscious mind with the proper input. The proper attitude and good thoughts influence the output of your subconscious mind because it does only what it's directed/programmed to do by your conscious mind. The subconscious mind is neutral and only carries out the conscious mind's instructions. Moral and value judgments are the responsibility of the conscious mind because the subconscious mind only carries out orders to the letter, whether immoral, moral, illegal, or legal. The job of the subconscious mind is to return to the conscious mind exactly what has been programmed into it.

The law of nature says that the ground will return to you exactly what you planted in it. You choose what you will plant in the ground. Your accepted thoughts water, fertilize, and take care of your mental planting. You have the power to plant whatever you choose in the ground of your mind. The soil will return your planted thoughts in abundance, whether positive or negative. The content of your subconscious mind is your seeds, and your subconscious mind is the soil. Your conscious mind, through negative thoughts, can plant seeds of anger, defeat, envy, failure, and resentment in your subconscious mind, which gives you exactly what you've planted. A person literally becomes what he or she thinks about because of the law of nature.

The only way to control your life is by controlling your thoughts. Monitor what you think about instead of just allowing yourself to think anything. Your subconscious mind responds to what you program into it. In order for your conscious mind to function properly, information storage takes place in your subconscious mind. Your conscious mind can't remember all past events, so every piece of information (everything you've read, experienced, seen, or been told) is retained in your subconscious mind in complete detail. The subconscious mind is a place of information storage for all past events, to protect the conscious mind from the bombardment of information. Most information is not required at all times, so the subconscious mind allows certain information to surface only when it's needed. Nothing is forgotten because all of your life (or life between lives) experiences are automatically recorded in your subconscious mind. A person can recall any life (or life between lives) experience when his or her conscious mind is regressed under hypnotism to a certain time frame. Sometimes your conscious mind can't recall something from the subconscious mind's memory because it was painful, distasteful, not important, or embarrassing. Recall is usually based on the amount of importance one attaches to an experience.

The Great Creative Process

What happens in the future is determined by the choices you're making in the present moment. Daily application of the principles of mind help one achieve success. According to your subconscious mind, whatever you believe is right. You control your creative law; your inner beliefs determine how you view the world and what you draw into your life. Multiple experiences are drawn to you based on the attracting force of your beliefs. You are a creative law unto yourself, which is why what you see is what you get, or, what you give your attention to you get more of.

The root cause of all experience is within. How you see the world determines your worldly experience. Your expectations, beliefs, and experiences create the lens through which you see the world. As you change this lens, your reality will change, since your lens creates your reality. The obstacles and problems encountered in life are caused by what's within, though most look without. All opportunities and perceived problems that manifest in our lives correspond to our thinking. The thoughts in your mind create your reality because thoughts are real forces. The thoughts that you're dwelling upon at this moment are creating your life. Your life is based upon the thoughts you're choosing to entertain. Your beliefs and thoughts are not just inner attitudes and perceptions, but real physical vibrations of energy.

Every thought, along with all physical reality, is made up of vibrations of energy. Everything is made up of the exact same substance: energy. Thoughts with corresponding emotion and feeling eventually make an imprint on your subconscious. All change begins within. The power of beliefs are reflected in your decisions, thoughts, and actions, becoming an inner vibration. We attract according to our beliefs, so each belief we accept should be carefully examined. The beliefs forming your inner vibration work in outer reality to attract or drive away people, opportunities, circumstances, or events.

The events of your life are interpreted through your belief lens. To the subconscious, your truth and reality (based on your accepted beliefs) are valid and real. Information or events not in agreement with one's preconceptions will be ignored by the conscious mind to a certain degree. It's important for us to see and understand the lens by which we view the world through because each belief will be validated. Your accepted beliefs take root within your subconscious, then are reflected back to you in the form of your life experience. These beliefs manifest in your outside world, making them real in terms of physical data. Your inner resonating beliefs repel or attract circumstances based on their vibration. Your beliefs can work for or against you, therefore you must free yourself from all undesirable beliefs. Since you have the power to choose your beliefs, take on whatever new belief you want.

You can create a new reality by simply working with your beliefs and thoughts between 5 to 20 minutes a day. Changing your thoughts and beliefs changes everything. Your current reality and possible future are created from your beliefs and thoughts. What you think and believe today determines your tomorrow. Your past experiences can't affect your current reality unless you believe they can. Changing your thoughts and beliefs will free you from past conditioning and change your future. Repattern your past by looking at it in a positive way. Searching the past with the same thinking lens will only create more of the same. Only dive into the past to find experiences to support your present idea.

Repattern, restructure, and reinvent your past from the present moment. You view your life through the lens you've constructed. You change your lens by changing beliefs. The lens you've accepted structures and filters all your past memories. Each mental lens produces its own different set of examples so that you will be able to justify your belief with proof. This is why whatever you believe is right. There are millions of diverse realities available to every individual, and the reality you accept is valid and real. Your accepted beliefs determine what you will attract, which is why all humans reap what they sow. Examine what you believe at all times.

Whatever you keep telling yourself, you're hypnotizing yourself into believing. You will begin to become what you believe because all habitual beliefs become self-fulfilling. Repetition reaches the subconscious mind and is how we've hypnotized ourselves with current beliefs. That which is repeated, written, or practiced over and over again becomes firmly imprinted into your consciousness. New beliefs can be permanently imprinted into your consciousness through the process of repetition. Repetition is the master key.

Five to 10 minutes a day, every day for 60 to 90 days is all that's needed to change your life. You can practice the mind power exercise of contemplation by concentrating your attention as vividly as possible upon a statement. Concentrate on any statement you decide to use and feel it. Each new day, bring your attention to and refocus on your statement. If you use the mind power technique of affirmations, feel the power of what you're saying, which makes your words become alive within you. You will absorb the message of whatever you repeat over and over.

Not only speak what you want, but channel your mental images toward your declarations. Neurological patterns are activated through mental or verbal repetition. New beliefs imprinted into the subconscious will naturally be materialized. As you repeat the mind power process daily, getting closer to what you're affirming will happen automatically. If you word your affirmations properly, it's possible that you may manifest spectacular results quickly. You may have to make multiple revisions before your statements feel right to you. Once you get your affirmations in order, continue saying them for a minimum of 60 to 90 days to permanently imprint your new beliefs. 90 days of commitment will change your life.

Act upon new beliefs and begin demonstrating your new reality. Take action toward your dreams by finding ways to demonstrate your changing reality. Inconsequential or small action is a huge step in the creation formula. Manifestation in outer reality comes from acting as if it were true. In your outer reality, you must take some symbolic action to indulge yourself somehow in your changing beliefs.

Only use the past to positively assist you in the present moment. Repattern your past by searching/finding past examples that will assist in what you're doing now and focus daily on them. For example, when I lost a good job in June 2003, I had to work hard labor construction jobs to survive. Family didn't help me and I was on my own. I registered with 5 different temporary day labor companies to keep money flowing in. Some of the jobs through Labor Ready were so bad that they would send out 60 people, then only 3 were left at the end of the job because the majority quit! Other jobs were so arduous that people were sent home for being unproductive, even though they tried their best. I did this strenuous work for 5 years and worked on over 300 jobs through construction temp. agencies. I took these jobs because they were easy to get; most people didn't want to do this type of hard labor. I was sent home on less than 10 of the 300 jobs I worked on. Since I was desperate for cash, I used my mind to assist me in not being sent home, or to the streets at the time. Instead of thinking about the few times I was sent home for not cutting it, I thought about all the times I wasn't sent home. One time, a slave-driver using the day labor service threatened to send me home 2 hours into a job but did not because I won him over with my relentless effort. So, while temp workers were fearful of the unfair hard labor jobs they were being sent to, I just thought of all the times I succeeded on grueling jobs in the past. I thought of the boss who wanted to send me home but changed his mind. I thought about a job where over 60 went out and I was one of the last 3 standing. I thought about a job that I survived where I decided not to come back the next day and the boss begged me to come back. He gave us extra hours, and was disappointed when I told him I had something else to do the next day. I think we were carrying 300 pound plumbing pipes for a new building. The point is, I searched for past examples to assist my confidence in the present. Each new day in the labor pool, I focused daily on my construction site HARD LABOR successes of the past. Thinking about positive experiences of the past creates a success vibration in the present. No matter what's happening in your life, focus on something positive.

Spend time every day imprinting new empowering beliefs supporting your goals in life. Follow your desires. If you have the desire to do something, you have the power to do it, for desire equals power. Desire supplies the needed emotion to your beliefs and thoughts required by the subconscious mind to translate thoughts into reality. The subconscious requires emotion, and desire is the catalyst supplying the needed emotion to your thoughts and beliefs. Desire will help you build your dream. A strong desire to achieve your goal will propel you to do things that seem crazy to others. Henry Ford went bankrupt twice, but his desire kept him from quitting. Thomas Edison failed over 10,000 times before he finally perfected the light bulb, proving to us that there is guaranteed success when you never give up.

The force of desire and determination draws upon the wisdom of the subconscious. Following your instincts is the way to success. You overcome all setbacks, problems, and disappointments through your burning desire. A strong desire doesn't recognize failure, it only focuses on what you've set your mind to. You will soon have whatever you desire intensely. The starting point for all achievement is a strong desire to possess what you're pursuing. Since something for nothing is an illusion, add skill, discipline, knowledge, and action to your burning desire. To create prosperity beliefs, write a statement to read over multiple times every day. Use mind power exercises upon rising in the morning, and again before going to sleep. Think about what you want whenever it comes to mind. Your strong desire combined with continuous action will attract to you the situations, people, and circumstances needed to successfully fulfill your goal.

Your consciousness, whether prosperity or scarcity consciousness, determines what you will receive more or less of. This is why Luke

19:26 says, "To them that hath ... more shall be given. To them that hath not, even what little they have will be taken away." Hard work, nor magic, causes success, only prosperity consciousness. Working hard while possessing scarcity consciousness will cause you to be sabotaged. Without the right state of consciousness, you'll be frustrated every step of the way. Things don't start to change until you begin vibrating with a new belief. Imprint new beliefs through affirmations, visualization, and positive thinking (directing your thoughts). As prosperity beliefs begin vibrating within you, you will begin attracting the people, events, and circumstances in agreement with the new consciousness you've created. A new life comes from a new mind.

Abundance is the natural law of the universe. Noticing all the abundance around you opens the door for abundance to come into your life. Everything in nature exists in abundance. One cannot count the blades of grass on a lawn, the stars in the sky, or the trees in a forest because nature is an example of plentiful abundance. Life points to abundance, and the natural conditions of life exemplify success. Abundance and success come into our lives based on how we use our consciousness. Attuning your consciousness to success and abundance imprints them within your subconscious. Recognizing success and abundance anywhere and everywhere opens the door for you to experience lavish/extravagant abundance and success.

Align your thought life with the greatest good, and keep your words in harmony with what you really want. Share your gifts with the world while developing your creativity and productivity. Others will be blessed and receive the benefit of you bringing forth your talents and succeeding in your calling. You manifest success in your calling by believing that you are talented enough to be successful. Believing in your own capabilities opens the door for Life to bring you opportunities to express and be compensated for your talents. The universal principle of unlimited potential means that any individual can grow, change, or develop any talent. The law of free will allows us to choose our beliefs, thoughts, and actions. Pursue any interest in whatever area you desire, knowing that universal law declares that we can do or become whatever we want. We are only limited when our thoughts are limited.

Your subconscious mind is the key to your success. Only the conscious mind has limitations, boundaries, and restrictions. The subconscious knows everything and has access to all knowledge and past experiences of humanity. Your personal reality and 5 senses don't determine the acts of your subconscious. As you properly direct your subconscious mind through the power of right thinking, it will give you guidance, insights, ideas, and plans. As you practice mind power exercises daily, your subconscious will reveal to you everything you need to know and warn you of what to avoid. Your subconscious mind is your access to knowledge, wisdom, and inspiration.

We hold within us Power, and it becomes our partner in success when we discover what it is and how it works. Within the subconscious, thoughts and beliefs mixed with emotion are transformed into physical reality. Your Power is in your knowledge of the interaction between your subconscious and conscious minds. You transform your life through the knowledge of the existence, power, and potential of the subconscious. Even if you don't make any effort to influence your subconscious mind, it continually functions day and night. Since the subconscious cannot remain idle, we must consciously attend to it. Negative beliefs work in your subconscious mind to draw into your life the corresponding experiences. It's your job to make sure that positive beliefs remain the dominating influence of your mind. Positive and negative thoughts can't occupy the mind at the same time because one or the other will dominate. Take control of your life by consciously directing your thoughts.

The subconscious mind can only be directed through the law of habit. Persistence is needed to form the habit of daily imprinting new beliefs. Your affirmations imprint upon your subconscious what you want it to do. The subconscious mind translates your desires into their equivalent as you daily imprint empowering beliefs. Your subconscious mind waits for you to create the blueprint for it to follow. Working diligently with your beliefs and thoughts every day gives your subconscious the proper instructions. Without a blueprint, the subconscious mind will create from the contradictory and limiting beliefs of the conscious mind. Your experiences in life mirror the habitual thoughts of your conscious mind. That which is allowed to remain in the conscious mind will eventually reach and influence the subconscious.

The decisions and actions of one affect all. What you do impacts your life and the lives of others. Every living human is forever changing and evolving. We are all 'becoming,' so it's wise to embrace change. This process of life can be used to our advantage by consciously creating the life we choose. As you change, everything changes because each part is connected to the whole. You are the programmer of your experience, therefore must write and activate a program. Thoughts of what you want will draw if from the reservoir within you. Thoughts of success will set your life in motion towards it. You will become what you envision yourself to be. Inner change causes all outer change. Assist inner change by using your imagination to see your life how you want it to be. Success is based on the mental program you've acted. Only the proper choices and beliefs can take you there. Once you've written a new mind power program, action is necessary.

The Art of Mental Imagery and Psycho-Pictography

Imagination is the most powerful force in the world. Imagine yourself in the most wonderful possible circumstances. There are no limits in the realm of thought. Only your imagination can limit you. Renowned scientist Albert Einstein said, "Imagination is everything; it is the preview of life's coming attractions." You will become who you imagine yourself to be because whatever you can imagine, you can achieve. What you see in your mind is reality, because your subconscious mind can't tell the difference between what's real and what's imagined. By imagining yourself being the person you want to be, you're using the mighty powers of your subconscious mind. Imagine seeing yourself as you want to be, then the Power of your subconscious mind will respond with thoughts and ideas to make your imagined activities true. Only see good in your mind's eye.

Emotional fantasies are stored as reality in the subconscious mind because there's no difference between a real experience and an imagined experience to the subconscious mind. Reinforce your mental picture with action and it will become more real in physical reality. Visualize with feeling, then take some action toward your mental picture. Action is the main ingredient. Even if the action you take is wrong, doing something is better than doing nothing, so get action going now! To be successful, you have to act in a certain way. All you have to do is try, then the law of averages will eventually cause the divine purpose of the universe to unfold.

Your imagination can work for you or against you. It can cause disease or make you sick if you use it improperly. Whatever you accept in your mind's eye will be so. Those who've imagined themselves to be sick developed symptoms of disease. All symptoms are imaginary in the beginning, then eventually manifest into real physical problems. Whatever your conscious mind believes to be true is transmitted into your subconscious mind, then your subconscious mind acts according to what you've programmed into it. Consciously direct your thoughts by practicing visualization or mental imagery. Never use your imagination and mental imagery to see (in your mind's eye) what you don't want to happen.

Force your conscious mind to concentrate totally on your goals, while completely disregarding input. Anything you repeat aloud impresses your subconscious mind. Whatever you concentrate on, you can expect to see more of in return. You program your subconscious mind with your thoughts and words. Think about what you want as much as you can throughout the day in a relaxed manner. Stop thinking about whatever you fear. You become what you think about, so work on concentrating entirely on what it is that you want. The worse things get, the more you must control your thoughts. You are in agreement with the Divine principle when you concentrate entirely on your goal alone. It's normal to think about the fear of failure or the fear of not attaining your goal. Positive thoughts only remain in good ground when you force fear out of your mind. Don't be worried about how you will reach your goal. Just know that it's yours the moment you begin to think about it and work towards it.

If you are mean to others, they will be mean to you. The reaction you get from other people is based on your own consciousness. Words aren't necessary to influence other people; as you change your thoughts and attitudes toward them, they will change. People treat you based on your thoughts and attitudes toward them, which is why: they'll be kind/courteous to you if you are friendly with them. Universal law says that you will always see your attitude reflected in the other person's behavior that you're dealing with. If you are hostile and rude to others, they will be hostile and rude to you. You can always change the reaction you're getting from other people by changing your attitude or programming your subconscious mind with thoughts of kindness toward others. The Law of Mind says, "as you think, so shall you become."

Write down what you want more than anything else and turn it into an affirmation. Write down on paper exactly what you want without showing or telling anyone what it is. Each written goal must be specific, clearly defined, and realistic. Look at your written goals frequently, while thinking about what you want throughout the day. Keep your goals at the forefront of your mind by thinking about what you want. The Law of Mind says that you must become what you think about, so what you are thinking about will soon be yours. You solve problems by concentrating on the solution. As you keep fear out of your mind and concentrate on your goal, your subconscious mind will use its powers to help you achieve your objective. Program your subconscious mind with the proper thoughts by never allowing the fear of failure to enter your mind. A burning perseverance and enthusiasm allow your subconscious mind to assist in the achievement of your goal.

There is always a price you must pay to get what you want. Your goals must be reasonable, realistic, and detailed. Don't give yourself an unrealistic deadline for your goal. Even if you don't meet your deadline, you will have made progress by using mind powers. Practice the system of giving yourself goals to attain, which gives the subconscious mind something to work on. The proper output from your subconscious mind comes from programming it with the right input of self-improvement or successful achievement. As your subconscious mind supplies the answers, you must follow through with sincere determination. Keep working towards your goals regardless of the obstacles you encounter. Either way, don't quit and never give up.

To live a productive life, you must decide exactly what you want to achieve and set a definite goal for yourself. Once your goal is set, let nothing interfere or get in the way of its attainment. The only way you can fulfill your vision is through an unswerving singleness of purpose. Get what you want out of life or die trying. Develop a plan with a realistic deadline for achieving your goal. If you have a sincere desire for whatever it is that you want, you've fulfilled the first law of gain. Some sort of action is ALWAYS required to be successful. Instead of just thinking about something, you must do something. To reach a goal, action is required and necessary. Take action after making decisions. Failing to act invites failure. When you're trying to achieve something, there's always consequences for your inaction; failure.

Success is the progressive realization of your goal, so you are a success if you're working towards a specific goal for yourself. A successful person is one who is deliberately doing what he or she really wants to do, independent of what others want him or her to do. Success is not easy and usually involves struggle, strenuous effort, and pain. To become successful in everything you do, eliminate failure ideas and channel your energy/efforts in the right direction. Override negative concepts stored in your subconscious mind by programming it with the right ideas. Refuse to accept any idea of failure and refuse to consider the odds against you. Everyone will suffer temporary defeats along the way to victory, but there is guaranteed success when you never give up.

All that's programmed into your subconscious mind will be recalled by your conscious mind when needed. Others or yourself can feed failure ideas into your subconscious mind, so you have to guard what you see, hear, and say. Negative ideas of failure and fear will destroy you because the output always equals the input. Negative concepts stored in your subconscious mind can be overridden by programming it with new success ideas. When you affirm new declarations for 60 to 90 days, your subconscious mind realizes that your conscious mind is no longer interested in failure. As you continue your affirmations, your old ideas and attitudes are buried deep into your subconscious mind, never to surface again unless your conscious mind allows them to. 60 to 90 days of repetition is the key to transformation.

Numerous temporary defeats are normal, but you must not accept temporary defeats as permanent failure. Regardless of what it looks like, you must continue to program your subconscious mind with the proper ideas. As you use the proper words to reprogram your subconscious mind for success, you will eventually succeed. To program your subconscious mind for success, you should never use words against yourself nor speak of what you don't want. Negative words create a failure picture for your subconscious mind and program it to work against you. Use positive words to reprogram your subconscious mind for success. Whatever you say after "I Am," you are creating. Use daily affirmations to constantly program your subconscious mind with positive ideas. As you program your subconscious mind with the right concepts, you withdraw its mighty powers to transform you into the image in your mind. Positive attitudes and concepts remove all the limits to your success which only you can place upon yourself. Never take yourself too seriously, which allows you to stay on the peaceful side of any situation. When you look on the bright side of things, you're programming your subconscious mind with the right input.

Refuse to allow others to program your subconscious mind with negative ideas. Others can program your subconscious mind if you think about or believe in what they tell you. Children can be improperly programmed if negative words are spoken to them consistently. Advertising people program your subconscious through habitual television watching. Accepting negative advice from others allows them to plant destruction in you. Your subconscious mind takes orders from your own conscious mind via daily affirmations. It will also accept suggestions from outside sources if you allow it. By not guarding the thoughts from outside sources entering your conscious mind, your own conscious mind is bypassed, and negative suggestion is planted in your subconscious mind. By training your conscious mind to reject all negative suggestion coming from without and within, you will not allow it to enter your subconscious mind. Consciousness is the relationship between your conscious and subconscious minds. The purpose of your life is to guard your conscious mind so that your subconscious mind will be programmed properly.

Develop an understanding of the inner workings of the conscious and subconscious minds. Those who play on other people's fears program the fearful one's subconscious mind to the benefit of the programmers. Some Christian evangelists do this through their 'hell-fire and damnation' preaching. Hell-fire preachers give vivid descriptions of the torture and agonies awaiting those who reject the Gospel of Christ. Hell is used to keep the church in business. 95% of religious believers only joined organized religion because they were told that they would be condemned for all eternity unless they became converted to the faith. Eternal salvation (according to religious dogma) is only available to those who accept Christ and repent of their sins. Religious fundamentalists only accepted organized religion after religious leaders programmed them with a sense of guilt, fear, and anxiety just short of a nervous breakdown. This intense fear produces greatly intensified suggestibility and a vulnerable condition only cured through conversion. Religion is built on FEAR, and the FEAR OF HELL is the only reason that the blind accept organized religion's theological message without question.

Most people don't realize that their subconscious minds are being programmed by outside sources. On rare occasions, this could be a good thing. A wife waited for her husband to go to bed and whispered in his ear, "stop smoking; cigarettes are bad for your health." She did this for several months, and right before she was about to quit, her husband said, "I don't know why, but I'm not going to smoke anymore. Something inside of me keeps saying that I should quit." No harm is done as long as what you're saying to another while sleeping is positive in nature. While another person is awake, the best way to program his or her subconscious mind is through praise. Children are always in a vulnerable situation because they are susceptible to programming from adults in authority over them. Parents and teachers are responsible for improperly programmed children because of their authoritative relationship with them.

Your conscious mind is supposed to be a gate to filter out negative or unwanted information from entering the subconscious mind. The conscious mind's job is to keep negative thoughts from entering the subconscious mind by refusing to dwell upon thoughts of what's unwanted. Only thinking about what you want protects your subconscious mind from outside influences and suggestions. The subconscious mind's susceptibility increases through fatigue. Worn-out or extremely tired people are more susceptible to suggestions from the outside sources of the external world. Your conscious mind isn't as watchful when you're tired and fails to protect your subconscious mind from outside influences.

NEVER accept negative advice from others. Reading the wrong books, listening to people who don't believe in your vision, or watching the wrong television programs is programming your subconscious mind in the wrong way. Act as if you can't fail and you will succeed. How you think of yourself, along with the concept of yourself in your subconscious mind, creates the outside conditions of your life. You will become what you think about, and your life will line up with your deepest held beliefs. James K. Van Fleet, author of 'Hidden Power: How To Unleash The Power Of Your Subconscious Mind,' published by Prentice Hall, says, "You know, in this respect, I am often reminded of the aeronautical engineers who can prove to you by aerodynamics and the laws of physics that the bumblebee can't fly. You see, they say his wing span is far too small for the size and weight of his body, so scientifically speaking, it is impossible for the bumblebee to get off the ground and into the air. The trouble is, they forgot to tell the bumblebee that, so he goes merrily on his way to the consternation of all those brilliant scientists who say it can't be done." The Law of Belief even works for insects! What you believe determines what you'll be able to do. If you listen to the bearers of bad news, you'll be defeated. Believe the impossible. Shut out all doubters. Only think thoughts of faith.

While working towards your vision, never compare yourself with others. Comparing yourself with other people programs your subconscious mind with failure ideas/attitudes/beliefs because you'll always find someone who's smarter or better than you are at something. Compete with yourself only instead of comparing yourself with others. Programming your subconscious mind with negative thoughts rooted in comparison will lead to more negative thoughts. Competing with yourself deactivates and defuses failure ideas and programs your subconscious mind for success.

To succeed like success, a goal to reach is required, then action. First make a decision, then take action. Inaction is the cause of failure. Use your intuition, accumulated knowledge, and past experience to make a decision. Your inner guidance is the powers of your subconscious mind assisting you. Some sort of action is required in order to keep the subconscious mind working on your behalf. Your subconscious mind becomes your greatest allie when you program it with the right input. On the journey toward manifesting what you believe, you will make some mistakes.

Mistakes build experience and reveal to you what doesn't work. Take this wisdom and concentrate your energy and efforts on what works.

Take a few minutes before doing something (like going to work) to make sure you're in the proper mind state. Evaluate yourself without being concerned about what other people think of you. Be who you are, not who others think you should be. Those who are truly free don't allow other people to act as the judge of their lives. Slaves to the world's way of life constantly worry about what they think other people may be thinking about them. You're not responsible for what other people think of you, which is none of your business. You're only responsible for what you think of yourself. Worrying about what other people think of you is a complete waste of mental power. You only become what other people think of you if you believe their thoughts. Universal law says that you become only what YOU think of yourself.

The Creative Power of Your Subconscious Mind

Work on eliminating all negative concepts of yourself out of your mind. Establish goals for yourself without allowing the past and the future to takeover your mind. Live in the ever-present now by focusing 90% or more of your attention on the present moment. A productive life comes from giving yourself current goals to achieve and staying busy with daily challenges. Don't get lost in the failures of your past, nor mourn over missed opportunities. Every day, stay aware of your present goals and what action you will take to reach them. Govern your conscious mind through self-discipline and perseverance to keep out negative concepts. Use affirmations to program your subconscious mind with positive concepts. See yourself as who you want to be because as you think, so shall you become.

Have confidence in yourself. The Power comes from within, not from without. Depict confidence beyond what you actually feel, which will cause you to glow with enthusiasm and project the aura of success. A relaxed presence of mind and a positive attitude are needed in the face of trouble. The person who remains calm in the midst of trouble maintains his or her Power, while the person who panics is doomed. As you remain confident of complete success, your self-confidence will inspire others. Enthusiasm for what you're doing withdraws the power of the universe to assist you. As you express confidence in yourself, others will be inspired to accept you as you see yourself.

Your subconscious mind will only work for you if you give it a goal to reach. Use your conscious mind to concentrate only on what you want or goals you're working toward attaining. Once goals are given to your subconscious mind to reach, it will reveal the methods necessary to achieve them. If you have the desire to do something, you have the power to do it because your abilities are related to your desires. The secret to happiness is achieving a worthwhile and challenging goal. Augustine, a leader in the early Christian church, said, "Happiness comes from the attainment of the right desires." People without goals fail because they haven't given their subconscious mind goals to reach. To have whatever you desire, you have to establish a goal for yourself. You will fail in life if you have no goals to achieve or no objectives to attain. Create a solid, specific, concrete, and tangible goal to shoot for, and when it's achieved, establish a new goal to strive toward. If you don't adopt this way of life, you will perish. The Bible says in Proverbs 29:18, "Where there is no vision, the people perish."

An athlete increases strength by using his muscles. Using your subconscious mind increases its power by way of you giving it goals to reach. Success begins with having a goal. After establishing a goal for yourself, believe that you have already received it and you will have it. Without knowing exactly what you want to attain, you're guilty of wishful thinking. Know specifically what you want, then give the exact information to your subconscious mind. When your goal is specific and accompanied by deep desire, your subconscious mind will reveal to your conscious mind the ideas necessary to make it come true. Once your goal is fulfilled, you must create a new specific goal to attain or else you will begin to stagnate. Practice this system of setting goals for yourself. The more ambitious and excited you are about a worthwhile goal, the more your subconscious mind will work for you.

Nonspecific, abstract, or vague goals don't inspire your subconscious mind to act on your behalf. You properly program your subconscious mind to help you achieve success by being 100% sure in your conscious mind of exactly what it is that you want. Goals must be measurable so that you can judge your progress on the journey toward attaining your goal. You will successfully reach your goal if it is specific and concrete. On your road to the fulfillment of your final objective, create intermediate goals, without taking your mind off your final goal. Use your mind properly by not thinking about where you were, where you are, but where you're going. Draw up plans to reach your goal within a definite time period, giving yourself a realistic time frame to attain your main objective. Recording your goal down in writing makes it concrete and specific. With no specifics, you're guilty of wishful thinking and fail to program your subconscious mind due to idle daydreaming.

Use your mind to visualize all the benefits you're going to gain after your goals are achieved. Most people think to themselves how difficult things are and try to use willpower only to change undesirable circumstances. Use your mind to only think about all the good things that will happen to you when you achieve your goals. Every life should consist of dreams, aspirations, and goals. While going about reaching a certain goal, keep it to yourself. Every individual will have different ideas about how he or she should go about achieving a specific goal, which is why 90 people could have 90 different opinions as to the right way of doing something. Therefore, discussing your goals, vision, or plans with others can cause confusion in your mind as a result of everyone's different ideas. Total chaos in your mind comes from listening to a bunch of people who don't see your way of doing things. You alone are to decide what you should do, based on what YOU want for YOUR life. Once you control your own mind, you will receive guidance and information from your subconscious mind revealing what you should do. Jesus gave some excellent advice in the Bible when he told certain people, "Go and tell no man."

Having one goal and concentrating on one point makes your subconscious work at its maximum. Discover one ultimate goal, composed of intermediate goals along the way to your final one. To become successful, you must concentrate on a single point and one purpose. All your energies and efforts should be directed toward one specific goal. The Bible points to a single purpose in mind, which is what Jesus was talking about when he said, "When thine eye is single, thy whole body is also full of light." Andrew Carnegie said, "Put all your eggs in one basket. Then watch that basket!"

Once you establish a goal for yourself, learn all the details necessary for its fulfillment. Once you do everything possible to achieve your goal and refuse to let anything stand in your way, your subconscious mind will give you everything that you need to reach it. As you program your subconscious mind by giving it goals to reach, know that their fulfillment is 2% inspiration and 98% action. You must make up your own plans for successful achievement and a deadline for its attainment. Keep your mind in an unswerving singleness of purpose by crystallizing your thinking. Planning your progress enthusiastically through organized activity produces power. Dedicate yourself to the attainment of your goal and think about it ALL THE TIME. Building mental pictures of yourself achieving your goal drives it deep into your subconscious mind. Your creative subconscious mind will then bring to pass whatever goal or desire you've programmed into it. Your desire for success produces a success consciousness. Success is yours with a positive attitude and the refusal to allow thoughts of fear or defeat stop you. Give no place to negative thoughts.

Think about and desire the things you want in life. Never give mental recognition to the possibility of defeat. Instead of thinking about your problems, obstacles, and negative circumstances, concentrate on your strengths. Ignore all criticism and follow through on your plan with determination. Don't give your attention to what other people think, say, or do. Work towards the fulfillment of your vision with concentrated energy, consistent effort, and controlled attention. Write down your goal, with a clear plan to reach it.

Though money is power, it doesn't always represent success. You can be very successful without being wealthy because success is the progressive realization of an ideal. Some people, like educators or underground spiritual writers (like myself), measure their success in intellectual or spiritual, rather than financial returns. Making money is the result of success; though success shouldn't be defined as the result of making money. Success can produce money, though money doesn't produce success. Defining success in terms of money only is limited thinking. Stop thinking only in terms of the accumulation of worldly riches.

Reprogram your subconscious mind with the proper success concepts and ideas of whatever you really want. You have God-given talents to do what you were meant to do. Successful people use their God-given talents/natural abilities to do what they're best fitted for. Usually, when you're doing what you really want to do, you're in the right profession. Do what's in line with your natural talents because you'll never become highly successful doing a job you hate. Anyone who doesn't love his or her job isn't doing what the Universe meant for him or her to do with his or her talents and will never reach the top. Instead of trying to make yourself into something that you're not/have no talent for, do what you're best suited for.

The majority of youths allow their subconscious minds to be programmed by their parents so that they think they have the desire/abilities for a profession they wouldn't normally care for. Most parents try to make their children into what they were never able to become or always wanted to be. When you force yourself to do a job you're not fitted for or don't like, you'll never be happy. Work the job while diligently looking for something else.

Happiness comes from following your inner guidance and doing what Life has given you the talent to do.

Accept your limitations while developing and using your real talents. Success involves specialized knowledge, so you must acquire all the specialized knowledge you can about the field you've chosen. Sharpen and improve your talents used in your profession by continuing to research, study, learn, and read. Become an expert and authority in your field by keeping up with your knowing; staying up to date with the latest developments in your field. Top experts never stop studying, even though NO ONE will live long enough to know everything there is to know about his or her profession. Keep on learning and continuing your professional education and development. If you are perfectly content with the job you have and how your life situation is right now, it's perfectly fine if that's what you want.

Use daily affirmations to develop your own self-image as a successful person. Universal law says that you can do nothing that is in conflict with your own image of who you are. It's impossible for you to become in the external world what deep down inside (the internal world) you don't really believe that you are. You act in agreement with the type of person you conceive yourself to be. This is why affirmations and visualization are used to create a successful self-image. Everything is consistent with the image you have of yourself, including your feelings, actions, and behavior.

Establish your own proper self-image, without copying or emulating another person. Many people submerge their own personality in someone else, trying to duplicate them. Since there is no other person on this planet exactly like you, it's impossible for you to copy someone else successfully. No other human is precisely like you, and you are not like any other individual. God doesn't make any carbon copies, only originals, so you're out of line when trying to be (or not be like) someone else. Develop 'your own' self-image by using your talents and accepting your limitations. Everyone has limitations, but they shouldn't be viewed as imperfections or defects, just limitations. Just use your thinking mind properly, which turns everything in your conscious mind over to your subconscious mind. Once properly programmed, your subconscious mind will give you the answer, guide you through feelings, and direct you through your inner guidance.

Do everything to the best of your ability, always make the extra effort, and never make excuses for any perceived failures. Be positive in all your actions and improve your mental attitudes. Be aware of how you're programming your subconscious mind by monitoring your habitual thoughts. Negative thoughts contaminate your subconscious mind as a result of jealousy, envy, bitterness, anger, or resentment. The thoughts you've accepted in your conscious mind set the course of the person you're becoming and the dominant personality you're projecting to others. Reprogramming your subconscious mind with positive thoughts will completely change your negative personality. Your entire life can be turned around if you'll keep your conscious mind full of thoughts of love, kindness, and whatever you want more of. The hidden power of your subconscious mind will only work in your life when you give your subconscious mind a goal to shoot for. Your goal will eventually be realized if you'll keep thoughts of bitterness, anger, jealousy, hate, resentment, and envy out of your conscious mind.

Most of the fear that people are in bondage to is imaginary. Some fears are based in good common sense, but psychological fear is the problem. New or unknown situations cause a natural fear reaction. Legitimate physical fear causes a natural physiological body response called the fight or flight syndrome. The fears that arise from negative programming are what must be dealt with by reprogramming the subconscious mind with positive ideas. Fear arising from new, different, unknown, or unfamiliar situations can be dealt with by gaining knowledge pertaining to your lack of knowledge. You are supposed to enjoy life, not live in fear. Programming your subconscious mind with positive thoughts will keep you from being consumed by uncontrollable fear. Never allow your mind to think about anything bad that may happen.

By consciously directing your thoughts, you'll keep fear in its proper place.

The majority of fears are not physical, but psychological. The greatest psychological fear is the fear of death. Death is inevitable and is no more than the opening into the realm of spirit. Death is the only way out of physical life and is the entrance into another dimension of existence. Evaluate your interpretations because misinterpretations cause psychological fear. Get free from the fear of what other people might be saying or thinking about you. Unacknowledged fear causes the most trouble for individuals, so ease the burden by admitting your fear TO YOURSELF. Unadmitted fear should be privately admitted, which is the first step in conquering it. Admitting fear causes the fear to lose its power. Justified fears can be resolved by simply doing everything possible to prevent errors. Most fears are unjustified, imaginary, and self-generated, but through thought discipline, you'll have freedom from fear.

You cannot control the world, so stop worrying about what you can't change. Control or conquer your fear because negative thoughts program your subconscious mind to work against you. Instead of concentrating on what you fear, create power over your fear by doing what you fear. Don't use your imagination to exaggerate fear in your mind. An active imagination keeps fear alive and helps manifest whatever you fear into physical reality. Whatever you fear will find you if you allow fear to take root in your mind. Job said in Job 3:25, "For the thing which I greatly feared is come upon me, and that which I was afraid of is come unto me."

19th century English author James Allen wrote, "As a man thinketh in his heart so is he." It's a fact that people become or get what they think about, whether good or bad. Think about not having enough and that is exactly what you will get, MORE circumstances of not having enough. You will attract to you whatever you constantly think about or concentrate on. You will project to others the essence of your habitual thoughts. Thinking about what you fear programs your subconscious mind with negative thoughts.

Concentrate on a solution to a problem instead of exclusively on the problem itself. Concentrate on and think only of the opposite of what you fear. Only listen to others if you've asked them for advice. Otherwise, avoid all unsolicited adverse criticism, which programs your subconscious mind with negative ideas, if you accept their negative thoughts. As you keep your attitude confident and positive, Nature will put the instinct and power in you to do what needs to be done. Everything will eventually work itself out if you'll control the content of your conscious mind. You will project whatever you think about. You draw to you whatever you concentrate on and constantly think about.

The Magnetic Power of Thought

There is a mind power exercise that will help you reflect on the direction of your life. Imagine that you are 90 years old, looking back over your life. Ask yourself, at 90 (in your mind), what you would've liked to see happen or what you regret the most. This period of futuristic reflection will help you get a clear picture of what you really should be working on in the present. By imagining that you are elderly, looking back over your life in a reflective manner, you will get a better idea of what you really want for your life now, to help avoid future regrets.

If you're convinced that something is impossible, it will remain impossible until something within you convinces you that it's possible. The Greater One within you floods new ideas and plans into your mind every day. If you follow the revealed plan, what was previously impossible will now be possible and probable. As you open up your thoughts, God speaks and opportunities open up. All you have to do is MAKE THE DECISION to do something, then the plans and ideas will be revealed. Wondering how something will happen or how you're going to do something accomplishes nothing. Once you establish your goals, the power of life itself will give you the power and means to achieve them.

Become inspired for some great purpose and allow your thoughts to go beyond current boundaries. You will become who you dream yourself to be. Once your mind transcends limitations, your current reality will begin to change. Right thinking releases the forces of the universe to assist you. Find something that inspires you, then align your mind and thoughts with it. As you get your mind right, everything else will fall into place. Seek ye first the Kingdom of God (the proper mind state), and all things will be added unto you. One of the founders of yoga in ancient India, Patanjali, author of 'The Yoga Sutras,' said, "When you are inspired by some great purpose, some extraordinary project, all your thoughts break their bonds. Your mind transcends limitations; your consciousness expands in every direction in a new, great and wonderful world. Dormant forces, faculties and talents become alive, and you discover yourself to be a greater person by far than you ever dreamed yourself to be."

Hard work is not the magic formula for success; one must work smart. Use your time and resources to the best of your ability instead of just working hard. You won't become more successful just because you're working harder. More often than not, the hardest working people in the workforce are the poorest paid. Believing that hard work alone will make you more successful will cause undue hardship and misery. Hard working people work long hours, are stressed, neglect their health, become stressed, and lose time with their families. The way of life is to work smart not hard. You receive what you believe. If you believe you need to work harder to be more successful, you will have to work harder in order to be more successful.

Instead of making sure that you're working hard, see that you're working smart, productively, and creatively. Use your time in the best possible way. Give yourself a time limit to accomplish each of your goals. Any task you set for yourself will expand to fill the amount of time you devote to it. Let me tell you about Arthur

C. Clarke, author of '2001: A Space Odyssey.' His physician told him he had less than a year to live. He thought about his wife and children because they lived off of the money he made as an author. He wasn't concerned about his life, he just knew that he had to keep writing to support his family. With less than a year to live, he knew that he didn't have sufficient time to write much more. Regularly, Arthur took a year and a half to write a book, but with new time restraints, he had to make a new decision. He figured out that he would have to write 6 books within a year in order to give his family adequate finances to fall back on. He made a hard decision to write a book in 2 months when it normally took 18 months, even though he didn't know how he was going to do it.

Arthur C. Clarke ended up writing 6 new novels! As he focused on his books instead of his ailment, a miracle happened. As he took his attention off of his one year death sentence and put it on his vision, he unconsciously cured himself of his illness completely. As a result of shifting his attention to his newly formed habit of writing a book in two months, a year later, there was no sign of his illness. As a fully cured individual, now that he had the time, he could've went back to spending 18 months on each book. When asked about it, Arthur Clarke said, "I liked my new productivity. And you know what? I think I write better this way."

Plan your work, organize around priorities, and start with the end in mind. What you do each day should contribute to the vision you have of your life. Keep a clear picture of your ultimate destination in your mind. Design a strategy to help you reach your health, financial, business, and spiritual goals. Working backwards from where you want to be will help you achieve your ultimate objectives. Use your imagination to see all the steps needed to reach your goal. Working backwards from your desired end gives you a blueprint to follow. To not stray off course, keep the overall image of what needs to be done in your mind.

Since your time and energy are limited, be most effective with the time available to you. You can't do 1,000 things in a day, so you have to decide what actions are more important than others.

Use your time wisely, and decide in what order you'll do that which will produce the best results for you. Manage and organize yourself by imitating actions which produce results. Don't forget the original game plan by allowing unforeseen developments, phone calls, or emergencies to sidetrack you. Work your plan by having an overview of what you want to accomplish daily, weekly, monthly, and yearly. Life is about setting and achieving goals.

Do whatever can be done immediately or today to move you aggressively toward your goals. Action is your vehicle to success, so always look for any action you can take toward your dreams. The Russian mystic Gurdjieff said, "Don't think of results, just do." Action makes a difference, since the strategies for greater success in life must be applied. As you take action, insights and solutions will automatically make themselves known. When you decide to act on a dream, you don't have to have everything figured out. Just get things moving and the greater wisdom of the universe will guide you along the way.

Rejection and the word no are part of life, but shouldn't direct our lives. Wallace Stevens said, "After the final no, there comes a yes." The laws of business say that no's lead to a yes, and the more no's you hear, the more yes's will appear. Salesmen know that for every thousand no's you hear, you'll hear a hundred yes's. You should celebrate every no you hear because a bunch of no's form a path leading to the yes's. The word 'no' is the sound of success in motion. No means that yes is around the corner, and the more no's you hear, the closer you are to a yes. Never believe that 'no' is the end. Michael Bloomberg said, "I've always had sympathy for a guy with an idea or two who doesn't take no for an answer."

The power of persistence always pays off. Keep your determination in the midst of discouraging circumstances or thoughts of discouragement crossing your mind. Rejection is just a temporary obstacle, but you won't view it properly without vision, desire, and persistence. Most people give up after the first rejection, but winners don't take no for an answer. Once you know clearly what you want, persistence is necessary. Those who possess persistence almost always succeed. The supernatural quality in persistence is the main ingredient necessary for success. Never quit, and ignore the 5 physical senses.

Your success and happiness depend upon your emotional and mental state. Thoughts of hatred and revenge destroy individuals and their dreams. Revenge and hatred have never worked positively for anyone. Carrying emotional baggage from a double cross incident only harms you because those negative forces are IN YOU. When someone double crosses you, forget about it and move on. People close to you will cheat you because the law of averages says that someone will cheat or double cross you sometimes. When someone does you wrong, take legal action if it's an option, then let go of it. Only allow that which is good to dwell within.

Take 5 or 10 minutes each day to imagine yourself doing what you want to be doing. Mentally practice any physical activity you'll be engaged in. If you truly want to be successful, you must make the time to work with the power of your thoughts. Acknowledge what you've already accomplished, while working towards new goals. There is knowledge all around you, so seek to learn from others. Emerson said, "Every man I meet is my superior in some ways, in that I learn from him and respect him."

Admiring others for qualities or talents they possess opens the door for your gifts to sharpen. Don't believe that you don't have anything to offer the world, for what you lack in one area is sharpened in another area. There's no gain without loss or loss without gain. What you lose in one area, you gain in another. For example, a blind man may have a remarkable pair of ears to compensate for his blindness. There is always a compensation for loss and another area that will develop extraordinary ability. What you believed to be a loss will prove to be an asset. Acknowledge and appreciate the area of gain compensating for the loss. Be determined to develop the gift which has been gained from a perceived loss and use it as an asset.

The pursuit of success involves hundreds of disappointments and setbacks, and thousands of difficulties. An overview of the situation reveals minor and major crises. Don't be surprised when you encounter resistance. Refuse to abandon your situation at the first setback. Draw upon insight, courage, and determination when you get knocked down. Everyone gets hit with their share. Know how to handle all loss or failure by getting back up. When you take whatever actions you can take in the midst of trouble, other options will present themselves. When all hell is breaking loose, the only productive alternative is to stay positive. Despair and helplessness do nothing for you. Thinking about anything positive keeps your mind working for you during tough times. As long as you direct your thoughts, you will recover. Guard your mind.

In the midst of horrific setbacks, there are options. Every human must weather setbacks and storms. People have recovered from major illnesses as a result of staying positive. People have lost their jobs and had to move onto 2nd, 3rd, and 4th careers. Move on without beating yourself up. There's nothing you can do to change all the things you could've or should've done. Even if things would've turned out different if you would've done this or that, there's no point in thinking about it. Mistakes are made by everyone, even by those with the best of intentions. Beating up on yourself or allowing regrets to remain in the forefront of your mind only saps your energy. Direct your energy into positive channels by only using the past to create a success vibration now.

Time heals all wounds and decreases the effect of damaging incidents in one's life. To be successful in life, you have to learn how to deal with trouble and extremely undesirable life situations. Get all the information you can about what you're going through, which will make your decisions more effective. Get advice and information from others who have gone through similar situations. Hold council with others who've had similar problems. It's helpful to learn about what they did and how they handled what you're going through now. With their knowledge, you will survive whatever situation you're going through. The trials and tribulations of life happen to all of us. How we handle what comes our way is what makes the difference. Those who live successful lives consistently rebound from disappointments and setbacks.

You don't have to know everything in order to be successful. All of us collectively know everything! When you explain your situation and what it is you need to others, they can help. You can obtain information by networking with others. Those who can't give you the information you need may be able to steer you in a direction where you can find it. Woodrow Wilson said, "I use not only the brains I have, but all I can borrow." Even if you 'falsely' believe that there's no one to help you, you can access a wealth of information via the internet and libraries. We live in the age of information technology, so you can find whatever knowledge you seek.

To be successful, one must know how to deal with others. People would rather do business with those they like. You and what you have to offer are one, so you're personality is either an asset or liability to your success. Your personality should be pleasing to others. If not, you can change it. You can change any part of you that you don't like and create your personality. A thorough self-examination will reveal what's needed to develop yourself. Your personality should be worked on because it can either attract or repel people.

Creating admired qualities within yourself can draw opportunities and people to you. An admired personality is one consisting of: a positive attitude, patience, confidence, and receptiveness. Operating high on the personable will cause startling changes in your life. You control your character and personality. You can resolve to change any parts of you that you don't like. Your personality is your own responsibility, so make the qualities you admire in others yours. You change your personality by changing your habits and thoughts. The evolution of your thoughts changes your personality for the better. Decide who you want to be, then become that person. Change is a part of life, so choose your changes and develop the qualities you admire in others. Who you are today is not who you'll be in the future or who you were in the past. We're forever changing.

True success is not measured by an accumulation of dollars and cents. Our life's journey should be an honorable one where in which we operate at the highest moral and ethical standards. Enjoy the joys and treasures of your life, and take time for leisure. Without giving yourself sufficient leisure time, your work will suffer. The problem isn't that people aren't working hard enough, they're not giving their minds a break. Relax, let go, and take a break from any deadlines or quotas. Creative ideas flow when the mind is in a state of relaxation.

Hard work is not the way to success. Many people work hard and still don't get anywhere. Balance is the key to all things. Failure is the result of hard work without the balance of leisure. Leisure time is necessary to be refreshed with enthusiasm and vigor. It's negligent to not take time out for reassessment and contemplation. The creative mind (your subconscious mind) advances during times of mental quietude to bring forth new ideas. Success is a balance of work and leisure. The Great Ones always knew this. 1997 Nobel Laureate Paul Boyer, while relaxing and overlooking L.A. from his house, said, "Getting away from it all, letting go, is more conducive to innovation than focusing continuously on your project."

Including more leisure time in your week will change your life. All you have to do is think about the things you enjoy doing and what gives you pleasure, then include them in your daily routine. Discipline yourself to have fun. Giving yourself quality leisure will help you do quality work consistently. Too much work causes burnout and what you're working on to suffer. If you love success, you'll give yourself quality time to enjoy fun activities or relax.

Believe passionately in what you're doing. Feeding others with positive messages makes them believe in themselves. We can all contribute to the world and make a difference. Make the time to do something positive, even when you're so busy that you really don't have the time. Do anything you can to help groups, individuals, and organizations that are making a difference. The decision to do things that help make this world a better place will bring you joy, satisfaction, and pleasure. Take the time to make a difference, despite your busy life. You came to Earth with nothing, and you'll leave with nothing, so your Divine purpose has something to do with assisting/helping others.

There are good reasons to take a positive perspective in all things. Your future will emerge based on the image you hold of it. There is no fixed future, and nothing just happens. The Creative principle (God) creates your future based on the energy of your images of the future. Positive thinking mixed with optimism guarantees a better future. All you have to do is believe that the future will be better. Whatever you believe, without doubting in your heart, you will eventually receive. How you create your future is your choice, based on how you use the forces of creation. Activist and writer Noam Chomsky said, "Optimism is a strategy for making a better future. Because unless you believe that the future can be better, it's unlikely you will step up and take responsibility for making it so. If you assume that there's no hope, you guarantee that there will be no hope. If you assume that there are opportunities to change things, there's a chance you may contribute to making a better world. The choice is yours."

Most people need to bring more fun into their lives. Awaken to the joy of fun by practicing having spontaneous fun every day! The mind needs variety and diversification, so mix fun into your daily routine. Enjoying a good song, reading, walking, or working out may be fun to some. The others should discover all the activities that are fun for them and include them in their daily living. We all should look for opportunities to have fun. Sometimes, when our minds are very active, we may not even recognize that we're having fun. Fun should be a part of every day of your life because it is beneficial, healthy, productive, and empowering. Fun gives you energy and refreshes you. When you incorporate more fun into your life, you will work better and be more effective at whatever you're doing.

Every person's life is unique and created according to his or her vision, courage, and understanding. Every individual born on Earth must learn how to live. Those who fall by the wayside categorize every event as positive or negative, good or bad. Myth says that Adam and Eve were kicked out of Paradise when they had the knowledge of good and evil. As long as they weren't judging life as good or bad, they dwelled in Paradise. All experiences are a part of life. Some things will make you feel good and some things won't. Life isn't always pleasant. Refuse to mentally label what you're going through as good or bad, just accept what is.

It's an illusion to expect life to always feel good and bring you everything you desire. Psychotic neurotics are those who believe that they should be fulfilled, happy, and stimulated every minute of every day. Some things you can control, but most things you cannot. You can't control everything that happens in your life, only how you react to it. We become miserly when we leave no room for pain, tragedy, and confusion. Most people reject anything unpleasant. God is Life. When we refuse to accept that which is undesirable as a part of our life, we've unconsciously rejected Life/God. The grand scheme of life unfolding involves failure, misfortune, and maybe sickness. Enlightened living is accepting life in its entirety.

Watch your mind to stop it from projecting and judging. Live in the present moment without being focused on future destinations. This very moment is filled with infinite treasures, but you won't be able to find them if your awareness is in the past or future. Make a conscious effort to live in the present moment. Living in the present moment is simply being totally immersed in what we are doing. Living in the present moment for just a few minutes a day is better than not at all. Being at peace with this moment is being at peace with yourself.

Part 2: The Bible of the Next Millennium

- The Laws of the Most High

- The Formula for Creating

- God Is (The Creative Principle of the Universe)

- The Teachings of the Ancient Wise Men

- Wisdom Teachings For the Inner Life

- Hood Christ

The Laws of the Most High

Always follow your dreams. Create a vision, then start working towards it. Control your mind while taking action, giving nothing less than your best. Create for yourself the most positive environment as possible, avoiding negative people. As long as you don't quit, you haven't failed. Staying open to change will help you make the proper adjustments necessary to be successful. Real success IS NOT measured in dollars and cents. You alone decide what success is for you!

Study Universal and Spiritual laws to make sure that the right principles are operating in your life. Most of the time, everyone is struggling to do the best they can. We should strive to do better every day and build on any success we've already achieved. If you're already doing well, sharpen your skills by hearing and reading about universal laws over and over again to ensure that you're operating under them. All the great spiritual teachers of humanity were explaining God's law, which is the real law. The mythical Jesus, Buddha, Patanjali, and thousands of other inspirational people all taught the exact same laws in different ways. The commonalities between all religions, spiritual teachers, and so-called holy books are what's true.

A fundamental spiritual law is the oneness of humanity. You are already living under universal and spiritual laws, but the key is becoming more conscious of them. Even if you aren't completely aware of them, you live under these laws, whether you're conscious of them or not. Understanding these rules of life are the process through which you will realize your dreams. Faith and dedication are more valuable than any college degrees, when it comes to your vision. Vincent Van Gogh said, "I dream my painting and paint my dream." In your mind, see your vision and stick with it no matter what your life situation looks like. Don't look to the educational system to make you a success because a degree alone doesn't guarantee success. A degree will open doors for you, but it should only complement, not compensate for, the spirit of faith and an imaginative mind.

All success starts as a vision in the mind of one who isn't afraid to dream. Your dreams will come to pass if you strongly believe in them to the point where you REFUSE TO QUIT until they become reality. Work to achieve your goals or die trying. Never let go of your vision. See the end result in your mind before you even get started. Once you get started, don't change paths or turn around (quit). All of us have been blessed with unique ideas; all we have to do is follow through on the ideas placed in us. God has already blessed you with power. All you have to do is listen to your imagination, which allows the universe to bring you a much more fulfilling life.

Visions are spiritual because they are God communicating to us what we are to be doing. People believe that they create their own visions, but more often than not, they create their own visions, but more often than not, they are originating from a Higher Source. Paramhansa Yogananda's 'Autobiography of a Yogi' says, "Your imagination is God itself." Yogananda was a spiritual leader from India, and like Jesus and Buddha, the essence of his teachings teach you who you are. The spiritual teachers of antiquity taught humanity to live by faith and not by sight. Faith is for the unseen, for if you could see it, you wouldn't need faith. Without faith, it's impossible to please God. The purpose of your imagination is to imagine the things of faith. Whatever you imagine, you can achieve through perseverance. Any worthwhile goal is going to take time to manifest. Just keep following your dreams.

You can either listen to your dreams or listen to haters. Haters are everywhere, which is why you shouldn't discuss your visionary plans with everyone. The world will speak negatively in your ear, but you must block it out. It's best to keep yourself in a position where you won't hear that negativity in your ear in the first place. Nothing matters but your vision. Harness your vision with faith, dedication, and focus, noticing how you feel about your inspirational ideas. If you're not on fire about an idea, or lose interest in it, most likely, it wasn't what Life/God wanted you to pursue. The universe guides you through the desires of your heart. Ideas and desires are given to you by God. When your passion is missing from something, it's a sign from Life that you probably should start focusing on something else. Follow your heart.

There are many roads to success in every industry, so never believe that there is only one path to success. Every path involves being clear in your vision and taking action. Always write out your plans, but stay flexible. Divinely-inspired (business) plans will always change or evolve. Your success is where your attention goes, so monitor your focus. Focus on one vision without moving on to the next challenge. Working on ten visions at one time makes it harder to manifest any one of them. You should never let your vision go. Important visions take years to come to pass. Follow your dreams, knowing that a passage of time is usually involved. Persistence and determination are needed if you are to follow your dreams because, most of the time, it will seem like they'll never be realized.

Your vision constructs your world. How you see the world determines the world you live in and your reality. Any dream combined with resilience and persistence will always become reality. Whatever you dream can become a reality through belief and faith. Whatever you really want, imagine yourself with it. Your faith makes your mental image a reality. Write what you want on paper with a willingness to compromise on the details. Often, plans will have to be abandoned or changed, but will require sacrifices to be made. A connection to the real faith inside of you is necessary to endure rejection and stay motivated to keep on moving. Struggle is part of the alchemy and becomes an important aspect of your character.

Passion is power, so if your passion is missing from the creative process, your Inner Being is guiding you to focus on something else. Stay true to who you are and what you feel you should be doing instead of following the trends of the masses. I write books that I believe in. Sales don't matter; I do it for the love for the art.

Even if I never sold one book, I would've still completed my 6 book series. Vincent Van Gogh is my hero because he only sold one painting while he was alive. If he looked at sales numbers and social acceptance, he would have thought, "No one cares about my paintings nor is supporting my creativity, so I should just quit and find something else to get into. I've only sold one painting my whole life, so maybe this just isn't worth it." Some people only follow their inner vision when they're receiving outer support from others. If you like doing something in the creative field, do it, whether people support you or not. Don't allow low or no sales numbers keep you from doing what you enjoy doing.

Do what you love, regardless of acceptance or rejection from the external world. Don't allow the opinions of the external world decide if you should keep doing something or not, provided you have the opportunity to keep doing it. Vincent Van Gogh is my hero because he only sold one painting while he was alive, yet kept painting anyway because that's what he loved doing! Do what you love, independent of the reactions of the external world. I don't sell many books and have very few readers. Every mainstream traditional publisher considers my career a commercial failure, but, I'm still here! I'm inspired by Vincent Van Gogh because he kept painting even though no one was buying his work. Most people would've quit, but he kept going. Some traditions say he sold no paintings at all, as in O!!! He didn't let this discourage him.

In today's society, if you release an artistic project that doesn't sell enough units, the big corporations will categorize you as a commercial failure and drop you. If people release a project that no one buys, most will quit and consider their efforts a failure. Vincent Van Gogh only sold one unit of his work while he was alive, and now, his work is worth MILLIONS of dollars. He could've easily quit, but he didn't. His attitude was, "even if the public doesn't support me, I'm going to continue to do what I'm doing because this is what I want to do. I want you to support me, but even if no one buys my paintings, I'm going to continue painting anyway." I like the fact that he never stopped and never quit, even though no one was buying his work. There is guaranteed success when you never give up, even if it's posthumously.

Van Gogh sold only one painting in his entire lifetime! He was poor financially and struggled throughout his lifetime. Vincent's brother Theo was an art dealer and ran an art gallery. Theo would buy some of Vincent's paintings with his own money, store them away, then lie to Van Gogh, telling him that someone bought his paintings. Historians say Theo did this to encourage his brother to keep painting and to help him make some money to survive. No one knows if Vincent Van Gogh ever found out what his brother Theo was doing. We do know that Theo was the only one buying his brother's paintings because after he died, the 'sold' paintings were found in his home.

Fine Arts students know, and it is common knowledge that Van Gogh sold either O or 1 painting. During Van Gogh's life as an artist, he thought he sold almost two dozen of his paintings, but his brother really had them. He sold O to 1, but didn't let low sales numbers discourage him. He followed his heart and kept doing what he was doing regardless of sales!!! It's about your love for the art.

Tap into the resources God has provided you by listening to the voice of God inside of you. Everyone has conversations with God, and taking heed is following the path the Universe has laid out for you. If you don't listen to your Inner Guidance, you'll end up following the world. Happiness comes from positively impacting the world. You will only be truly happy while doing God's work, which is fulfilling your divine purpose. When you're not doing what you are meant to be doing, you won't be happy. When you do exactly what you came to Earth to do, there will always be people who won't understand you or disagree with your decisions. Listen to your own heart and stay in touch with your higher self. Being afraid to go against the grain will keep you doing things the same way and helplessly conformed to the ideas of the world. You decide what's best for you.

When you establish your vision, it should be your only focus.

You may have to work on it for several years. Breakthrough usually happens when it seems like you're making little to no progress and have exhausted all your possibilities. Success frequently takes years to develop. Start following your dreams today. Today you will start, for the day you start, you're already closer to the fulfillment of your vision. It's never too late or too early to start something new. Whatever you want, take it yourself now instead of waiting for someone to hand you something. Each of us has a variety of ideas and resources, so do the best you can with what you have at this moment.

Everyone is special, with numerous talents, some of which haven't been realized yet. People become stagnant and unhappy when they don't use the skills God has blessed them with to pursue their dharma (life's purpose). Pay attention to what your inner voice tells you. Notice the ideas that come into and go out of your mind. Observing your mind will help you identify your true passion. Once discovered, put all your energy into it and pursue it with everything you've got. Ignore all difficulty because no goal is so difficult that you can't start working on it now. You can pursue a new dream at any age, for it's never too late to start a new path in life, except maybe in physical fields like sports and such. With a strong mind, physical fields can remain attainable.

Age, wealth, or poverty aren't to determine whether or not you should set out on a new path in life. Decide what you want, then take whatever steps you can to achieve it. Buddha decided to become a penniless monk (after being a rich prince) when he was almost 30 years old. At this time in history, thirty was deep into middle age. Colonel Sanders of KFC didn't start building his franchise until he was in his sixties. Taikichiro Mori, a wealthy Japanese builder, didn't start his construction business until he was in his fifties. Rodney Dangerfield didn't get into comedy until he was 42. Anthony Burgess, author of 'A Clockwork Orange,' didn't release his first book until he was 39. Eckhart Tolle was 49 when his first book 'The Power of Now' was published. Mother Teresa, born Agnes Gonxha Bojaxhiu, didn't start the 'Missionaries of

Charity' in Calcutta, India until she was 40. Twenty years later, she became well-known internationally for her humanitarian work of ministering to the poor, helpless, sick, orphaned, hungry, and dying.

Don't wait for the green light from others to follow your dreams. You are the master of your own life, therefore, don't need any outside approval to go after what you want. Live as if you're already where and who you want to be. Fake it until you make it, ignoring your external reality. Make the time to pursue your vision instead of waiting until you have more free time. Don't focus on or talk about how things are right now. Work hard without looking for someone else to put you on.

You may have to struggle for years before someone else in power is willing to bring you to the next level. Those at the top of the industry you want to get into usually don't express interest in the work you haven't done, but will be willing to invest in you based on being impressed by the work you've already started. Don't sit around waiting for someone to hand you something, work now! It may take many years for your breakthrough, but every little step you take brings you closer. Start following your dreams today instead of waiting for someone to deliver you from obscurity. Work on your art for free instead of trying to get someone to pay you first. As you keep working hard, people will eventually notice you.

The Christian scriptures teach that 'you will have what you say.' Jesus says that if you speak in faith, believe that you receive, and have no doubt in your heart, whatsoever you say shall come to pass. The metaphysical principles hidden in religious holy books are the only reason they're worth reading. In the Bible, God created the Earth and everything in it by 'his' words. If we are created in 'his' image and likeness like the scriptures say, then we are to use our words to create also. As soon as you put your word out there, the idea you're speaking of will begin to take a life of its own. Whatever you speak of, you're putting into the air. Speaking the same words over and over again gives them power to mature into actual facts. Words can pave the path toward your dreams and take your idea to the next level. Once you decide what you want, speak it into existence on the spot. Only speak words that will work for you.

Everyone receives initial inspiration from the Universe. We must immediately act on what's received. Life is about pursuing your dream. Success begins by taking baby steps toward what you want. Action of some sort is needed to get the ideas out of your heart into the world. Throughout the creation process, you have to live your life as if you're already where you want to be. As you fake it until you make it, opportunity will present itself. It's your job to pursue any opportunity that presents itself. If nothing is happening where you are, go where the action is. Most people don't want to relocate because they're afraid to submit themselves to the unknown. The world is filled with uncertainty and opportunity, and they usually go hand in hand.

Many lives are filled with past failures, but enlightened living is letting go of the past. Just keep working now towards your future goals. Vince Lombardi said, "The dictionary is the only place where success comes before work." Since work comes before success, you must never give less than your best. Success in life comes from dedication and hard work. Working your hardest is the key ingredient to success. Hard work is a spiritual practice. Worldly success comes from a commitment to hard work. Doing good work is a process by which you can obtain wholeness and happiness. Some people don't have a disciplined approach to work and self-sacrifice because they're working a dead-end job, even though there's no such thing. Put in hard work every day, regardless of what kind of work you're doing. Mental focus and hard work make improbabilities more probable. Create a set of rituals to follow every day to keep your mind focused. Dedication to these rituals (affirmation, visualization, and mind power exercises) set a positive tone and feed your motivation and inspiration. The power of these daily rituals will keep you focused on the creation process and positively influence your subconscious mind. Only what you do daily influences the subconscious mind.

Depression comes from a disconnection to your higher self. Listen to the higher voice inside of you, which is God speaking. God is not what's described in religious holy books, but the Higher Self. Get your mind toned and in shape through self-study and reflection. It's more important to have your spiritual self in shape first, before being concerned with your outside look. Getting your mind in shape produces a clear and focused mind. Originally, our minds were perfect when we were born, due to the fact that our minds were blank sheets created by God. This pureness inside of us was corrupted by the world outside of us, and even now, we all struggle with the external world. You overcome the struggles of life through an awareness of your connection to your higher self. Being spiritually minded allows you to hear the God inside of you. Most people listen to the world (media, religion, educational system) instead of the God inside of them. The voice of God inside of you is always speaking. You just have to listen to the God that's in all of our hearts for yourself instead of following someone else's vision of what God is.

Enlightened living is staying disconnected from the Judeo/ Christian/Muslim way of seeing the world. The real God has nothing to do with organized religion. The only reason religious fundamentalists get results is because of their strong faith, which withdraws the power of their own minds. Religious scriptures are only good for their deeper meanings. Jesus and other religious heroes revealed themselves to show you what you can do. You realize that potential when you substitute religious holy book characters with yourself. When you really study various spiritual books, you'll discover that the holy heroes didn't reveal themselves to prove what they could do, but represent what God-realized humans can do out of the same state of consciousness.

The signs of God are all around you, but you have to live in the present moment in order to see them. Try to be a little more present than you currently are, which helps you stop thinking about life's distractions. Being (intense present moment awareness) frees you from the entanglements of the world. Organized religion, specifically Christianity teaches that we are born with a void that only God (Jesus) can fill. The emptiness some feel is attributed to the lack of a religious savior in one's life, but in reality, the void is filled by a union with God and your higher self. God is within, so religious holy books, religious dogma, and attending the meetings of religious institutions aren't needed. There's no need to worship anything outside of yourself.

Spend a few minutes in meditation each day. Going into a peaceful, reflective state should always be an essential part of your daily routine. Even five minutes a day will connect you to divine answers within. Trying to do better every day is a journey for all of us, and silence will help us. The less you talk, the more you'll be able to hear everything God is trying to reveal to you. Stop talking, sit in silence, and start listening to your higher self. Meditation clears your mind of distractions and helps you to watch the world instead of being overwhelmed by it. Watching your thoughts gives you control over them. Keep your mind on God and reflect on all the things you have to be thankful for. Don't use your mind to focus on the dark side of life. Only think about good things.

Religious prayer based on the teachings of religious holy books is a HOAX! Prayer, based in organized religion, is a religious scam due to its narrow limited concept. In reality, everything you think and say is a prayer. There's no need to set aside a time for religious prayer because everything is prayer. Real prayer is really what you're thinking and saying every day. Living in the light is realizing that you're talking to God every day, every time you speak. Since your thoughts are prayers, use them to create more positivity in the world. Positive actions come from focusing on the positive, and the more positivity you put out, the more positivity the world gives back to you. Negative actions come from thinking about negative things, which is negative prayer. Your words and thoughts are your prayer to God. You're always having a conversation with God, whether conscious or unconscious.

Create daily rituals to help you stay focused on the work in process. Universal law says that your dedication to hard work will pay off. People who work hard at everything they do will be noticed and rewarded for their dedication. Even if they don't get a financial reward, they will get something. The value of your hard work will help you to rise up. Some people may be stuck in a job they hate and believe isn't worth their energy. Thinking that you're too good for a job hinders your connection to the Power of God. Humility is needed to realize that any job you may have to work for survival purposes is worth your while. Great things arise from small things honored. You have to be faithful with the few before you can be elevated to a ruler over much. The Book of Proverbs says, "All hard work brings a profit, but mere talk leads to poverty."

Focused effort brings results. When trying to get into something new, you may need to work your hardest for free until those in authority notice your dedication and effort. Work your hardest to make the most out of any opportunity that comes your way. Hard work, dedication, and faith are needed to succeed because nothing is going to just fall into your hands. Start today instead of waiting for something to happen for you. Before taking action, get your spirit right first by overcoming mental barriers. Poverty or prosperity is only in your mind. Everyone is pretty much doing the best they can in life, so never condemn yourself or others. Block all past failures out and get fully engaged in what you're doing now. Your dreams can come true if you'll invest all of your effort into them.

Worrying about the past or future does nothing. Nothing good in life will ever come from worrying. Faith is the answer. It's impossible to please God without faith. Faith is believing before seeing or faith in the unseen, which wouldn't be needed if you could already see or already have what you want. Faith is for those who don't already have what they're believing for but choose to use their minds eye to see those things that be not as though they were. Mark Twain said, "Faith is believing what you know ain't so." So if your vision isn't a reality, faith is needed to bring it into this dimension. Legitimate faith is believing what isn't so, despite what circumstances claim. Real faith believes without proof and knows what you haven't seen yet. I'm not talking about religious faith here. Religious faith is for those who can't think for themselves and have no ideas of their own. Organized religion is rooted in blind faith, but doubt will get you a real spiritual education.

Be aware of the people you allow to surround you. Being around spiritual and hardworking people will make you spiritual and hardworking because you will become like the people around you. To achieve your goals in life, you must also listen to the right people. People will usually share what they've gone through, which will help you from getting tripped up. Those who've experienced obstacles which you haven't experienced yet are available to share knowledge with you to save you time, energy, and mental anguish. Every day there are people around you available to share their wisdom with you, which is why we have two ears and one mouth. Opening yourself to the experiences of another person will help you find an easier path in life.

Accept the blame for any life condition you're experiencing instead of pointing the finger at some external force. When you believe that someone else is responsible for your position, you'll fail to look within to discover the true cause. Only by taking responsibility can you improve your condition. No matter how bad things are, resilience and hard work will change things. Never give up no matter how often things don't go your way. Sri Swami Satchidananda said, "There is something good in all seeming failures. You are not to see that now. Time will reveal it. Be patient."

Highs and lows are a part of every human life. All life paths consist of obstacles. People want to quit every time they suffer a perceived setback, confusing it for a failure. Setbacks are part of one's journey to success. The only reason people don't reach the finish line is because they quit due to a setback. When something doesn't work, you've gained knowledge as to what not to do the next time. You've only failed by quitting. Holding onto your mistakes hinders your path and fills your mind with worry and fear.

Universal law says that you will overcome as long as you never quit. The human experience involves running into walls. Mistakes are learning opportunities when you acknowledge them. Good and bad experiences are your teachers. Learning from your failures by analyzing and understanding what you've done wrong gives you wisdom and knowledge. Actually, failure is a myth and there is no such thing. Dennis Waitley says, "There Are no mistakes or failures, only lessons." As you accept your mistakes and learn from them, you will be more successful as a result of building on 'perceived' failures. As long as you don't give up, you'll do better. Colonel Sanders was rejected by 1,000 financial backers before his Kentucky Fried Chicken restaurant found a financial backer. When you believe in your vision, you won't be distracted by how many times someone tells you "no." Most people would've given up before 1,000 rejections, but Colonel Sanders looked at massive rejections as an obstacle to be overcome. When you really believe in your vision, you won't look at yourself as a failure when someone turns you down.

Other people will attempt to talk you into failure, but you must listen to your dream instead of the negativity coming from dream-killers. No one will just waltz through life, for every life consists of obstacles. Robert Tepper explains this principle in his song 'No Easy Way Out.' It's a comforting belief to believe that everything is just the way God planned it. Detach yourself from the emotions of worry and fear. Take risks and pursue your passions. Work towards what you want without being attached to the result of your effort. The concept of detachment is the only sane way to live. You'll realize your dreams after you detach yourself from the fear of failure. Giving up attachment to the results is a part of the creation process. Deepak Chopra says in his book 'The

Seven Spiritual Laws of Success,' "In order to acquire anything in the physical universe, you have to relinquish your attachment to it. This doesn't mean that you give up the intention to create your desire. You give up your attachment to the results."

Don't feel guilty about any honest mistakes you've made in life. Detach yourself from the things of the past and focus on what needs to be done in the present. Detach yourself from guilt, then focus on getting back to where you want to be. The process of life involves making progress and slipping backwards. No one is ever going to get things right all the time. Staying persistent is what will make your dreams come free. All perceived failures are a test of your resilience. Success doesn't happen overnight, and nothing is going to happen on your timetable. Unforeseen disappointments are a part of every day life. Only those who refuse to quit will be rewarded and kept moving forward in life. Universal law says that the world will always reward individuals who don't quit. Persistence is strength, and you will posses it if you really believe in your idea.

The Formula For Creating

Everyone has beliefs deeply ingrained within their subconscious minds. Negative beliefs sabotage your efforts at creating anything positive. Through religious institutions, the mainstream news media, and bearers of bad news, people mistakenly take limiting beliefs upon themselves. Religious programming has convinced some to accept untrue beliefs about money that are unproductive. So what, money can't buy happiness, neither can poverty! Happiness comes from within as a result of creating a life that has meaning and value. You can be happy and successful with or without money. The wealthy aren't all greedy; for all economic levels consist of both greedy and generous people.

Adopting faulty beliefs about money makes one out of balance. It's usually not money, but the lack of money that's the root of most problems. Some religious fundamentalists believe that money is unspiritual because of the biblical quotation, "The love of money is the root of all evil." Riches by themselves are neither good or bad, it's the consciousness behind the riches. Money is a form of energy and is not bad in spiritual terms. In the right hands, the energy of money has incredible potential for good. Having a lot of money or not having money is good. There are some cultures and spiritual traditions that view poverty as a blessing (they take a vow of poverty to avoid identifying with the material world). On the other side of the money debate, King Solomon was the richest man in the world during his time. Christ spoke highly of King Solomon, and numerous biblical passages speak of him in the highest esteem.

What you create in your own life adds to the whole. You can only create and manifest according to your understanding. The love of money is loving the good that money can do. Those who manage and use money well should have a lot of money because they have an enormous potential to do good with money. Anyone who recognizes social responsibility will naturally find themselves dispersing money in ways that will help/benefit others. Most of the good works on Earth are a combination of money and vision. Mother Teresa personally took a vow of poverty, but her foundation raised millions of dollars for shelters and hospitals. The only reason her work did not have a minimal effect on the poor and homeless is because of the abundance of money flowing through her foundation. Money is good, but don't be a slave for it.

Money affords one the benefits of freedom, material comforts, self-expression, and other good reasons to have money. As you appreciate and acknowledge the good that money can do, the law of abundance will begin working in your life. Failure helps no one, but your success helps many people. Feel good about having lots of money. If you don't view money properly, you're unlikely to have it. The amount of money you'll eventually possess will be determined by your beliefs about it. Convince yourself that you are successful and prosperous. Entertaining the thought of anything else will sabotage you. The secret to abundance is to feel good about wealth, money, and success.

If you have a really strong desire to accomplish your mission in life, you'll refuse to recognize the word impossible. Living the life of your dreams is not easy because while working towards it, those around you will label you as unrealistic or a dreamer. Use your mind to imagine your new life as true, while continuing to search for opportunities in the external. Success only comes to those who are able to rebound again and again from habitual rejection. People who've searched for financing for their business visions have been turned down multiple times daily for months to years. Those who've succeeded approached numerous organizations, being turned down by all of them until one finally agreed to undertake their project. Let not your heart be troubled.

Vision and persistence are needed to devote yourself to the outcome of your faith. Hold your vision clearly in your mind while doing whatever is necessary to attract new conditions to you. Don't allow yourself to entertain any thought of what you don't want. Get rid of all faulty and limiting beliefs. Daily mind power exercises ensure that you're programming yourself for success. Condition your mind by repeating your affirmations daily for 90 days without missing a day. Allow your self-talk to assist you immeasurably. Throughout the day, repeat both to yourself and others how things will go down. Create a statement that represents what you want to happen in your life and repeat it like a mantra. It helps to notice what you're repeating over and over again to yourself. Everything you say is either encouraging yourself or putting yourself down. What you say is either filling you with thoughts of confidence and inspiration or fear and worry.

The inner voice of God is talking to you all the time. Everyone has conversations with God every day. In addition to listening to the voice of God, use positive self-talk for moral support. The phrases you mentally repeat to yourself are talking you into that exact situation. Talking about anything that you don't want to happen is programming yourself to fail. Expecting the worst causes it to occur. No matter how bad your life situation looks, use your self-talk for an empowering effect. Only speak that which reinforces your belief in yourself.

Throughout the day, take a few minutes to repeat positive statements. The way you talk to yourself is what's most important. Spiritual law says that you will believe whatever you repeat to yourself often enough. Whatever you tell yourself enough times you'll eventually believe. You'll accept that which you tell yourself over and over and over and over again and again. As a human, you have the power to decide what you say. Many people have changed their lives by saying things to themselves, writing out affirmations, or writing out their goals 15 times every day. Once you choose your own mind power practice, follow through with it no matter what happens or how disappointing the circumstances are.

Choose the thoughts that go through your mind. You will become what you think about all day long. Be selective with what you think about and say to yourself. Negative self-talk is the source of failure and most negative experiences. You will become what you're habitually describing to yourself. Take some time to create empowering beliefs to say to yourself, then begin saying them for 90 days. The principle is the same, whether your affirmations take the form of writing or speaking to yourself. As you imprint new ideas several thousand times, unexpected things will happen to you all the time. How you think of yourself determines what happens in your life.

Success is a powerful vibration of energy. Once you build a success vibration, it will attract more success to you. Recognizing yourself as successful creates a success vibration. You create your own success vibration by focusing only on your positive qualities, acknowledging past success, and giving your attention to your past and present achievements. We all have negative and positive qualities, but should regularly focus on the positive qualities we possess. Most people have the habit of putting more emphasis on their negative parts. Neglect of positive reinforcement creates a failure consciousness, which attracts more failure.

Create more success by letting your mind concentrate for several minutes on any success you're already experiencing. A success vibration can be built by doing mental exercises for 5 minutes every day! All past and present success is a potential source of power for you when you re-use success energies from your past achievements. Focus regularly on your past achievements again and again, even if they happened many years ago. Focusing on any past achievement in the present moment creates success energy in the now to assist you to further success. Create a success vibration by remembering your past success.

Life consists of successes and failures, victories and defeats. Our failures and defeats shouldn't be focused upon, while our successes and victories should be relived to empower us. Examine your life to discover anything that makes you feel successful or victorious. Acknowledge everything positive and anything that makes you feel good about yourself. Always have your goals in your mind and think about succeeding. Keeping your attention on the positive side of life will keep you from being intimidated by setbacks or when other people attempt to discourage you. As you keep your mind on past and present successes and victories, you're creating a vibration of success.

You have to have the right attitude for success. Charles Schwab said, "A man can succeed at almost anything for which he has unlimited enthusiasm." Enthusiasm means to be inspired. The word enthusiasm comes from the Greek word 'enthous,' meaning 'inspired.' When you become inspired by Life/God to do something, your whole being becomes charged with confidence. Enthusiasm makes it hard for you to fail. People around you will feel your enthusiasm and be influenced by it. Enthusiasm flows naturally when you're excited and inspired by what you're doing. Take steps to create enthusiasm by becoming more excited and inspired about your goals. Your thoughts and beliefs are the source of your enthusiasm, which comes from within. Your enthusiasm is birthed from an inner conviction that what you're working on is valuable, good, and important.

Become inspired and excited about your goals. Keep your mind on the positive side of life by taking a few minutes every day to think about all the joys and blessings that life affords you. Acknowledge and give thanks for everything good in your life. Be grateful for all positivity: friendships, passion, music you enjoy, health, intellectual stimulation, the beauty of nature and art, and free will. Thinking about why it's good to be alive or why it's important that you are successful in life keeps your mind thinking properly. Philippians 4:8 says, "Finally, brothers, whatever things are true, whatever things are honest, whatever things are lovely, whatever things are of good report; if there be any virtue, and if there be any praise, think of these things."

Your inner state of being affects how others respond to you. When you're convinced, others will become convinced. When you say what you sincerely believe in your heart, others will believe what you're saying. Begin by imprinting key points into your consciousness. Anything can be achieved by harnessing your mind. The imprinting process can help you achieve what you previously thought unattainable. Enthusiasm allows you to accomplish almost anything and opens the door for intuition to flow to your conscious mind. As you practice mind power daily, you'll regularly receive inspiring ideas and divine guidance to assist in the achieving of your goals.

Whatever you want to do in life, opportunities are everywhere. Opportunities exist in abundance in unexpected places. You have to open your inner eyes (your intuition) to discover them. Your ordinary eyes will miss opportunity, but your inner eyes know that there's more out there. Opportunities are rarely noticeable and are usually disguised as inconsequential events, problems, or difficulties. Opportunities hidden in unusual places won't be found until you attune yourself to expect, look for, or see them. Great change brings new opportunities, but you have to follow your instincts in the same places where others found nothing.

You will receive what you believe in all areas of life. Mark 9:23 says, "Jesus said unto him, If thou canst believe, all things are possible to him that believeth." If you believe that there are no opportunities left, you won't find any. When you believe that opportunities are everywhere, you'll look (take action) until you discover them. Your inner eyes and instincts will recognize opportunities when they appear. You can use your words to program your mind to believe that abundant opportunities are everywhere. The idea of no opportunities is a myth. Opportunities are everywhere, and there's money to be made (almost) anywhere. Millions of people have turned their inspired ideas into fortunes. Unusual and new ideas have made people millionaires many times over. Jeff Bezos believed that opportunities were everywhere and left his high-paying hedge-fund manager job to found Amazon. com. It doesn't matter what age you pursue opportunities; Colonel Sanders of Kentucky Fried Chicken fame didn't reap financial abundance until he was in his 60's.

Ignore what others want for you and follow your passion instead. Shakespeare said, "This above all, to thine own self be true..." National polls reveal that over 80% of the working population don't enjoy their jobs. Work consumes much of our lives, so we should do what we love. It's a tragic statistic that the majority of workers don't enjoy what they're doing. The achievements of the successful are related to the enjoyment they derive from the work they do. Success comes from doing a job you enjoy working in. You are more likely to prosper when you find your passion and devote yourself to it. Working at an occupation you dislike makes it harder for you to get ahead. People don't usually make fortunes doing what they dislike. Explore life and choose something to pursue that you believe in and are excited about.

Forget what others want you to do. Follow YOUR dream. You will succeed when you find something that feels right that you can do with conviction. Follow what you believe in passionately, even if there are hundreds of other (worldly) reasons why not to. Your calling is in areas where you're best suited. People stay in positions they hate due to a lack of self-confidence. Without passion for what you're doing, you won't succeed. It doesn't matter what your current mental state is because you can create a daily program designed to build self-confidence or whatever is lacking. When you make your mind power exercises your first priority, your perspectives and vibration will change.

We all have talents and strengths. Stay away from that which has no interest to you, while following your inclination toward specific subjects. Notice the activities that you disdain and the ones that bring you pleasure. Try to work your way out of doing what your heart isn't into. For awhile, you may have to work a job that you don't enjoy to make ends meet. You most likely will need money to pay off debts or get started in something new. All you have to do is stay open and receptive to new opportunities and they will manifest. The only boundaries are those that exist in your mind. Don't be afraid to dream. Leave your mind open to various possibilities and options.

Your subconscious mind is powerful and will guide you as you take the proper action. Think about all the activities that give you pleasure. Examine yourself to discover your mental strengths and assets. Create a success vibration by focusing upon your past and present accomplishments. If money were not an issue, what choices would you make? Follow the careers that sound interesting to you. Don't look at outer circumstances by wondering if you have the opportunity or talent to pursue a new direction in life. Trust your instincts while following your dream. Give your all to what you passionately believe in.

Get away from any job that robs you of your spirit and is stopping you from fulfilling a dream. No amount of money is worth living your whole life remaining on a drudgery job. While working your way out of a job, move in a direction that you have a passion for. Life is about following your heart and instinct. Every human has his or her own mission in life that can't be replaced or done by anyone else. Discover your own uniqueness and look for opportunities to implement it.

Observe your choices and opportunities, then devote yourself to what you're passionate about. Following this advice fulfills your contribution to the world and brings you personal fulfillment. Joseph Campell says, "Your whole physical being knows that this (following your passion) is the way to be alive in this world and the way to give the world the very best that you have to offer. There is a track just waiting there for each of us, and once on it, doors will open that were not open before and would not open for anyone else."

Don't believe in the idea of one career in a lifetime. To survive in the world of materiality, you must learn, change, and always be willing to re-invent yourself. Author Alvin Toffler said, "The illiterate of the 21st century will not be those who cannot read and write but those who cannot learn, unlearn and relearn." Every year we should rethink our present situation carefully and make any necessary adjustments. Adapt to change and equip yourself with new skills and talents. Obtain all the information you need to quickly learn new skills. Knowledge is power, which is why learning new skills provides future opportunities. Behavioral psychologist Thomas Spencer said, "the average worker of today will probably have to relearn his job five different times in his career." Intelligently learning makes one well positioned for the opportunities that change is bringing. Marshall McLuhan said, "The future of work now consists of learning a living rather than earning a living."

Doing mind power exercises every day of your life will literally transform your life. Your subconscious mind picks up on whatever you say more than twice. How you perceive and frame your life situation in your mind is being imprinted into your subconscious. Notice what you're thinking or saying to yourself. Speaking and thinking about what you don't really want gives the subconscious a very dangerous imprint. What you hear yourself say daily is programming your mind with what to believe. Your life situation is never the problem, only your perception of it. No matter how bad things look, never use your thoughts, words, and imagination against yourself.

One of the basic foundations of human living is the power of choice. Every life contains options and choices at every moment of time. Any choice you make can change the direction of your life for better or worse. Some choices are made unconsciously or with much deliberation, but either way, we must become conscious of our choices. What makes us human is our ability to choose and direct our lives. To live a fulfilling life, we must direct our thoughts, use our mouths properly, and make the right choices.

Go for what you want out of life. Helen Keller said, "Life is either a daring adventure, or it is nothing." To really start living, establish both where you are and where you're going. Hoping and wanting to achieve something without setting up a plan to achieve it doesn't work. Lecturer and author Dennis Waitley said, "The reason most people don't achieve their goal in life is because they didn't have any in the first place." Everyone wants success, health, happiness, money, and thousands of other things, but most haven't created blueprints to achieve their desired objectives. The world is full of people working hard and trying to advance in life. Most people fail at things because they don't have clearly defined specific goals on how to get there. Serious self-reflection is needed to determine what you want out of life. If possible, take time off to make certain that the direction of your life is moving in the right direction.

Create goals for yourself that reflect YOUR vision and passions, not someone else's. Only pursue those things that are in your heart. Try not to make the wrong choices in your life. Once you've set goals for yourself, they will determine the new situations and circumstances of your life. Pursuing your goals determines the direction you're life will go. Get clear on your goals by pondering the most important things you want to achieve in YOUR life. Discover what's truly important to you and what you'd like to see happen. Keep a clear picture of what you really want to be doing in your mind.

God Is (The Creative Principle of the Universe)

God is the creative principle of the universe; the Force who is the Source of all things. God is not male or female, but the divine principle; the spiritual source. Man made God is his image and created religious gods who are no more than projections of the human mind. The gods written of in religious holy books are all man-made and failed attempts of male humans to define the Divine. God is not a man, nor a male with a Son, but the Highermost Creative Principle. The unlimited creative power in the universe is god waiting to change your reality based on your own thinking. We are all divine creations and can utilize the power of God (the creative principle). As extensions of God, we can create via our thoughts and beliefs.

The Bible is symbolic and represents universal principles. Religious interpretations of scripture only lead to bondage and oppression. Religious scriptures are only beneficial for their esoteric meanings. Avoid religious dogma and interpret all ancient holy scriptures esoterically. John 8:32 says, "And ye shall know the truth, and the truth shall make you free." Jesus wasn't talking about some sort of shallow truth, such as a religious doctrine, but the truth of who you are beyond your name and physical form. The highest truth of mankind is knowing who you are in essence, which frees you from the cares of this world. You overcome the world by living through your timeless invisible indestructible nature and working with God (the creative principle). Sin is symbolic for unconsciousness, or not knowing who you are beyond the physical. Only knowing the world of form is sin, or unconsciousness, because you're not living through your eternal indestructible essence. Once the truth (of who you are beyond worldly identifications) makes you free, through knowing it, you'll be conscious of your Divinity and express it. Christianity isn't the only path to God and eternal salvation. Those who misinterpret Jesus worship him as the savior and only Son of God. Jesus isn't the only savior. Jesus represents an enlightened being and the embodiment of the Christ

91

consciousness (awareness of one's inner Divinity). Even now, I'm one of the thousands of people functioning as a savior in the Earth. My books are designed to show you the Way, the Truth, and the Life. Following the principles therein makes one the Light of the World.

Interpret all religious scriptures esoterically, or else you'll miss their deeper meaning. Father in the Bible means the Highermost Creative Principle. God is the spiritual source. The Devil, is there such a thing? No!! Satan is symbolic. The Devil is your own mind when it operates against you through its own belief and thought power. Using your thoughts and words against yourself is 'demonic activity.' Through misuse of mind power, you become your own devil. God is the only Divine power in the universe. There is no other power than God; the divine principle symbolized in the Book of Isaiah. Isaiah 45:5 says, "I am the Lord, and there is none else, there is no God beside me." Esoterically speaking, the Creative Principle is the only Power. The Devil is simply your misunderstood or misused power coming back to you as a result of negative thinking.

John 1:1 says, "In the beginning was the Word, and the Word was with God, and the Word was God." Your word is your God. Your word IS ALSO any thought, feeling, or idea. Every life situation and circumstance begins with your word. All conditions in your life began in your thought life, mouth, and feelings. The law of the effect of the Word says that your thought, feeling, and word precede physical manifestation. John 1:14 says, "And the Word became flesh,..." The word always becomes flesh. Your word is everything. Everything you say, think, and feel is always manifesting into form as your life experience.

In the Bible, I Am is God (Exodus 3:14). I Am is the nature of divine principle, which declares that you will become whatever you add to the I Am. The Law of I Am says that whatever you put "I Am" in front of, you become. This is why the Bible says in Joel 3:10, "let the weak say I Am strong." 'I Am' is the name of the Lord in the Christian scriptures. Lord, esoterically, means spiritual law;

symbolic of the Principle of Life. You reap according to the words you sow after "I Am." One of the 10 Commandments says, "You shall not take the name of the Lord your God in vain, for the Lord will not hold him guiltless who takes his name in vain." Taking the Lord's name in vain is symbolic of one who is unconscious of his or her power. Watch your words.

The Lord is the great Law of Life. Instead of trying to define God based on religious holy books, leave God nameless. God has nothing to do with organized religion. Religious institutions serve a man-made god, created for the benefit of religious leaders, those in authority, and businessmen in the Temple. All of the world's major religions (3) serve a false god. Believe in the God in you; for all are God in the flesh. The life purpose of every individual is to become conscious of his or her Divinity and express it. You don't find God by turning to institutionalized religion. You don't know God because you're familiar with a religious holy book attributed to the authorship of God. Eckhart Tolle, author of 'Gateways to Now,' published by Inner Life Experiential Audio, says, "God, or Love, is the essence of who you are. God is not an entity that somehow is in space and controls everything. God is the essence of your Being. If you go deep enough, you find that essence." Since God is your innermost essence, you don't need to seek God in holy books, religious meetings, and religious rituals.

We are all divine creations and extensions of God. What Christians believe about the divinity of Jesus is true of all human beings. We are all God in the flesh. God is the Divine Intelligence; not one of the gods written about in some religious holy book. The Divine Intelligence is limitless and is who you are. Trust in the inner divine part of yourself; for 'God is' within. Live through the sacred part of yourself, knowing that the outer reflects the inner. The Divine Mind doesn't differentiate between the inner and the outer. Changing your 'inner' beliefs changes 'outer' form. All change begins on the mind-level. Your body responds to your beliefs and is a construct of the mind. All bodily diseases exist in the mind of the personality and can be healed instantly by changing your thoughts and beliefs. Become a master of your own mind. A fundamental law of psychology says that 'you will get more of whatever you focus on.' Toxic thoughts produce toxic results. The entire universe is only energy shaped and formed into matter through the power of one's thought. Sin is the conditioning of your mind, so free your mind to only create good in your life. By directing your thoughts, you're working with God/the creative principle of the universe. The Lord is the unlimited creative power. Praise the Lord!

Nothing is impossible except that which you haven't believed or thought of yet. Once you think about a goal and believe it's possible for you to achieve it, it becomes possible. Everything (within the realm of possibility) is possible if you 'could' or 'would' believe it. Extreme belief and expectation is the root of all miracles. Your God power is your ability to change reality based on your own thinking. You can't create what you didn't first conceive in your mind. The only way to open yourself up to new miraculous possibilities is through the willing suspense of disbelief. Your belief settings set the course of your life. Anything that you don't feel worthy of you can't have. You can only bring into your life whatever you're in resonance with. Therefore, to know God is to know the creative principle of the universe. Now praise the Lord – spiritual law symbolizing the Principle of Life.

The Teachings of the Ancient Wise Men

Faith is not needed for what you can see. If you can see it, you don't need faith. Faith is the evidence of the UNSEEN. You will see it when you believe it. If there's something in life that you want but cannot see, employ faith! When it looks bad is the time to utilize faith. When you make faith (believing before seeing) a part of your life, you will never be in a hopeless situation. You will only see what you believe, so believe the impossible. Don't use the force of faith against yourself. Saint Augustine of Hippo, 4th century theologian and bishop (354-430) said, "Faith is to believe that which you do not yet see, and the reward of this faith is to see that which you believe."

Examine your life for doubt, the enemy of faith. Doubt keeps what you want from coming to you. Doubt and fear both produce results. William Shakespeare, 16th century English playwright, said, "Our doubts are traitors, and make us lose the good we oft might win, by fearing to attempt." Any doubt within you is working against you, so eliminate it when discovered. If you allow doubt to remain in your mind by not controlling your thoughts, your mind will become your enemy. The world is all mental, so you must direct your thoughts away from doubt and fear. The Bhagivad Gita, 5th century B.C. Hindu text, says, "The mind acts like an enemy for those who don't control it." A fulfilled life comes from keeping your mind focused on the things you love.

You have to believe that something is possible before it becomes possible. All possibilities are based on your thinking. The direction of your thought life determines what's possible for you. Mark 9:23 says, "Jesus said unto him, If thou canst believe, all things are possible to him that believeth." Whatever you believe becomes possible for you once you've convinced yourself of its reality. If you're not convinced that you can have what you want, you won't get it. You don't have to worry about how something will happen, just convince yourself of the possibility and it will happen. Once you're convinced, you're unstoppable. Charles Haanel said, "Remember, and this is one of the most difficult, as well as most wonderful statements to grasp. Remember, that no matter what the difficulty is, no matter where it is, no matter who is affected, your have no patient but yourself. You have nothing to do but convince yourself of the truth which you desire to see manifested."

Life is about following your heart. J. Paulsen said, "The cost of not following your heart is spending the rest of your life ... wishing you had." Most people don't follow their hearts for financial reasons. If you're a slave to money, you'll rarely go after your dreams. When you have a desire, go after it. God put that desire in you to fulfill the divine purpose of the universe. Ralph

Waldo Emerson said, "You wouldn't have the desire if you didn't have the ability to receive it." Notice your desires, and view them as direction from God. Your desires are really instructing you as to what is really yours. A proper relationship with your desires allows them to manifest. Neville Goddard, 20th century 'New Thought' author, said, "All you could possibly need or desire is already yours. Call your desires into being by imagining and feeling your wish fulfilled."

You can only have what you want from life if you can imagine and feel it first. You will receive whatever you think and feel. A life lesson is to imagine and feel that you already have what you want. Spend every day imagining and talking about what you want. If what you want is big, don't see it in your mind as big. When you think of big things as little things, the power of the universe will work on your behalf. Control all outer life situations with your inner thinking. How you view circumstances with your thoughts affects their outcome. The proper method is laid out in the Book of Arda Viraf, 6th century Zoroastrian religious text, which says, "Taking the first footstep with a good thought. The second with a good word. And the third with a good deed, I entered paradise."

Spend at least 7 minutes a day imagining and feeling what you really want in life. Never imagine the worst in life nor contradict your desires in word. Do everything you can to stay focused on the positive side of life. Prentice Mulford said, "A person who sets his or her mind on the dark side of life, who lives over and over the misfortunes and disappointments of the past prays for similar misfortunes and disappointments in the future. If you will see nothing but ill luck in the future, you are praying for such ill luck and will surely get it." Bad feelings and dark thoughts will come, but they don't have to remain. When you feel bad, work on getting back to feeling good. Bad feelings work to bring you what you don't want. Changing how you feel about a subject changes the subject. Examine your thoughts to make sure that they are more positive than negative.

Life is about having fun. When you take life too seriously,

the flow of life will force you to take life too seriously. Life isn't as serious as we make it to be. Gautama Buddha, 5th century B.C. founder of Buddhism, said, "A wise man, recognizing that the world is but an illusion, does not act as if it is real, so, therefore, he escapes the suffering." Accept that which you have no control over, and do not resist what is. Non-resistance connects you to the power of the universe. Whatever you don't resist, you take the power out of. Resisting gives power to what's resisted. Some ancient masters have advised to "resist nothing."

Imagine and feel your dream. Work on building feelings of excitement for what you want. How you feel determines if you're creating good or evil. If you feel good, you're creating good. If you feel bad, you're creating what you don't want. Your feelings are your guide, revealing what's to come. Chanakya, 3rd century B.C. Indian politician and writer, said, "Your feelings are your God." Always pay attention to your feelings.

Say yes to your feelings and excitement. Bad feelings push away what you really want and bring you more things to feel bad about. Life presents things to you for you to choose what you want in your own life. What you see in your personal life is Life making a presentation to you. When you feel good about what someone else has, you are choosing those things for you. When you feel good about the good circumstances in someone else's life, you're bringing the exact same good things to you. When you see good things happen in someone else's life, Life is trying to bring those things into your life. When you greet the good in another's life with the bad feelings of envy and jealousy, you're stopping those good things from entering your life.

In the midst of trouble, find anything to be grateful for. The power of gratitude changes situations and circumstances. John Henry Jowett, 19th century Presbyterian preacher, said, "Gratitude is a vaccine, an antitoxin, and an antiseptic." All you have to do is think of things to be grateful for throughout the day and Life/God will rearrange your life. A rasta friend would always say "give thanks" many times a day before and after every conversation.

A life of holiness is a life of thankfulness, NOT following the religious man-made edicts of false holy books. If you express gratitude and give thanks daily, you are holy. Meister Eckhart, 13th century Christian theologian, said, "If the only prayer you say in your entire life is 'Thank You' that is enough." Find anything in life to be thankful for.

The power of love and gratitude will change anyone's life. Only talk about, think about, and do what you love. Be grateful for anything good in your life. Make it your daily practice to use gratitude every day. The power of gratitude MULTIPLIES whatever you're grateful for. If you think hard enough, you can find at least one thing to be grateful for. Dietrich Bonhoeffer, 20th century Lutheran Pastor, said, "In ordinary life, we hardly realize that we receive a great deal more than we give, and that it is only with gratitude that life becomes rich."

Your thoughts, feelings, and beliefs form your reality and life experience. Your health is affected by your mindstate more than by what you eat! Jesus says in Matthew 15:11, "Not that which goeth into the mouth defileth a man; but that which cometh out of the mouth, this defileth a man." The New Living Translation of Matthew 15:11 says, "It's not what goes into your mouth that defiles you; you are defiled by the words that come out of your mouth." Your thoughts and words affect your health more than what you eat does. Your emotions even have more control over your body than what you put in it. The 100 trillion cells in your body are following instructions from your thoughts, feelings, and beliefs. We give food all this power when the mind is directing the body! Thomas Tutko, contemporary sports psychologist and author, said, "Your emotions affect every cell in your body. Mind and body, mental and physical, are intertwined."

Controlling your mind is the key to successful living. How you see things in your mind determines their outcome in the world of materiality. Your inner thoughts affect your outer reality. How you view your past affects your outer reality. How you view your past affects your present and future. Your life situation is based on your thoughts about it. Confucius said, "He who says he can and he who says he can't are both usually right."

Success comes from never giving up. Work on your goals without being attached to the results. Enjoy the journey more than the outcome, which will affect the final result. Do what you love out of your love for the art, and never let outer circumstances make you quit. Keep working on your vision while studying to master your intention. Albert Einstein said, "Anyone can be a genius if they pick just one specific subject and study it diligently just 15 minutes each day." Knowledge is needed to succeed in any field, so be committed to a life of continual learning. Don't allow mistakes and failures stop you, for they also teach you success. Those afraid to fail or make mistakes will not achieve success. Benjamin Disraeli said, "The secret to success is the constancy of purpose." When you continually work on something, you will eventually succeed.

Perseverance is the key to success. Plutarch (C.A.D. 46-C120) said, "Perseverance is more prevailing than violence, and many things which cannot be overcome when they are together, yield themselves up when taken little by little." When you fail and make mistakes, forgive yourself and let it go. We make mistakes in all areas of life. Publilius Syrus (1st century B.C.) said, "How unhappy is he who cannot forgive himself." The only thing that matters is what's going on in your mind. Plato (428-327 B.C.) said, "When the mind is thinking, it is talking to itself." We are the products of our continual thinking. Gautama the Buddha (560-480 B.C.) said, "What we are is what we have thought for years."

There are no limits in the realm of thought. This is why Solomon (10th century B.C.) said, "As a man thinks in his heart, so is he." Your thoughts determine what is and what is not possible for you. The Roman poet Virgil (70-9 B.C.) said, "They can do all because they think they can." You take control of your life by taking control of your thoughts. Plato (428-327 B.C.) said, "Take charge of your thoughts. You can do what you will with them." It's not what happens to you that troubles you, but your mental interpretation of what's happening. Epictetus (C.55-C.135) said, "Men are not troubled by things themselves, but by their thoughts about them." Mind is all; the director of your life. Marcus Aurelius Antoninus (121-180) said, "Your life is an expression of all your thoughts."

Believe in yourself. Confucius said, "What the superior man sees in himself is what the small man seeks in others." Ignore your present reality and go after your dreams! Alexander the Great said, "You must live as if you will live forever and die tomorrow, both at the same time." As you chase your dreams, know that you are already rich. When you're content with what you have, you're creating a strong foundation to work from. Lao Tzu said, "Be content with what you have; rejoice in the way things are. When you realize there is nothing lacking, the whole world belongs to you." When you work from the base of contentment and watch your words, you will succeed. Socrates (Ancient Greek philosopher, 470 B.C. – 399 B.C.) said, "Such as thy words are, such will thine affections be esteemed; and such as thine affections, will by thy deeds; and such as thy deeds will by thy life."

Be willing to change. Winston Churchill said, "To improve is to change; to be perfect is to change often." Learn from others so that you don't have to go through what they're going through. Aesop said, "Better be wise by the misfortunes of others than by your own." Do your best and God will step in to assist you. Aesop said, "The gods help them that help themselves." This is the origin of the common phrase, "God helps those that help themselves." Aesop was very wise and said things like: "Be content with your lot; one cannot be first in everything." "The injuries we do and the injuries we suffer are seldom weighed on the same scales." "Appearances are deceptive." "I will have naught to do with a man who can blow hot and cold with the same breath."

Don't live a life thinking that you need more. Believe that you have enough. Enlightenment is lightening your load. The value you place on worldly possessions should be very small. Having a lot of money is not a testament to success. The less you have, the better. Live more like Gandhi. Russel Simmons, author of 'Super Rich: A Guide to Having It all,' published by Gotham Books said, "I've read that when Gandhi died, all of his worldly possessions could be counted on two hands: a pair of dinner bowls, a wooden fork and spoon, his diary, a prayer book, a watch, a spittoon, a letter opener, and a set of porcelain monkeys acting out the "see no evil/hear no evil/speak no evil" motif. That's it. He was one of the most influential men in the entire world, but those were the only things he owned. Gandhi kept it so simple because as a highly enlightened individual, he wasn't interested in chasing worldly things."

Wisdom teachings For the Inner Life

Every culture and religion around the world teaches a version of the law of Karma. The law of Karma is a Hindu term referring to the law of cause and effect. This universal concept is found in all religions and outside of religion. Religious holy books point to the fact that 'you reap what you sow,' while non-religious belief structures say things like 'what goes around comes around.' The results of your actions go beyond this lifetime because lifetime to lifetime is about learning lessons until you get it right. The law of cause and effect points to the fact that everyone in the world is connected, and everything an individual does affects someone else.

Learning life lessons on Earth allows one to enter a state of pure enlightenment. Religious fundamentalists are afraid of judgment and punishment from God for wrong actions. Bad karma doesn't bring down punishment on you, it just stands in the way of your enlightenment. On Earth, we usually stay stuck in cycles until we get it together and get things straight. Your actions affect all people. Use your mental energy to focus on the good you can do in this lifetime. You bless or curse yourself based on the seeds you sow. A good seed is responding to all negative situations with positivity. You curse yourself when you respond to negative situations with more negativity. Negative situations will always present themselves. You can't always control what happens, but you can control your reaction and response to it. The only thing you have full control over in life is your actions. We can only control our own lives.

Patanjali said, "You are your own best friend as well as your own worst enemy." Only your own actions determine your future. Every action you take in life will either move you toward the light or toward darkness. Religious holy books will only help you if you ignore the religious dogma and discover the universal concepts hidden beneath. Most spiritual practices are really teaching the importance of human beings not harming each other. As you work towards always planting good seeds, your success will begin improving. Abstention from attachment to possessions and becoming more conscious about the quality of the food you're putting in your body are examples of good seeds. Correcting your own issues instead of judging other people is sowing a good seed. Since we are all connected, you lift yourself up when you lift up others. Universal law says that everything you do will come back to you, which is why we should strive to only plant good seeds with our actions.

Work hard and think big. Stay positive and only listen to your own heart. Don't always expect to see instant results from your work. Struggle helps us to realize the divine in ourselves. Be a blessing instead of waiting for someone to bless you. You can only get ahead by giving back first, therefore, giving is your job in life. The law of giving means that you have to help someone else first before you yourself can receive, making everyone's basic job to give. God is inside all of us, which is why the process of giving keeps one inspired and happy. A lot of people who think they're taking are actually giving. When you create and sell a product that helps or has a positive influence on others, you're not taking, but practicing these laws already. Your purpose is to serve, and serving is a rewarding way to use your life. Service of others isn't always charitable work, for if you serve others to the best of your ability on a job or such, you are practicing the law of giving. Gandhi said, "The best way to find yourself is to lose yourself in the service of others."

There's nothing wrong with living in abundance and owning a lot of material possessions. True success involves a constant flow of giving AND RECEIVING. We aren't to hoard what we've been given and must let what we've received flow back into the world. Failing to outflow your inflow causes your energy to become stagnant; one of the causes of sickness. The religions of the world discuss the Law of Abundance in their own unique ways. Laksmi is the Hindu goddess of prosperity and generosity. Though money doesn't equal happiness, it can be a symbol of victory over the struggle. To the other extreme, you have renunciants who reject all material attachments (to keep them from getting lost in the world). The true way is the path between austerity and indulgence, what the yogis call 'the middle way.' You shouldn't give away all of your possessions, just downsize.

Don't fall for the world's definition of success and happiness. Giving unlocks happiness and stops our blessings from being blocked. Once you have complete faith in your mission, create out of love instead of creating for money. Practice a giving model by using your gifts to uplift others. Use your resources to give back, whether giving money, inspiration, or service. The main purpose of every individual's life is to give back to the world. Use what Life has given you to make others' lives better. It's your intention, not whether you give a lot or a little. You can give things without spending any money, like a hug, smile, encouragement, knowledge, or a compliment. No matter how hard you're struggling, there's always things you can share with the world.

Everyone hears the voice of God inside of them. Your purpose is to make positive changes in people's lives. Giving is the key to life, leading to success. When we give compassion, support, love, and other good to the world, the world will give us good back. Giving the world something good causes the world to bring more good into your life. You receive what you give, so if you give the world anger and violence, expect to receive the same back from the world. You empower yourself through empowering others. Whatever you do to others, you do to yourself. Empowering others generates blessings for yourself. Being sympathetic to the needs and struggles of others has a positive impact on your spiritual well-being and success in the world. Trying to help others in any way possible is in your best self-interest. Look for ways to give instead of take. The spiritual investment of empowering someone else FIRST, usually precedes financial empowerment and is the most important step you can take to change your life situation. Your individual life's purpose is to help others.

We are all One. Anything that promotes the illusion of separateness should be avoided (organized religion, religious holy books, and saved/unsaved ideologies). Enlightened living is embracing and respecting diversity. No one is going to hell just because they don't ascribe to your religious belief structure. You advance spiritually when you stay open to things, ideas, and philosophies that seem different from you. You become wiser when you deal with different people with different perspectives. We are more similar than different, so we should focus on our commonalities. Ignore that which divides, and give your attention to what brings people together. Without religious dogma/doctrines, we will experience the love and unity of all people.

If you study the various spiritual scriptures, what's the same in all of them is usually the only bit of truth in them. Racial and religious baggage holds down humanity. There are many paths to God; no religion has a monopoly on the truth. Get rid of all things that separate people from each other. The spiritual teachings of all religions teach some of the same spiritual principles and revealed some of the same truths. The problem is the religious dogma that claims that its religion is the only one inspired by God, and anyone who doesn't follow it will burn in hell for all eternity. Those who think their religion is the only spiritual teaching inspired by God and separate themselves through religious holy books are actually wrong. There are as many paths to God as grains of sand on a beach. Most of the religious prophets all taught the same thing, but you wouldn't know that unless you stay open to all the messengers and messages. If you're a religious fundamentalist who claims that only your prophet or savior was right, then you're a lost soul!

The division and finger-pointing of the religious community leads to violence. Fundamentalist Christians, Jews, Hindus, and Muslims are the main 'human' problems in the Earth and fought in the name of their religious gods. People separate themselves through religious holy books because they believe God wrote the one they ascribe to. The division caused by religion leads to violence on behalf of extremists. Believing that God wants you to kill for 'him' is not real spiritual faith, but the mental insanity of organized religion. The real God only wants us to fulfill our potential. Humans who worship a false man-made god of a religious holy book believe that they must convert others and protect their faith. Conversion is a human thing, and faiths don't need to be protected. God isn't pleased with mosque, church, or synagogue attendance, nor with those who kill in the name of god. Giving and leading a non-harmful existence is the Divine way. Religious extremism isn't the holy life. Ditch religion and be extreme about following your vision, giving, practicing good karma, and living in the present moment instead.

Whatever you do to others you do to yourself. Use whatever resources you have to help people empower themselves. Take care of your body and keep your mind right. Don't get lost in this physical world. Everything that 95% of the population lives for can't be taken beyond this world; you only take your mind, personality, thoughts, knowledge, and other MENTAL things with you. When it's time to leave planet Earth, you can't take your health, money, or looks with you. The fact that you came with nothing and leave with nothing means that your purpose has to do with helping others. Life teaches Earthians that life isn't about the accumulation of worldly/material riches, which is why many in the history of humanity have had it all and then lost it all just as quickly. Luke 12:15 says, "And he said unto them, Take heed and beware of covetousness: for a man's life consisteth not in the abundance of the things which he possesseth." The 'Bible in Basic English' translates Luke 12:15 as saying, "And he said to them, Take care to keep yourselves free from the desire for property; for a man's life is not made up of the number of things which he has."

Though the material world isn't as important as we make it, we should still learn how to live successfully in this realm. Smiling and conscious breathing are alternative methods of healing. Mental, spiritual, and physical senses of disempowerment can be healed by focusing on your breath. All problems only exist in your mind. Consciously focusing on your breathing takes you beyond the thinking mind. Smiling and breathing helps you overcome every difficulty you'll face in life. Breathing helps one get past physical obstacles and is used in yoga and all physical sports. In Karate, they teach us to breath during every strike, which is why we make sounds to ensure proper breathing. In my book 'The Awakening of Global Consciousness,' I said that I regretted having to quit karate as an orange belt. Well, in February 2011, through the power of my mind, I was financially able to relocate and join AmeriKick again. I went from purple to blue belt, and am on my way to a black belt in Goju/Kempo karate.

In life situations where you'd normally cry or curse, smile and breath instead. Substitute panicking with conscious breathing because things won't seem as painful as you focus on your breath. I unconsciously practiced the 'smile and breath principle' in the past when things fell apart in my life. Many people asked, "why do you smile when bad things happen?" It was perceived as smiling inappropriately, even though I was smiling about what was happening in my own life! Since then, I've learned that smiling is an alternative way of dealing with perceived problems and emotional obstacles. Smiling is a healing force.

Train your mind to take whatever the world throws at it. Knowing how to properly use your mind will give you a healthier life, both spiritually and physically. Everyone hears God's voice and can realize their dreams with focus and hard work. Living without fear harnesses the Power that's inside of you, while worry dilutes it. Focus, meditation, and confidence are the keys to success. Meditation is simply bringing total awareness to an action. Intense present moment awareness is necessary to bring more consciousness into what you're doing. Without 'consciously' living in the present moment, you'll make more mistakes, and some mistakes take a lifetime to make up for.

Anyone can achieve what they want in life with dedication, faith, and hard work. If possible, unite with other like-minded individuals because incredible power is possessed collectively. Separation prevents the harnessing of this power, which is only available when 2 or more work together on a common agenda. An open exchange amongst individuals will make each individual wiser. A free exchange of ideas and opinions is how we are to live because EVERYONE has a strand of truth in their teaching/message. The Wise Ones listen to every opinion, while those in darkness think they've got all the answers (usually religious fundamentalists following religious holy books). You should always listen to others' truths and perspectives before forming your own persuasive arguments. Listen to all sides and hear everyone out.

You don't need to attend religious meetings and services to find God. Religious holy books aren't necessary; God didn't write them and they're no more than collections of unholy lies. The truth is already inside of you, so listen to your higher self. The essence of all faiths are one. There is not one particular faith that only knows the path to God, for God is in everything, everyone, and everywhere. Organized religion is a religious scam that created the concept of believer and unbeliever. Religionists are in a state of serious mental illness because of their groundless faith in unverifiable beliefs. The Buddha said, "Do not believe in anything simply because you have heard it. Do not believe in anything simply because it is spoken and rumored by many. Do not believe in anything simply because it is found written in your religious books. Do not believe in anything merely on the authority of your teachers and elders. Do not believe in traditions because they have been handed down for many generations. But after observation and analysis, when you find that anything agrees with reason and is conducive to the good and benefit of one and all, then accept it and live up to it."

Look for ways to give instead of take. Happiness and sustainable success come from living under the laws discussed in this book. No matter what you're going through, live life completely focused on pursuing your dreams. Ignore the low notes of your life and keep pressing on. Surround yourself with the right people by cutting off all those who don't believe in nor support your vision. Most people will be faced with seemingly overwhelming obstacles, but attention must stay focused on what's wanted. Instead of looking up to religious leaders and such, focus on your higher self. No matter what it looks like, never quit following your dream. Be willing to die for what you believe in. Martin Luther King said, "If man hasn't discovered something that he will die for, he isn't fit to live." I'm willing to die to be able to release my books to help others. That's how I released my first book 'World Transformation' from the streets of Washington, D.C. with little money and no home. Even when your vision appears to be far from becoming a reality, you must continue to have faith in it. Detach yourself from fear, worry, and doubt. The Bhagavad Gita says, "The doubter is the most miserable of mortals."

The fear of death is the most fundamental fear in humanity. Fear drives humanity to religious enslavement. The 5 Kleshas of yoga lists the fear of death (Abhinivesha) as one of the five obstacles (Kleshas) to human liberation. Your physical body is your temporary home, and when you leave your physical frame, it's your spiritual essence that remains alive and well. The Bhagavad Gita says, "These bodies are perishable: but the dwellers in these bodies are eternal, indestructible, and impenetrable."

Those afraid of death spend their entire lives trying not to die and usually turn to organized religion for safety. From a religious perspective, the concept of reincarnation seems to be the way, the truth, and the life. The concept of reincarnation is found in

Christianity and many other religions. Christ said that John the Baptist was the prophet Elijah in his previous life. The church rejected the concept of the cycle of life, along with many other ideologies that promote an easier path through life. Originally, the early church accepted reincarnation, but in 553 A.D., the Christian church decided to ban the doctrine of reincarnation. They had to ban the concept of reincarnation to keep the hell-fire and brimstone teachings strong.

Death just means that someone moved on. Religionists bound to the fear of death never live because they're enslaved to religious dogma; rules and rituals that God has nothing to do with. If religious fundamentalists weren't afraid to die, they wouldn't follow religious holy books attributed to the authorship of God. Henry Van Dyke said, "Some people are so afraid to die that they never begin to live." Fear of death is the nucleus of religious thought, which is why organized religion uses hell-teachings to convert others through fear. Socrates said, "To fear death is nothing other than to think oneself wise when one is not. For it is to think one knows what one does not know. No one knows whether death may not even turn out to be the greatest blessings of human beings. And yet people fear it as if they knew for certain it is the greatest evil."

In the physical world, you can't experience gain without loss or loss without gain. It's impossible to lose without gaining something; what you lose on the level of form you gain on the level of essence. A Sufi aphorism says, "When the heart weeps for what it has lost, the soul laughs for what is has found." Death isn't really a loss, but an opening into another dimension, the realm of spirit. The Buddha's view on life and death is, "Everything is changeable, everything appears and disappears; there is no blissful peace until one passes beyond the agony of life and death ... Even death is not to be feared by one who has lived wisely." The fear of death is worrying about the future. If you truly live in the present moment, you won't live in the past nor anticipate future troubles. The Buddha said, "The secret to health for both mind and body is not to mourn for the past, not to worry about the future, or not to anticipate troubles, but to live in the present moment wisely and earnestly."

Your view of death will determine if you'll fear it or not. Mother Teresa said, "Death is nothing else but going home to God, the bond of love will be unbroken for all eternity." Enlightened humans throughout history have had some amazing views on death. Only organized religion programs one to fear death, judgment, and an illusory eternal hell. Walter Scott says, "Death—the last sleep? No, it is the final awakening." Some believe that death is an illusion (created by the thinking mind). Henry Miller advises, "Of course you don't die. Nobody dies. Death doesn't exist. You only reach a new level of vision, a new realm of consciousness, a new unknown world." Overcome the fear of death and dying.

Religious dogma causes us to fear death, giving judgment day a religious basis. Religious fundamentalists are restrained by fear of punishment, following religious scriptures in hope of reward after death. This isn't enlightened living, but religious programming. Albert Einstein knew better, which is why he said, "A man's ethical behavior should be based effectually on sympathy, education, and social ties – no religious basis is necessary. Man would indeed be in a poor way if he had to be restrained by fear of punishment and hope of reward after death." The Native American view on life and death is that you leave your body to return to your true home in the spirit. White Eagle said, "You live on earth only for a few short years which you call an incarnation, and then you leave your body as an outworn dress and go for refreshment to your true home in the spirit."

Hood Christ

Instead of getting lost in the cares of this world, set aside time for philosophical and spiritual guidance. An individual can be a profound presence on earth, even with no money or possessions. Souls never stop training or learning, for that is the purpose of life on earth. After death, we return to our soul groups. These are usually the people you meet for the first time and feel like you've known them forever. Since death is an illusion, you may have known them forever. The Bhagavad Gita, 5th century B.C. Hindu text, says, "There has never been a time when you and I and the kings gathered here have not existed. Nor will there be a time when we will cease to exist. As the same person inhabits the body through childhood, youth, and old age, so too, at the time of death, he attains another body. The wise are not deluded by these changes."

The Lord of all the Worlds dwells within, for Christ is your inner eternal essence. Sometimes the fourth dimension, which is time, causes humans to get lost in form and forget who they are. Most are not aware of their inner Divinity and lose consciousness of their Divine presence. Knowledge and wisdom give birth to this understanding. Knowledge is the foundation of all things, and wisdom is the manifestation of knowledge. Your life should consist of the intelligent application of learning. You don't have to get it all right at this moment, just journey towards the Light. Lao-Tzu said, "The journey of a thousand miles begins with a single step."

Your present enemies can become future allies, and blessings can arrive as a curse. God can help you through other people. The one appointed by the universe to help you will take a liking to you for some reason. As you direct your thoughts, things will eventually work themselves out. The answer may have been available the whole time unnoticed. Some things won't make themselves visible until you're truly ready to see them.

Students and teachers never stop learning. Failure is an illusion because pain and disappointment birth wisdom and understanding. Life lessons are revealed in all people and all moments. Wisdom comes with pain, and joy comes after the pain of childbirth. Failure is not failure if you've learned something from it. Failure and mistakes are a part of life. Gain and loss go together. People lose and fail all the time, but that doesn't make them failures. I've never had a commercially successful book, but I haven't failed because this is what I love doing. When you enjoy the journey more than the destination, you'll be fulfilled, whether the project succeeds or fails. If it fails, you'll gain knowledge and wisdom for the next project. Your new knowledge, wisdom, and understanding from life experiences will help you achieve success in the future if you're willing to work hard.

Go after your dreams at all costs without being attached to the results. Even if you go from next-to-nothing to nothing while chasing your dreams, your life is fulfilled. The half-lived life of ignoring your innermost desires will bring future torment. The horror of not trying at all is worse than trying and failing (though failure is just a mental perception). Herman Melville (1819-1891) said, "For as this appalling ocean surrounds the verdant land, so in the soul of man there lies one insular Tahiti, full of peace and joy, but encompassed by all of the horrors of the half lived life." Don't live out the horrors of the half lived life. You won't have peace and joy by living a half lived life of not going after what you want. Don't think of how it will turn out, just do it! The rapper Canibus said on his Rip the Jacker album, "...movement in any direction is progression." Think positive thoughts, do the best you can, and take action in the direction of your dreams.

When going after your heart's desire, you may succeed or you may fail, but at least you persued it. Failure and success are a part of life. You won't always know exactly when each manifestation will appear, though on a soul level, you've set it up that way. In 2011, many people failed on a commercial level; hopefully they enjoyed the journey more than the destination. The movie Rum Diary, starring Johnny Depp, grossed $19.1 million worldwide on a $45 million budget. The movie Mars Needs Moms grossed only $39 million of its $190 million production budget. The 3D film Conan the Barbarian only grossed $48.8 million worldwide on a $90 million production spend. The movie Your Highness grossed $25 million on a $50 million budget. The movie The Dilemma only grossed $69.7 million on a budget of $70 million. The movie The Thing only grossed $16.9 million domestically and $19 million worldwide on a $38 million dollar production budget. I'd rather try and fail then not try at all. At least these visionaries brought their visions out of their hearts and into our world. Plus they have more knowledge and experience to succeed (on a commercial level) next time. Releasing a project alone is a form of success, regardless of sales and profits. The rapper Canibus said, "A wise man sees failure as progress. ...A movement in any direction is progression." Fulfill your dreams or die trying!

Work and meditate to achieve peace, happiness, knowledge, wisdom, understanding, and freedom. Knowledge of self is knowing who you are beyond name and form: God in the flesh! Wisdom is the reflection of the knowledge of your invisible indestructible God-essence. Understanding is acting on wisdom and freeing your mind from ignorance. There is a reward or penalty for your actions, so make sure that your thoughts and words are going in the right direction. Only eat mental food from the tree of life, which is food for your mind. Protect your mind from the lies and corruption of the outside world by guarding what you see, hear, and say. Faith and a guarded mind can transform your surroundings. When you don't let situations and circumstances lead your mind, even if your life is hell, your mind won't be in hell.

God is within all members of mankind. God is you and inside you. You will only know this when you educate yourself and seek knowledge on your own, independent of religious businesses. The Bible can lead you to God, but only if you understand how to read it. Eastern thought, Christianity, and other spiritual or religious groups ALL have truths. You don't need any religious holy books or spiritual books to learn of God. The best way to gain spiritual knowledge is through sitting quiet and alone, contemplation, and meditation. All necessary knowledge will be revealed to you by the universe when you're ready. There's an appointed time and place for every kind of knowledge you need to flourish in your life's purpose. The ancient Chinese philosopher Meng-Tzu said, "Truth out of season bears no fruit."

You can learn the ways of God from the wisdom of Eastern,

Western, scientific and religious thought. Christians make the mistake of believing that the Bible is God's word. Anything that doesn't agree with the 'Word of God' is rejected, meaning that Christians have made the Bible God. Therefore the real God has been replaced by a man-made book attributed to the authorship of God. Religionists have made the Bible their God. Religious fundamentalists believe that they know God just because they believe in religious texts. The only true way to get to God is to find God within yourself. God doesn't need any holy books to teach anyone. All one has to do is look, listen, and observe. Internalizing the lessons from God/Life will transform you and strengthen your mind. Life is about knowledge, wisdom, and understanding, and those who reject them are mentally dead.

Your will and determination will cause you to succeed, not statistics, strategy, probability, or mathematical insight. Your obsession to win will help you triumph more than organizing and planning. Find focus and refuse to give up. When others count you out, ignore them. Stay focused on what you're doing in the midst of confusing things going on around you. The power of focus will overcome all adversity.

Life will put things in your path to light a spark in you to guide you in new directions. Follow your interests, and pay attention to new desires. Your desires are part of God's truth within you. You are one with the universe and one with God. Don't look for God in organized religion or religious holy books. All religious texts are only good for their esoteric ideas. For example, Jesus symbolizes an individual in tune with God. Following his example of consciousness of oneness with God will bring you the Kingdom of God on earth. Jesus is symbolic of one who has found the Kingdom of God as a result of being in tune with God. The savior god ideology is a misinterpretation of the esoteric message beneath the religious dogma. God and religion aren't one.

The world is mental, so you can change all things mentally. Use your mind to assist you. You can draw energy from the Earth through your mind. Use your breath and mind to draw God's energy through you. God is in all of us, so on an individual level, we must each take our place as God (of ourselves). We're all one and have the potential to become like God. Every true spiritual path points to your own Divinity. When you're lost in the ways of the world, it'll be harder for you to discover your Christ Consciousness. Psalm 46:10 says, "Be still, and know that I am God." You find God in the stillness, not religious services or books. Ho Shang Kung, an ancient Taoist, said, "A dragon is still, thus it can constantly transform itself. A tiger is busy, thus it dies young." The key is to not get consumed with worldly accomplishments and achievements. Instead of getting lost in one dimension, blend all the dimensions. This is what it means to be 'in the world but not of the world.'

To advance in life, have the will and courage to do something difficult. God may be leading you to do what you're trying to do and will guide other people to assist you. The same Divine Spirit is in all of us. God is the source that connects us to one another and the universe. God will bring you knowledge, and your reward or penalty will depend on how you use it. Let wisdom drive your decisions, not fear. Fear comes from delusions. Rejecting wisdom causes an overdose of pride because you're trusting your own limited knowledge and rejecting other knowledge. Pride got many of the heroes in Greek epics killed. Seek knowledge and understanding to assist your faith. All praises due to the universe!

God is alive within you; faith summons its force. Light expels darkness. The Light of Knowledge should be the driving force of our lives. God is the Life underneath all the forms of life, and life has no beginning or ending. Every individual has knowledge of what he or she should do from God. You dispel the darkness with the light. It doesn't matter how dark your life appears to be, for out of darkness the light was produced. The light of knowledge will change any situation. Once you embrace knowledge, you become the Light of the world.

See through the world and resurrect yourself. Be a seeker and giver of knowledge. Dedicate yourself to freedom, justice, and equality. Study to see through religious, political, historical, economical, and spiritual lies. The world is dominated by DECEPTION at this moment. Only knowing the truth shall make you free. The truth always exists and can never be eliminated. The 10% who deceive and exploit the 85% lie to those who don't know the truth, but the applicators of the lies know the truth. Only 5 percent of any given society know the truth about politics, religion, and the world's system. Even less than 5% will speak the truth freely without personal gain. Religion and spirituality are BIG business, and less than 5% of the leaders in these movements will do anything for free. The business of Jesus is all about money, and most teachers are only about personal and financial gain. Any teacher who won't do anything without being paid is a false teacher. You don't have to do everything for free, but are responsible for making no strings (dollars) attached contributions to humanity. If you're a starving artist like me, do what you can without putting yourself in a position of great loss. I can do things locally, but if I'm invited to another country, I can't go unless I receive the necessary funds. However, it's not about money. Money isn't my motivation and is only solicited when truly needed. A rich multi-millionaire teacher should volunteer here and there across country and to other nations for the good of humanity. Everything shouldn't be done 'only' for a buck.

The majority of people don't know much and are easily misled by politics, organized religion, and the mainstream media. Over 85% are misled and deceived by the Global Elite and have been PROGRAMMED with foolishness. Those who know the truth, like media people controlled by the shadow governments, use it to deceive and exploit. About 10% know what's really going on, but use their information to exploit the 85%. The rulers of this world and those who work for them will not reveal their inside information for the benefit of humanity. Anything they reveal through their news broadcasts, religious institutions, and academic structures is for their own benefit. The 10 percent take advantage of the 85 percent, who are slaves to the media, religion, and politics.

Only 5% of the population are seekers and givers of knowledge. The 10 percent are everywhere and the 85 percent are everywhere. The 85% are usually the worker-slaves that I talked about in the Gospel According to Jawara King. The 10 percent are usually the slave masters of the 85% and the executives of the world's big businesses. The educational system directed by the 10% programs the children to join the 85 percent. The 10 percent in control of all media, politics, entertainment, and religion continuously program the 85% to remain robots and have no knowledge of self.

Money is the god of this world. People (85%) are willing to remain worker slaves and dumb as long as money is coming to them. Money isn't good or bad, it's just a tool. Money is either positive or negative depending on how it's used. Money is keeping the 85% in darkness because as long as they have money, they take their thinking caps off. Money only gives you economic freedom, but doesn't free your mind from lies and ignorance. Money is the main motivation of the inhabitants of this world and their god. Use money, but don't let money have power over you.

Forces in the world try to fight against what the universe puts in your heart to do. Bearers of bad news will always be around to discourage you. Don't believe them. Look inside and listen to your true self. It's not always good to have a lot of people around. It's always good to be alone and quiet. Take a break from the world by sitting in silence for 20 minutes so that you can hear yourself. The things of this world's system (religion, politics, entertainment) are designed to keep you away from your true self. This culture works hard to keep you from looking inside yourself.

Ask the universe for help, and practice being by yourself. Prayer is asking for whatever you're looking for. Practice any form of prayer that you choose. RZA, author of 'The TAO OF WU,' says, "Martial arts are a form of prayer—they're why Da'Mo taught the monks Kung-fu." I use Affirmative Prayer. To enhance your life, all you have to do is find a form of prayer and do it. Whatever form of prayer you choose will attract positivity and put you in harmony with God. Studying lessons, reading books, and doing what you love are excellent forms of prayer. The worst form of prayer is religious prayer because religionists have been tricked into believing that God wrote their holy books. Religious fundamentalists are praying to and putting their trust in man-made myths and fables.

Aristotle said, "What we learn to do, we learn by doing." This was the case with my books. I learned to write as I was writing in 2003. The first book came out in 2006, and I am only getting better. The point is: take action towards what's in your heart, even if you don't know exactly how to make it happen. Zig Ziglar said, "You can have everything in life you want, if you will just help other people get what they want." Therefore, help other people get what they want while taking action towards what you want. Use positive self-talk to assist you. It will appear to others that you're talking to yourself, but you're really talking to your higher self and God.

Meditation will bring you the light of wisdom and help you see in a new light what the next step is. Meditation will help you get in touch with the part of you connected to God—your true self. There are many definitions for meditation, and they're all accurate. Meditation is simply bringing total awareness to an action. It is to be fully here, now in this moment. Intense present moment awareness is a productive form of meditation. You can even meditate without being still or closing your eyes. All you have to do is be aware of your inner and outer self. Walking meditations and such aren't to create, but reveal something. Affirmative prayer, creative visualization, and affirmations are to create something. Meditation is for revelation purposes, to reveal your designated path. The RZA, author of 'The TAO OF WU,' published by Riverhead Books, said, "When Da'Mo was meditating for nine years, his future self came back and talked to his current self. His current self said, "Who are you?" his future self says, "I'm you." And Do'Mo says, "What do you mean?" His future self says, "I'm what you're going to become." Da'Mo had attained a state in which he could see that time is linear but life is eternal."

Serve others in life, for those who are able to serve are able to lead. Share your wisdom with the world and do things out of love, not for money. Follow your burning passion, even if you're in a starving artist situation. I did a lot of legal and illegal things in the past to raise funds to publish my second book. Even though I was temporarily involved with negativity, I didn't do anything with a negative heart. I only used my illegal and legal money for positivity, and am now a law-abiding citizen. We all have many faces and must be detached enough to notice the good and bad in ourselves. The key is not to judge the bad in yourself, and strive toward perfection.

Monitor what you say and make sure that the whole energy of each word itself is good. Be willing to lay everything down for what you want in life and work all day and night if necessary. At this moment, I'm working hard on this classic book until it's finished. Thoughts and words must be aligned with what you want, but you must also be willing to put in hard work. The RZA, in his book 'The TAO OF WU,' said, "In photos of me back then, I look older than I do now. The prince had become a funky-smelling workaholic down in the lab three days straight, not bathing, not eating. I was like Frankenstein, because I didn't care. I thought it was worth it."

The RZA said, "Scientists have said that it takes ten thousand hours of practice to become a master." I believe I'm a master at certain things in life. On a physical level, there's a beginning and end of physical things. This moment will pass away, and all physical matter will run its course. However, the spiritual is eternal. Realize your eternal essence; the existence of God in yourself. You are God born into existence. Enlightened living is being conscious of your connection with all of creation.

Do the right thing (what you're inspired to do) with your time and creativity. Freely give knowledge and wisdom to others. Summon the forces that no one can control. Refuse to believe in failure and defeat. Those who live through defeat are not defeated, for they've acquired new levels of wisdom and understanding. If you've been beaten down by life, you're still a successful winner if you've acquired wisdom. Don't believe in the judgments of the mind. Mythology tells us that Adam and Eve were kicked out of Paradise after they ate the fruit of the tree of the knowledge of good and evil. As long as they weren't judging things as good or bad, they remained in Paradise. Once they started labeling and judging, they were thrown out of Paradise. The esoteric meaning of Genesis 2 and 3 is to not judge things in your life as good or bad; they just are. Your mind's projections of reality are an illusion. All the mind sees is shape and form, not true essence. The mind mistakes illusions for reality, which is why the Buddha said, "All is illusion."

When we follow what the universe places in our hearts, we are doing the work of God on earth. We are extensions of God's hand. Through our minds, we have Power to manifest what God has placed in our hearts. You can only be limited by the power of your own mind and spirit. The power of God to create good flows through positive thoughts, words, and actions. God is good, and good will triumph over evil. Good things will manifest in due time if you'll work towards them. Right thinking will manifest in its own good time and place. Patience is the narrow path leading to God (manifestation). It takes time for thought to materialize into our three-dimensional world, so HOLD ON. Ignore your external reality and never give up.

We are here to attain wisdom. Don't use your thoughts and words against yourself. No one can harm you as much as your own thoughts. You and God are one, and your life on earth is God Almighty expressing a different part of itself. At this moment, you can free yourself from the ways of this world, redeem yourself, and become great. If you don't have control of your thoughts, you won't be able to come out of the low periods of life with your mentality intact. You can't control everything. Most things in life will be out of your control. All you can control is your own body and mind. Accepting what you have no control over is submitting to God's will.

As you learn about the real God, who has nothing to do with institutionalized religion, you'll gain more wisdom and enlightenment. There is some truth in the belief that you're God. Psalm 82:6 and John 10:34 say, "ye are gods." All life forms are a part of God; for God is the life within all the forms of life. Some spiritual/religious groups have the true Gospel of God correct. The people in 'the Nation of Gods and Earths' call themselves and each other Gods. They know that they are Gods of their own cipher, which is the physical body, family, and home. You are the God of yourself, your body, family, and home. You can only control your own thought and cipher. This is knowing God, not submitting to religious dogma. You are God. The RZA said in his book 'The TAO OF WU,' "...you're God himself. That's because there is some truth to it. If you were to compare to God an ocean, you could say that each one of us has a drop of water in us. In one sense, the drop of water is not the ocean. It's just a drop of water. It doesn't have the magnitude of the ocean itself. But on the other hand, in that one drop of water, you can find the vastness, the magnitude of the ocean. So in that sense, you are the ocean." Like Jesus, we are ALL God in the flesh.

The narrow way is the path of wisdom, knowledge, and understanding. Those who've turned to sources outside of themselves have turned off that road. Jesus said, "Enter by the narrow gate; for wide is the gate and broad is the way that leads to destruction, and there are many who go in by it." The wide road is the path of the majority all around you, who seek to drag you down it. Those on the broad road to destruction follow political and religious leaders, not knowing that they're all pawns in the larger scheme. Politicians and elected officials rarely work for the good of humanity. These false leaders are part of the 10% who exploit and deceive the 85%.

Habakkuk 2:4, Hebrews 10:38, Romans 1:17, and Galatians 3:11 say that the just shall live by faith. Faith is believing before seeing. Faith is to be employed when things aren't going your way. Faith must be practiced and put in action. When you don't practice and exercise it, it will go away. Use faith to change what can be changed. The things that can't be changed must be accepted fully as if you've chosen them. Work to change what can be changed while accepting what can't be changed. Peace comes from accepting what you can't change. Wisdom is everywhere and means to act on what you know. A Mother Goose rhyme advises, "For every ailment under the sun, there is a remedy, or there is none. If there be one, try to find it. If there be none, never mind it."

Your mind can possess you if you don't know how to use and direct it. Be conscious of your connection to God and yourself. Use your spiritual tools correctly. Discipline your thought process and utilize your will. Your will is part of the Armor Of God and can withdraw certain spirits from the other side to help you. To increase yourself, erase what you know. Don't coast through life only doing what you know how to do. When you listen to a spiritual teacher talk about something you're already familiar with, clear your mind to accept the information as if you're hearing it for the first time. He that hath ears to hear, let him hear.

The pains of life affect everyone. Trouble your trouble by utilizing the power of right thinking. Through your mind, you can set yourself in Heaven at once. Ignore the forces of darkness and tune out the voices that are set against you. Ignore the forces trying to pull you away from your dreams. Living in the past makes one blind to the gifts of the present. Focus on what's right in front of you and ignore the bad experiences of the past. Rumi said, "Past and future veil God from our sight; burn them both up with fire."

Only see good. Only speak of good. All returns to calm after the aftermath of the storm. Religious ministers tell religious believers to "go through the storm with God." The mistake they make is believing that the God of the Bible is the real God. God is within you. Religion and holy books are unnecessary. The devilishment in the world is the result of man, not some Devil. Man functions as God and the Devil on earth. Men are functioning on the earth as devils and won't be able to conquer Hell until they deal with the evil (unconsciousness) in themselves. Don't look to religious institutions to bring you closer to God; you find God by looking inside of yourself.

Change your thoughts and the source of negative thoughts. Devilish thoughts attack everyone, which is why we must learn the right way to think. Avoid the things or people that make you think the wrong way. We all radiate thoughts and can build or destroy with them. Our personal thought lives must be correctly mastered and executed. The world is all mental, which is why our thoughts are the governing, dominating power on earth. The man-made creations all around you came from the thoughts of people. Do what you love, and the power of the universe will assist you. Without doing what you love, you'll have no sense of purpose.

Part 3: Knowing the Truth Will Make You Free

- Peace Be Still!

- A New Way of Thinking

- Conspiracy to Overthrow the Mind

- Mass Mind Control, Social Engineering, & Media Manipulation

- Be Not Deceived!

- Vaccines Kill, Steal, & Destroy

- Save the Children!

- Hell on Earth

Peace Be Still!

When the trials and tribulations of life kick in, trust that you will be okay. We are responsible for our own happiness, which comes from controlling our thoughts. You can't stop thoughts from entering your mind, but you can stop them from remaining there. Work at being comfortable with life as it is by casting out all thoughts posing a threat to your inner peace. Stop struggling with how you wish life would be. Accept what is because some things won't come into your life until after you surrender.

You have to live life a certain way in order to live a life of inner peace. Become comfortable with not knowing. When you acknowledge and accept that you don't know, the power of life itself will bring people to share their wisdom with you, open new doors for you, and guide you into new places. God is always teaching, so pay attention to the knowledge that comes simply from being alive. Live your life without judgment. Remember, Adam and Eve were kicked out of Paradise after they judged life as good and bad. Eating of the Tree of the Knowledge of Good and Evil is mentally judging "I like this" or "I don't like that." When you think 'this is good' or 'this is bad,' you will be kicked out of mental Paradise. You live in Paradise by accepting what is, going with the flow of life, and not labeling the situations and circumstances of life as good or bad.

Look at life without judging yourself and your life situation. On a higher level, there is no such thing as right or wrong choices. Every choice one makes is simply his or her own path to wholeness. Everything you go through is what you need for the evolution of your consciousness. Don't make things rougher by judging your life. All choices are different paths to wholeness, whether you perceive them as good or bad choices. Some of our paths to wholeness are arduous. There are no mistakes, believe it or not. The greatest works of personal development come from our 'perceived' mistakes.

In the midst of hell on earth, some people find comfort in

religious belief structures. Religion can be both good and evil, and usually helps people psychologically. The only truth in organized religion is that which is included in all spiritual paths. Many faith traditions teach the same message and help people improve their lives. Institutionalized religion has a good and evil side and can be used for both good and evil. We have an inclusive nature and are one with each other and God. All religions point to the dysfunctional state of humanity and give guidelines to help us on our path to wholeness. We are all ONE and should therefore bear witness to each other's struggles. Don't deny any part of your own reality or anyone else's. Metaphysically, what one person goes through, we all go through. We should help each other because when one suffers, we all suffer. An ancient Upanishad says, "When a blade of grass is cut, the whole universe quivers."

Peace comes from becoming comfortable with not knowing. What you're going through is your path to wholeness. Embrace the beautiful struggle and find beauty in the midst of darkness. Surprise blessings are found in our struggles toward wholeness. Acceptance is the key to peace of mind. Work towards becoming comfortable with life as it is. Accept your life the way it is, and from that state of consciousness, work towards change. Your way of walking through the world isn't to be judged by anyone else (provided that you're following all state and federal laws). Instead of yielding to the opinions of others, trust yourself.

Obstacles are opportunities to climb higher in spiritual advancement. People who appear to be in trouble are simply stumbling their way toward wholeness. Everyone is here to evolve and advance on a soul level, and what we go through helps us do that. Stories of joy and pain are part of everyone's path. The process of becoming comfortable with life as it is makes a troubled life easier to bear. On your journey, you decide what is right, based on what's comfortable for you. This is your journey, so you alone must decide what will work for you. What works for me is found in all my books. I am the Light of the world.

Those who aren't comfortable with life as it is usually carry around their pasts or worry about the future. Some people replicate the past or desperately reject it. Living in the Light is living in the present moment. Fully accepting this moment is not judging this moment. The painful and the good are part of living. It may take years to let go of certain feelings and judgments. Time heals all wounds. The circumstances and conditions of your upbringing are a part of you and may still have an effect on you. Exercise your faith by believing that you'll be alright, no matter what happens or where you come from. You can make a sound choice to live differently and free yourself from the past. Your childhood affects your adulthood and is the source of many buried feelings. The experiences of the past can affect your present if you keep reliving a negative childhood or dwell upon the life circumstances of the past. You may have lost your past markers of success and are fretting endlessly about losing what you were accustomed to. You're already defeated when you believe that money is the defining factor of life. Commit to enjoying your life without the benefits and luxuries of this world.

Through the power of your upbringing, your early life may have an influence on what you do and how you feel as an adult. Some feelings from early childhood stay with you well into adulthood. As adults, we can more readily bring ourselves out of the identities our families have established in us. No one can go back in time and change the forces that shaped them. We can only choose how we'll go forward with them until we liberate ourselves fully of their influence. We can change ourselves, but we can't change the people who affected us. In dealing with people who attempted to destroy us, we can only change how we feel about them and ourselves. You can't change other people, so changing your feelings toward them is the best you can do.

To become comfortable with your life, you'll have to give up the image of life that was programmed into you since childhood. There are other valid choices than what the world promotes to you. Become comfortable with your limitations, and develop other talents. When you abandon the family script and stop living to please others, you'll discover your own passion in life. Even if you achieve YOUR passion, you may never become the successful person your family had always imagined. Some things aren't discovered until later in life, so don't condemn yourself if you haven't found your life's passion yet. Just live in the present moment and accept what is. In this state of consciousness, your life's purpose will be fulfilled. Learn to trust your own mind and heart. This is your life, not some other person's. The world's system measures the success of one's life based on how well he or she follows the universal script. This is why unconscious people ask others questions like: "What do you do for a living?" "Where did you get your degrees from?" or "Where do you live?" People ask questions out of ego to test if you're living up to the world's status quo.

To follow your heart, most likely you'll have to throw out the script and start over. Most people are blindly following along with worldly conditioning because they don't 'consciously' know the script. They think that it's just the normal way to live. The majority follow the script because the structures of the world are set up to keep us from trusting our own instincts, insights, and answers.

Accept your pain when it appears; for every life has its share of pain. Since life consists of feeling pain, try not to inflict more pain on yourself through wrong thinking. Pain is inevitable, so make peace with suffering. Our own pain may not be understandable to others, and their pain may be incomprehensible to us. Never judge another person's pain. What's painful to them may not be painful to you, and what's painful to you may not be painful to others. A man's pain is his own, so no one else has the right to judge it.

Accept yourself without approval from the world. Those who are lost in the world's system always have problems accepting themselves as they are. The world programmed the weak-minded with false ideologies about life. Every day, the controllers of the worlds programmed way of life bombard humanity with input and advice about how they ought to think, be, act, and look. The manipulators tell us what we need to do to be considered successful according to the world's system. 95% of people have been programmed as to what cars they ought to drive and what clothes they ought to wear. Most people work hard to accumulate material possessions to show other programmed humans how successful they are. Clothes, money, cars, education and such don't symbolize 'real' success. Those who don't fit the mold suffer on the inside if they're not conscious. Programmed humans tease others for being different. The structures of the world teach us very early how important it is to conform. The consensus reality teaches everyone to strive after an image that is almost impossible to achieve. Stop living for and to please the world.

Don't attempt to conform to standards that don't fit who you are. Make peace with yourself and the world by honoring the differences in others and not judging them. You get back what you give out. How you act with other people will determine how they'll tend to treat you. Hopefully you won't have to be taught through the school of hard knocks. As we accept ourselves as we are, and accept others as they are, we're living in the light.

Practice self-acceptance by allowing yourself to be who you are. In order to allow life to be as it is, you must let go of all expectations. Surrender isn't giving up, just accepting the present moment as it is. Becoming comfortable with life as it is means accepting the things you cannot change and accepting all moments as they come. This is the only state of consciousness from which to change the things you can. Understanding will help one live by this process of accepting. In the midst of trouble, some will run to organized religion for relief. If you feel compelled to turn to God, use open spirituality instead of religious God-talk. Go to the God within, not the man-made false gods of religious holy books.

The only constant in life is change. Peace comes from remaining flexible with life and moving with grace from one life situation to another. Life can change in the blink of an eye. To live a life of inner peace, we must live by the process of accepting transitions from one way of being to another. Modify your life if need be, and accept any new limitations life places on you. An ever-deepening connection to the Divine will help you see life as it is. Without it, you'll be unable to accept your situation. Non-acceptance is a decendant to hell that will make your life extremely undesirable.

Acceptance is needed when dealing with the loss of a dream, physical ability, person, or other type of loss. Grieving and letting go are a part of dealing with loss, so give yourself time to do so. Dealing with loss may involve suffering great pain. Some pain, only time can heal, and some scars will still remain. These scars allow you to help others who are going through what you've been through.

Find your own way to acceptance. Pain doesn't have to be kept buried. All we have is the present moment, so acceptance can only be done now. When moments we wish we had never experienced manifest, we're only in control of how we respond. Things change, and there's nothing you can do about it. Accept your feelings, other people, and limitations the way they are before taking action. Figure out what you can change and what you cannot. Sometimes the only thing you can do is accept.

Coming to acceptance can be very hard work, especially if what you're going through is totally unacceptable to you. Accepting the unacceptable will put you in a position to do something to change it. Some things are not possible until you accept where you are. Those who are incompatible with the world's system must accept their otherness. Reject the need to blend in to the woodwork. Accept yourself as you are, and accept any wrong choices you've made. Forgive yourself all the time. Make acceptance your way of life. Of course there may be something that you may want to change, but action must be taken out of the right state of consciousness. Once you accept what is, you can do something to change it.

Getting lost in life is often a gift. Life changes demand a great leap of faith. When the forms of life dissolve, we are given a chance to discover our strengths. We learn from our intuition when the external world offers no solutions. When you are forced to do something new in life, adjust by doing something that you like to do. If you feel that you haven't done anything in life, abandon that problematic belief structure. Many people don't start doing what they're on earth to do until they're in their fifties or older. Trying to be important to the world is the cause of needless suffering. Many people make up stories in their heads to separate themselves from 'perceived' losers and feel important. Be open, accepting, and truthful about who you are now. Trying to live up to the expectations of others only causes unnecessary pain.

We've all walked tough roads. Knowing how to deal with trouble will give you peace in the midst of hell. Misperceptions and misplaced anger will cause one to make up stories that have nothing to do with the real circumstances. A troubled mind comes from troubled thoughts, not life circumstances. You can change your mind. You get to decide how you will feel at any moment by directing your thoughts. Give up resentment. Be grateful for whatever is left in your life. If nothing is left, be grateful for the present moment. Each moment is all you have and can be sure of. Any extremely undesirable life situation can be changed when one truly appreciates each day. Live each day as a new life by accepting each moment fully.

Embrace all the change that WILL enter your life, for the only constant is change. Accept what is because it is. Your experience is neither right or wrong, it just is. Your life story is always changing and evolving. As you navigate life, never take things too seriously. Allow things to be as they are and let things unfold naturally. Clinging to what is is not letting life unfold in a natural way. Impermanence is a mandatory fact of life, so allow things to be as they are. Don't get hooked on outcomes. You avoid pain by not taking your thoughts so seriously while crying on the inside. Acknowledge all difficult feelings instead of covering them up. Use laughter, fun, or listening to music as a tool for comfort. Stay in tune with the Divine by following your inner guide and trusting your feelings.

Our inability to control the world is why we must master our minds. Surrender to what is without giving up. Work towards finding your place in life from the state of consciousness of accepting yourself. Take in only what fits for you by monitoring your words, what you see, and where you place your attention. Abandon judgment, and don't try to fix everything at the same time. Getting less busy is the path to peaceful living. All stress is created in your mind and then moves to your body, creating illness. You deal with stress by finding time to take care of yourself. Giving yourself a half-hour every day just for you is the path to healing. You can take a nap, read a book, sit in silence, or whatever you want while alone. Create a balance between paying attention to and ignoring your life situation. Instead of dwelling on what's wrong, focus on what's right with your life. Surrender to what is while acknowledging symptoms of decline. Trust both yourself and others whom you surrender to for help. Things fall apart in everyone's life. Figure out what works for you because this is not a one-size-fits-all world. Make the choices that put you first because only you know what works for you. No one gets out of life without dying, but you can choose not to suffer.

Loss is a part of life. Grieving is a normal and slow process that's sometimes life-long. Once you go beyond the state of constant grief, the pain of what you've gone through is never far away. You can suffer enormously and still rise again. Practice attitudinal healing. Those who are going through great pain are on a painful journey to wholeness. When things are falling apart, think about what anchors you or helps you regain stable ground.

Being around certain people, breathing, meditating, writing, walking, practicing rituals, or going to certain places may help you regain your energy. Pay attention to and notice what you're doing. Be careful and watch yourself (your mind). Falling down and getting back up is something that we'll have to do many times throughout life. Don't be troubled by setbacks. When things fall apart, take time to recover and assess your life. Do whatever you can to become comfortable with your life (acceptance). Joy and peace will return to any life that accepts what is.

The life you know may disintegrate under your feet, leaving

you searching for stable ground. No one can always anticipate or foresee the crisis that will befall them. We can't control our fate, and are only in charge of our reactions. We are responsible for how we respond when life pulls the rug from under our feet. We may have to sit a long time with the changes that come with the most difficult situations. It may be awhile until we have the strength to move forward. The troubles, pains, and trials of life will pass quickly after we come to a place of acceptance. Accept what is as if you've consciously chosen it. Surrender to life and resist nothing.

Some people go through uncomfortable or undesirable life experiences better by finding community. This is why people run to churches during times of trouble. Religious, social, or work-related communities help people because they fulfill man's psychological need to belong to something. Being a part of a community for years (like a church) helps form you. Your chosen community imprints itself upon you. Communities give humans security and comfort in this world because most people have a need to belong somewhere. Community can be anywhere more than two people are gathered together around shared interest. This companionship can be an environment where people take care of each other or share skills and resources. Communities help share the burden of one going through problems and difficulties. Some communities act as protection from harm because they disseminate protective information. Usually, either circumstance or choice brings us together in community. Any community that robs your individuality is harmful, and that's what religious groups living by holy books are doing. No God wrote any holy book! Most people only go to church out of habit and fear of retribution anyway.

Throughout life, be willing to change your mind. Some people haven't accepted the fact that it's all right to change your mind. It takes faith to give yourself permission to change your mind. The spiritually free change their minds and direction at any time without seeking outer validation. Don't stay in the same religion, job, or marriage if the mental, physical, or spiritual cost is no longer comfortable. We are to be comfortable with life as it is, but are still allowed to change our minds on major decisions.

Out of the state of surrender, give yourself permission to change jobs, follow a different spiritual path, or leave an unhappy marriage. Allowing flexibility in your life opens new doors unexpectedly. It may not be easy to give up what you're used to. One must learn to stay flexible, open, and let go of rigid expectations. People give other people excuses for their own lives instead of giving themselves the option of changing their minds. Give yourself permission to live your life as you choose. If not, you'll pay the price of stubbornness. Inflexibility causes great pain and suffering. Consciously work through suffering and pain to completion by having the courage to change your mind. Fear of making a mistake keeps some people unable to admit that they'd like to change their minds. When you know you're not stuck with your decisions, something will start to shift inside of you. You can plan, but remain willing to change direction if needed.

Instead of filling your mind with thoughts of 'what if,' live in the light by accepting 'what is.' Honor others, but don't let their expectations and disappointments keep you in a rigid box. View all choices without outside influence, and allow yourself to change your mind. You can listen to what others have to say, but make your own decisions. Many are stuck in jobs they hate or joyless marriages because they refuse to change their minds. Making a new choice is usually stepping into the unknown. Things improve when we're willing to venture outside our safety zone and trust life. In the midst of so-called hopeless situations, choose to trust. Believe and have faith no matter what.

Not being flexible to change may cause physical problems. This is usually when health declines and physicians are unable to put a finger on the problem. Spiritual advisors know that the mental, spiritual, and physical are all connected and affect each other. Our thinking causes illness. We can think our way out of everything. This is why working with the mind changes all areas of one's life. Meditation allows yourself to reflect and discern what the Divine has in store for you. Noticing your breath takes you out of mind and into the present moment. Present moment practice is about noticing the present moment, so when lost in mind, go back to your breath. Be with what is, right now, and give yourself time to breathe and be.

Learn from each event that takes place in your life. Some things happen to wake you up. We don't have perfect lives so we'll have to accept some things we don't like. No one is going to fix your life for you so it's wise to become comfortable with life as it is. Your choices determine your degree of comfort or misery. Surrender to the things you can't control. Surrender or go crazy. Surrender to the irritations of life and that which you can't fix. Surrender when you don't know what's coming next. Continue to have faith. Every life is marked by pain and filled with challenges. Life is a difficult journey which will test your faith to the extreme.

Find whatever brings comfort into your life. Live each day with gratitude. Your current life situation provides a great breeding ground for the evolution of your consciousness, which is why you're going through what you're going through. On this path called life, you have to trust that you'll be okay. There are so many things we can't control in this life, so surrender is the only sane way to live. We are not in control of every day life and can only choose how we respond to it. You're not in charge of everything. Give up fury and frustration. Accept the things you cannot change. Change 'YOUR OWN MIND' by changing your attitude toward something or someone that you can't change, or asking for some changes that will make things more satisfying.

A New Way of Thinking

Healthy psychological functioning comes from understanding the nature of human relationships. As enlightened humans, we must understand thinking, moods, feelings, and separate psychological realities. Live in the present moment and accept whatever manifests in your current reality. A fulfilled life comes from properly directing your thoughts. Pick and choose which thoughts you will accept. Be aware of your habitual thoughts because everyone produces a steady stream of thought 24 hours a day. Dismiss negative thoughts, which produces positive thinking. When you're feeling bad, positive feelings will return as you disregard negative thoughts. All negativity can be stopped on the level of thought. Control your thoughts.

The Wise Ones know how the mind works and functions. Don't take your thoughts too seriously, nor believe everything you think. When you understand the nature of thoughts, you'll say "it's only a thought" when a negative thought attacks. Every day thought attacks are common in our troubling world. Those without the proper understanding of thought will lose the battle with their thought attacks. Never allow your thinking to ruin your day. Your mind is the key to happiness and works for or against you in every moment. James Allen said, "All that you can achieve, and all that you fail to achieve is the direct result of your own thoughts." Realize that there is a relationship between your thought life and present reality.

Contentment brings a fulfilling life. Those who aren't content will struggle with problems. You can still go after your goals and dreams, but do so out of the state of contentment. Be content with who you are and what you have now. Cicero said, "If you have a garden and a library, you have everything you need." You get to contentment by counting your blessings. Look for the good things in your life to put the focus on what you do have. Aristotle said, "Happiness is self-contentedness."

Contentment isn't being content with your life situation and never attempting to improve it. You can be content with what you have and still work to improve your life. Those who aren't always trying to improve have given up on life. The wrong outlook on life is a major contributor to unhappiness. The conditions of your life don't make you unhappy, but your choice of behavior, attitude, and thoughts. Unhappy people focus on all the bad things in their lives. Inaction to change your situation eventually brings depression. Happy people ignore problems and focus on the good things in their lives. No matter what's going on in your life, you can find good things to put your attention on. When things aren't looking so good, counting your blessings will turn things around. Simplify your life, use the power of your words, and do what you love in life. Appreciate what you have at this moment and do things that make you happy.

Find contentment in what you already have instead of wishing for something else. Choose to be content now. Become happy by doing more of the things that make you happy. Be content with less instead of always wanting more. A simpler life is better than a life of always acquiring more and never being content. Stop acquiring and start enjoying, for you don't need more. Don't try to change others, rather accept them for who they are. The people around you will be happier when you don't try to change them. Those who change for you will become unhappy, affecting your relationship with them.

Change whatever you're unhappy with, while being content in other areas of your life. Discontented people are usually complainers and negative. The goal is to be content with life in general. You can strive for change while remaining content with a positive outlook on life. Gandhi said, "Man's happiness really lies in contentment," and "Healthy discontent is the prelude to progress." Healthy discontent is positively seeking to change that which is undesirable. Inner contentment as a person will give you the inner power to face outer challenges. Gandhi taught his fellow countrymen to make the best of what they had in India. He taught people to be content with simplicity. Gandhi's life teaches us to be content with our personal lives, but not content with any system of oppression around us. We can begin changing any system for good by learning to be content with what we have and freeing ourselves of our dependence on the world's system.

Reflect on the good things in your life on a regular basis. Create a daily gratitude session. Think of all the things and people that you're grateful for. Thank people in your mind for any good that they've done for you. Enjoy the simple or free things in life instead of allowing the world's system to seduce you into buying expensive things. There are many awesome things in life that don't cost much. Elise Boulding said, "Frugality is one of the most beautiful and joyful words in the English language, and yet one that we are culturally cut off from understanding and enjoying. The consumption society has made us feel that happiness lies in having things, and has failed to teach us the happiness of not having things."

George Santayana, 'The Irony of Liberalism,' said, "I like to walk about among the beautiful things that adorn the world; but private wealth I should decline, or any sort of personal possessions, because they would take away my liberty." Earthians must learn to not get lost in material possessions. The less you have, the better. Lin Yutang said, "Besides the noble art of getting things done, there is the noble art of leaving things undone. The wisdom of life consists in the elimination of non-essentials." We should all work to simplify our lives. Henry David Thoreau said, "As you simplify your life, the laws of the universe will be simpler; solitude will not be solitude, poverty will not be poverty, nor weakness." Real wealth is being satisfied with what you already have. The Talmud says, "Who is rich? He who rejoices in his portion."

Vernon Howard said, "You have succeeded in life when all you really want is only what you really need." A life filled with worldly possessions is not living in the Light. Henry David Thoreau said, "Simplicity, simplicity, simplicity! I say, let your affairs be as two or three, and not a hundred or a thousand. Instead of a million count half a dozen, and keep your accounts on your thumb-nail." People work so hard for worldly foolishness, when a life of simplicity would make life 50% easier. Edwin Way Teale said, "Reduce the complexity of life by eliminating the needless wants of life, and the labors of life reduce themselves." Socrates warned, "Beware the barrenness of a busy life." The busy life is usually to increase worldly goods. Donald Horban said, "We don't need to increase our goods nearly as much as we need to scale down our wants. Not wanting something is as good as possessing it." So if not possessing something is as good as possessing it, you have overcome the world by NOT wanting much!

Disappointments are a part of life. They are fruitful if you learn from them. Mistakes and failure give one degrees of wisdom and understanding which couldn't be obtained otherwise. Henry David Thoreau, 19th century transcendentalist author, said, "If we will be quiet and ready enough, we shall find compensation in every disappointment." Don't expect to never be disappointed in life, because we don't have power over other people or events. Many things in life will be out of your control. The only thing you can control is your mind. You can't control every situation and circumstance, but you can control your thoughts. In extremely undesirable life situations, controlling your mind may be the only thing to keep you sane. Don't condemn yourself for any mistakes you've made because once you've learned from them, they are no longer mistakes.

Your inner desires are God directing you in the direction the universe wants you to go in. Life puts desires in people to fulfill the divine purpose of the universe. You must work to fulfill your and God's desire. As you work towards manifesting your desires, it's important not to contradict them in your day-to-day actions. Even though God placed desires in you, you must utilize the power of right thinking to bring them to pass. If your thinking is not in order, even that which you are supposed to have won't come to you. This world is all mental, so everything is based on your thinking. Your thinking works for or against you every moment. Always make mental adjustments. Pay attention to what's going on in your mind and dismiss all thoughts against what you're creating. Only think about what you want to happen. Use your mind to focus on good things.

Thought is the originator of your life experience. We must always observe where our thoughts are focused. Thoughts can pull one away from happiness. Understanding the laws of mental dynamics will help you understand the origin of your feelings.

141

Thoughts consumed with the future produce worries and concerns in your mind. Thoughts consumed with the past produce regret and cause one to relive past hurts. Living in the present moment is the only sane way to live. Present-moment awareness is the key to mental health. Guilt, anxiety, worry, and regret come from living out of the present moment. Don't believe every thought that enters your mind. Thoughts can only hurt you if you give them significance by refusing to cast them out. When you feel angry, depressed, or frustrated, your thinking is usually dysfunctional. Your feelings let you know when you're thinking in a dysfunctional manner. Allow negative feelings to guide you back to where you want to be. Sheila Crystal said, "You are only one thought away from a good feeling."

The past in your mind only exists as the thoughts you have about it. Even though the past really happened, in the present, it's all thought and memory. The wrong memories allowed to remain in the mind can be very harmful to healthy psychological functioning. Memories are simply harmless thoughts passing through your mind. The past doesn't exist now, but is re-created through your thinking. If your past is painful, negative, or harmful, don't recreate it in your mind. The Constitution of the Universe says that no thought can hurt you without your consent. Stop allowing destructive thoughts to hurt you. The worse your life situation is, the more you'll have to bring your attention and thinking back to the present moment. Stop reliving old wounds and frustrations. Controlling your mind is the key to peaceful living.

Thinking determines your misery or happiness. Those who live lives of calmness and those who live in turmoil are both living the result of their thinking. It's a fact that your thinking, not what you're going through, determines how you feel. Being bothered, frustrated, annoyed, stressed, or upset comes from what you're thinking. Situations and circumstances are just self-justifications for your behavior. A Course In Miracles says, "I am never upset for the reason I think." Discover and release all thoughts that take your good feelings away. One thought can produce a nice feeling. Abraham Lincoln said, "People are just about as happy as they make up their minds to be."

Don't expect things to always go your way. Life isn't always comfortable. Rapper William 'Booth' Cooper says, "Comfort is the enemy of progress." Whether life is good or bad for you right now, keep all thoughts in perspective. Extremely undesirable life situations bring forth growth and development.

Your thoughts are the cause of your suffering. To maintain a sane mind, you must not become preoccupied with your thinking. Don't spend a lot of time thinking about what's wrong. We disrupt our own lives with our own thinking. Don't think about things that bother or anger you. If you're miserable, it's your own thought system that's creating your own misery. The only way to change your experience is to change your thought structure. Negative thoughts will pull you off track if you don't deal with them. Stress only exists in one's own thinking, based on his or her perception of a situation. A peaceful life comes from taking your attention off of whatever you're thinking about that's negative. Control your mind.

Negative and positive feelings come from your thoughts. Your feelings reveal the direction of your thinking. Your feelings are reflections of your thoughts. All suffering is caused by your thinking. Pain that manifests in this moment is to be accepted and surrendered to. You can experience pain without mental suffering. Thinking, not life circumstances, are the cause of your feelings. You can't control other people, situations, and circumstances, but you can control your own thoughts. The thoughts about your life situation determine your experience. In reality, it's your own thoughts that upset you, not your experience. Thoughts can only upset you if you allow them to.

Your feelings are based on your thinking. Use your feelings to show you how you're thinking. Your thinking shapes your experience. Thoughts alone cause distress and unhappiness. Any thought that upsets you needs to be eliminated. Mental health is determined by our relationship to your own thinking. Everything that crosses your mind isn't worthy of your habitual thinking. Cast out all negative thoughts immediately. Choose not to think about the dark side of life. Positive thoughts feel better than negative ones and create positive feelings. A happy life comes from embracing positive thoughts. Negative feelings are created by your thoughts and will go away when you take attention off of them. Focusing on and analyzing negativity will deepen your negative experience. Happiness independent of your circumstances comes from controlling your own thinking.

No thought in your mind is reality. Every thought is a tiny perspective out of many. Your thought life shapes your reality from the inside out. We use our thoughts to make sense of what we see. When you understand the nature of thinking, you won't disrupt your life with your own thoughts. Each thought is no more than an interpretation of reality, not reality itself. Wrong interpretations damage the quality of one's well-being. The mind interprets circumstances in the context of what it believes to be true based on past conditioning and programming. Your own thought system determines your interpretations of life and your beliefs. You interpret life based on what you've put in, which is why what you hear, say, and see is so important. We see what we see based on our own conditioning and beliefs, which is why the mainstream corporate media is so dangerous. The main purpose of television programming is to take over our thought systems and condition us.

Your life is based on the content of your thoughts. Everyone lives through their own individualized thought system, which interprets everything that happens in their lives. Never be a slave to your thought system. Stay open to other interpretations of life. Slaves of their own thought system dismiss all new information that's against their existing thought system. Everyone will not see everything your way because they have their own thought systems. Enlightened living is not expecting others to see things your way. Successful human relationships come from having an understanding of thought systems. Without the understanding of thought systems, two people with a difference of opinion won't see eye to eye. An argument is simply two thought systems combating one another. The solution is to not misinterpret others' thought systems.

Everyone's life consists of low moods and high moods. Conscious living is knowing how to function in high and low moods. While in a high mood, no adjustments need to be made. You know you're in a high mood when you're in a positive feeling state. While in a low mood, you should question your judgments. In this state, you'll take things too seriously and want to have serious discussions with other people about your problems with them. When someone is in a low mood, he or she will try to think, force, or look for a way out of the mood. They will usually unjustly accuse others while in a low mood and say things they later wish they hadn't said. It's a fact that while in a low state, absolutely nothing is seen in true perspective.

We all see life differently in different moods. Conscious people acknowledge when they're in a low mood and take their attention away from what they're thinking about. Life always appears differently while in a low mood. The worse you feel, the less seriously you should take your thoughts. When two people have trouble with each other, it's usually mood related. In a low mood, you'll see the darker side of life and want to confront others. If you don't understand the characteristics of one in a low mood, you'll interpret his or her actions as negative and pessimistic. Negative thoughts about life are produced in a low mood. When you're having a low mood reaction, notice it and don't make any serious decisions. Don't judge others when you notice they're in a low mood. Have mercy on their illogical arguments and say to yourself, "of course they see it like that in a low mood."

Most problems are caused by taking someone else's low mood actions too seriously. Allow what is to be and accept what is. Allow others to be in a low state of mind. Allowing others to be in their low mood helps them easily come out of it. Questioning or arguing with them, which most people do, deepens their mood. Troublesome situations resolve themselves when people give each other space in a low mood. Everyone has their share of low and high moods, for life consists of up and downs. 100% of the time, troublesome words and actions emanate from a low mood. When you understand the power of moods, you will not take what others say while in a low mood seriously. Not paying attention to others' mood levels is an invitation to problems. Instead of judging one's low mood actions, let them be.

Mental health is understanding the mind and the psychology of moods. Your life doesn't change, only your moods. Those who understand moods in general will have a better perspective on life. It's an indisputable fact that people say things differently based on the mood they're in. Your mood determines how you feel about something. In different moods, what you're going through looks different. Your mood is behind your outlook on life at this moment. In a low mood, you lose your perspective and see the problematic side of your life situation. Wait until you feel better before you start dealing with things. People want to solve problems while in a low mood, but they should wait and solve all problems in a high mood. The low mood will try to make you think that you have to confront someone, but it's wise to wait for positive feelings before you consult another.

Don't believe everything you think while in a low mood. When you're feeling down, take yourself and your thoughts less seriously. Always be aware of the state of mind you're in. Usually, when people are in a low mood, they take things too seriously and blow them up in their minds. In a low mood, you'll see life in a dysfunctional manner and generate negative thoughts. Negative feelings reveal that one is seeing life in a negative way. In this low mood, don't trust your distorted thoughts. In a low mood, your thought system works to keep your mind occupied with your concerns. God's way is to only solve problems when you feel good. In a low mood, people say and do things that they wouldn't do in a high mood. Never take others' low moods seriously. To get along with others all the time, you must never judge what they say or do while in a low state of mind.

Falsehoods come from the negative thoughts generated from a low mood undealt with. If you try to confront someone in a low mood, they'll be non-receptive and defensive. People want to express their negative feelings while in a low mood and are driven to get down to the bottom of a situation. Confusion and resentment come with a low mod, along with distorted perception. Don't take your thinking too seriously while in a low mood. Low mood thinking is a distortion in thinking. Give less attention to low mood thinking instead of trying to analyze your thoughts. Understand thought and its influence on you. When you don't understand the dynamics of your own mind, you'll be tormented by thoughts taken too seriously.

Low moods are a part of life, and we should take it easy while in one. When you're in a low state of mind, don't take your opinions and point of view too seriously. The majority of individuals will be full of concerns and want to deal with problems while in a low state of mind. Have mercy on those in a low mood. People are not receprive to information while in a low state of mind. When you find yourself in a low mood, work towards a positive state of mind. Control and direct your thoughts. Happiness doesn't come from a set of circumstances but your state of mind.

Don't believe all your thoughts, for all thought is relative. Thoughts accepted as reality are the cause of all of humanity's suffering. Many people are victimized as a result of thoughts accepted as reality, not the circumstances of life. To maintain a sound mind, you must examine your relationship with your thinking. Thoughts produce thought attacks when they're unconsciously accepted. Whatever you think about grows in your mind, so make sure that you only think thoughts of what you want. Stress originates in one's own mind from wrong thinking. Since stress doesn't come from outside of yourself, it can be eliminated from the inside out. All change begins within.

The Principle of Separate Realities states that people see, act, and do things differently. Conflicts amongst humans come from expecting otherwise. When dealing with others, keep attention off of your personal expectations. Anais Nin said, "We don't see things as they are, we see them as we are." Everyone has his or her own interpretation of life. Separate realities are a fact of life. We all see life from our own separate reality. Others will not see everything precisely as you do. The 'joy of differences' can only be experienced when one understands the facts of separate realities.

The law of individual thought systems declares that individuals will not see things the exact same way that someone else does. Respect the other person's position by listening without judgment. Don't expect everyone to agree with your individual viewpoints. An understanding and appreciation of separate realities will help you get along with ALL people. Know that everyone will not see life as you do. Every human being has his or her own version of life. You will not see eye to eye with other people and shouldn't expect to. You don't have to agree with anyone either. Those living in the Light overlook their differences with another.

Your thinking is behind how you feel about others. How you think about others creates your feelings toward them. What's inside of you affects those around you through the law of resonance. Refusing to allow other people to be as they are is the cause of negative thoughts toward them. Accept that individual perceptions of life vary. We all see life differently and live in separate realities. Welcome disagreements; for divergent points of view are the way of life.

Light-bearers understand the low mental state, which helps them not to focus on the negative aspects of a person. If you're a slave to your habitual thought system, you won't be able to accept those in conflict with it. Thoughts and beliefs must be kept in the proper perspectives, for they are one aspect out of many. Beliefs come from past conditioning, and no thought contains the entire truth of the matter. Accepting a thought or belief as the one and only possible reality makes you a slave to your version of reality. Belief systems seek to validate their interpretation of life, so if you're a slave to them, they'll grow while causing conflicts with others. No one thought contains the entire truth.

You should never allow your mind to cause suffering and difficulties for you. An understanding of life will alleviate much mental anguish. French born American author Anais Nin, 1903-1977, had a thorough understanding of how life works. She said, "Life is truly known only to those who suffer, lose, endure adversity and stumble from defeat to defeat." This is the story of my life, but I'm fulfilled because I'm doing what I love doing. All the suffering, loss, adversity, and defeats throughout my life have been extremely undesirable, but have brought me wisdom and understanding. Whatever you're going through is for the evolution of your consciousness. We come to earth to learn our life lessons through experience. Anais Nin said, "There are very few human beings who receive the truth, complete and staggering, by instant illumination. Most of them acquire it fragment by fragment, on a small scale, by successive developments, cellularly, like a laborious mosaic."

We all come to earth for soul development. To help others, we should accept them as they are now. Anais Nin said, "We do not grow absolutely, chronologically. We grow sometimes in one dimension, and not in another; unevenly. We grow partially. We are relative. We are mature in one realm, childish in another. The past, present, and future mingle and pull us backward, forward, or fix us in the present. We are made up of layers, cells, constellations." Life involves suffering, error, and losing, so don't get upset if things aren't working out at this moment. Anais Nin said, "I postpone death by living, by suffering, by error, by risking, by giving, by losing."

Live your life as you want to live it and express yourself through it. Anais Nin said, "Creation which cannot express itself becomes madness." Avoid organized religion at all costs, which will try to tell you how to live your life. Institutionalized religion is against critical thought and freedom of expression. You can't be who God wants you to be when you deny your will to what's written in religious holy books that God didn't write. Don't be a slave to organized religion. Anais Nin said, "When we blindly adopt a religion, a political system, a literary dogma, we become autonomous. We cease to grow."

Conspiracy to Overthrow the Mind

Network television is used for mass mind control. When you watch television every day, your thoughts are not your own. Countless American people go with the illuminati agenda because of television programming. So many people call for a police state control grid and other globalist agendas because of the corporate mainstream media. The modern science of social engineering and mind control is used for governmental and corporate corruption. People watch the daily news as if politicians are really working for the good of humanity. What the so-called news presents isn't in your best interest. Watching the mainstream media is nothing more than spending time with the enemy of humanity. There are stacks of documentation revealing that this world government isn't working for the greater good of humanity. Sooner or later, you'll realize that the government is the enemy.

90% or more of humanity have no idea of what's really going on. Most people would rather remain asleep than investigate what Light workers are talking about. Entertainment, sports, reality shows, and other distractions are designed to keep people choosing to remain asleep. Some Earthians were at least partially awake at one time, but the temptations of the world's system drew them back into self-deception (money, media programming, institutionalized religion, politicians, etc.). Anyone who feeds on television programming for many hours a day, every day, will return to the slumber of dreamland. Money is the god of this world, so as long as people have money coming in, they don't care about what's going on behind the scenes. As long as the masses can eat, pay their bills, make money, and feed their families, they ignore what the mainstream news media IS NOT talking about. 95% of television PROGRAMMING is garbage.

What you watch on television is a carefully crafted design. It's no accident that, most likely, your thoughts are not your own. The purpose of network television is to dumb down the populations of planet earth so that their thoughts are not their own. Mass mind control is a classic art that existed before the creation of the United States. The entertainment industry keeps people distracted from understanding and deciphering the systems of control. Your favorite news casters and media personalities are all the magicians of influence and propaganda. We will not be able to defeat our enemies and dictators as long as we are addicted to network television. When you understand the ruling establishment and what they believe in, you'll be able to spot all the mass mind control going on all around you.

Mind control is the way of our society. Project MK-Ultra is an example of overt mind control. It's an advancement of an earlier secret program called Bluebird. The Bluebird program was formed to keep up with the Soviet advances in brainwashing. The CIA had many objectives with the old programs and are going for the home run with the new programs. The earlier aim of the first programs was to study multiple methods 'through which control of an individual may be attained.' The manipulators have mastered narco-hypnosis as a result of many years of secret experimentation. Narco-hypnosis dominates our society, but humanity is too lost in the world to see it. The blending of mind altering drugs with various forms of hypnotic programming is how narco-hypnosis works. The global elite use their resources (doctors, network television, trusted personalities, etc.) to get as many people as possible on mind altering drugs, then use sports, entertainment, and the TV for hypnotic programming.

For many years, CIA teams have tested new interrogation techniques along with various drugs to erase the victims' memories. Marijuana, LSD, sodium pentathol, heroin, and all manner of narcotics were regularly used to keep the subjects from remembering being interrogated and programmed. The CIA can program you for their purposes, then use narcotics to erase your memory of what they've done. This is not a conspiracy theory, and if you believe so, you're a victim of mass mind control. Even now, CIA-sponsored mind control programs are flourishing. Who controls your mind? If you watch network television every day, your thoughts ARE NOT your own.

The super-secret Project MK-ULTRA was birthed on April 13, 1953. You can be a government employee and still not know what's going on. Only those in the upper echelon of the CIA were privy to the Knowledge of Project MK-ULTRA. The scope of Project MK-ULTRA is broader than anyone ever thought. According to official CIA documents, MK-ULTRA is an 'umbrella project' with 149 'sub-projects.' 95% of the population are victims to many of those 149 sub-projects. Network television will make sure that you don't know about this or anything else that's really going on. A lot of these sub-projects dealt with electronics, activating the human organism by remote control, testing illegal drugs for field use, and brainwashing individuals to function in a certain way. These mind control projects brainwash individuals into becoming couriers and spies for the ruling establishment. 95% of the population are working for the global elite without their knowledge. When you repeat a lie you heard on the mainstream news, you're a courier for the NWO. When the corporate news establishment tells you to report those who speak out against the government, and you do it, you're a spy for the NWO. Without your knowledge, you're a courier and spy for the globalist agenda if you watch and believe in what the mainstream media is reporting. You're a spy because when you hear people speak against your media programming, you defend the official position presented on network television. The TV news lies!

The CIA was formed in 1947 and was originally only authorized to operate overseas per Congressional stipulation. The CIA was forbidden to have internal security powers of domestic police. The MK-ULTRA staff broke all the rules and began testing on unwitting American citizens. CIA rules according to Congressional stipulation were just a show to make it look like the CIA was controlled by political oversight. No one will ever know exactly how extensive illegal testing became then, but it's still going on now. Over 90% are deceived and living in deception.

Richard Helms was the CIA Director and chief architect of the MK-ULTRA program. Before leaving office in 1973, he ordered the destruction of all MK-ULTRA records. The documents that were misfiled resurfaced in the late 1970's. The spy agency's MK-ULTRA program became widespread knowledge, and a few civil lawsuits followed. This form of behavior modification was just the beginning and small stuff compared to what's going on now. MK-ULTRA is not the most expansive mind control program. The types of covert thought control going on now are the most dangerous in the history of humanity. Guard your eyes and ears when possible, and don't speak the lies promoted by the mainstream news media.

During the formation of this country, the founding fathers, through the bill of rights, laid the groundwork for a free society. Even though they didn't know of the technological advances that would be made, an article in the bill of rights specifically prohibits the government from engaging in thought control/mind control. The 4th Article in the Bill of Rights promises our protection from the government. It says, "The right of the people to be secure in their persons, houses, papers, and effects, against unreasonable searches and seizures, shall not be violated, and no warrants shall issue, but upon probable cause, supported by oath or affirmation, and particularly describing the place to be searched, and the persons or things to be seized." People are starting to realize that the US Constitution and its Bill of Rights are now worthless because our supposedly elected officials won't enforce them.

The television set is the most common example of mind control. Our so-called civilized and free society has been hijacked and manipulated with the advent and usage of the television. Most of the things on TV are geared towards brainwashing you, and the small amount of good stuff helps cover up the television's destructive qualities. Westinghouse (CBS), General

Electric (NBC), and the largest media corporations control all of the programming on television and use it to accomplish their purposes. The manipulators behind media programming have interests in defense contracts, which is why they use the daily news to promote war. The mainstream daily news is the reason why Americans get behind these bogus wars.

All the networks employ techniques of brain washing and have multiple ways to make lies the truth. Radio is a part of the same mind control program. Radio has been proven to have the ability to brainwash any population into submission. On the night before Halloween in 1938, the global elite conducted an experiment in psychological warfare on six million American subjects. Mercury Radio broadcasted Orson Welles' radio adaptation of H.G. Wells' War of the Worlds at 8 p.m. CST to test unwitting subjects. As an experiment, the book's story was presented as if it were breaking news. Realistic bulletins caused one million people to falsely believe that the world was really under attack by Martians. The theatrical presentation caused thousands to succumb to panic, and many fled during the night in an attempt to get away from the alien invaders. The outright panic caused by this experiment in psychological warfare caused many not to wait to hear H.G. Wells' explanation at the end of the program. He was going to reveal that this whole thing was nothing but a Halloween prank, but most people were already gone physically and mentally before he explained what was going on.

Media owners ran the 1938 psychological warfare experiment to confirm the power of the broadcast media. The broadcasting of Orson Welles' radio adaptation of H.G. Wells' War of the Worlds on Mercury Radio was a research project. Researcher Mack White said, "Psychologist Hadly Cantril conducted a study of the effects of the broadcast and published his findings in a book, 'The Invasion from Mars: A Study in the Psychology of Panic.' This study explored the power of the broadcast media, particularly as it relates to the suggestibility of human beings under the influence of fear. Cantril was affiliated with Princeton

University's Radio Research Project, which was funded in 1937 by the Rockefeller Foundation. Also affiliated with the Project was Council on Foreign Relations (CFR) member and Columbia Broadcasting System (CBS) executive Frank Stanton, whose network had broadcast the program."

Merciless men working for the ruling elite head the news divisions of all networks and are the chairmen of the boards of all major corporations. Radio and television programming incorporate all of the effective techniques of mass brainwashing. The corporate news media is the propaganda arm of those who've hijacked our government in the early 1900's. The dawn of television is the propaganda apparatus for the shadow government, who rules the world from behind the scenes. The effectiveness of psych-political operations (propaganda) is increased the more you watch network television. Free yourself by cutting your television-watching by 80%. Stop watching the mainstream daily news completely. The only safe news is the news behind the news (alternative and independent news sources).

Herbert Krugman conducted experiments on the affects of watching television. His work revealed that brain activity switches from the left to right hemisphere while watching television. The left hemisphere is where logical thought takes place. The left hemisphere of the brain breaks down and critically analyzes information. The right brain uncritically processes incoming data and makes emotional instead of logical responses. Television watching causes a shift from left to right brain activity, causing endorphins to be released. People become physically addicted to watching television because of the body's own natural opiates, endorphins, being released from habitual television watching. Numerous studies have validated this hypothesis, which explains why most people aren't able to get rid of the television habit. Cut the TV off!

Network television raises and teaches the youth today. If they watch hours of television every day, by their early teens, they'll be intellectually dead. Anyone who watches network television every day is intellectually dead. The television is used by the ruling establishment for the dumbing down of humanity. Watching television causes many shifts in the brain, not just the release of endorphins. Watching television causes activity in the neo-cortex and the higher brain regions to diminish. Activity in the limbic system and lower brain regions increase from habitual television watching. Brain activity in the lower brain regions is associated with primitive mental functions. The reptile brain refers to activity in the lower brain regions, where the fight or flight response functions.

Network television increases activity in the reptile brain, which is unable to tell the difference between reality and simulated reality. To the reptile brain, the simulated reality of television looks real, so it's real. On a conscious level, the reptile mind doesn't know that the daily news is only a staged theatrical presentation. The created scenes put together by media manipulators cause physiological reactions like the heart beating faster or a shift in one's emotions. I'm not referring to the traffic reports, weather updates, crime reports, etc., just the programming aspect. The little bit of real information that comes through news programs is designed to make you trust the whole media presentation. The totality of each new PROGRAM is designed to manipulate you on a conscious and unconscious level.

The effect of habitual television is powerful because the mass mind control operates on the deepest level of human response. The programming is unconscious, which is how media manipulators can make us feel how they want us to feel (if we keep watching TV). The reptile brain allows us to survive as biological beings, but leaves us open to propaganda techniques. Television activates the reptile mind (activity in the lower brain regions), leaving one open to the manipulations of television programmers. The manipulators behind the media tap into your emotions and use them to control you. The news distorts information to move you in certain directions. The mass mind control through network television is usually undetected and takes place in the subconscious. Why sit in front of the TV and listen to a liar every day?

Journalist Walter Lippman and psychologist Edward Bernays (Sigmund Freud's nephew) codified and applied scientific techniques scientifically in the early 20th century. Bernays and Lippman were hired by President Woodrow Wilson to be a part of the Creel Commission. The purpose and mission of the Creel Commission was to manipulate popular opinion in favor of going to war on the side of Britain. The Creel Commission provided themes for the brainwashing speeches read at public functions by charismatic personalities. The Creel Commission pushed for the censorship of the American press and set the framework for the mass mind control going on today. In 1928, Edward Bernays wrote a book called 'Propaganda.' Bernays said, "The conscious and intelligent manipulation of the organized habits and opinions of the masses is an important element in democratic society. Those who manipulate this unseen mechanism of society constitute an invisible government which is the true ruling power of our country."

Lippman and Bernays created a war propaganda campaign to sway intense anti-German hysteria. They exposed the power of propaganda to control public opinion, and the mainstream media hasn't been the same since. American business was impressed, and through the Creel Commission's example, Adolf Hitler and many others learned about manipulating the public through large-scale propaganda campaigns.

Betrays and Lippman ran a public relations firm in the first half of the 20th century and set the framework for the use of propaganda as a weapon of war. Bernays came up with the important concepts used in all propaganda work. Lippman and Bernays' work is the foundation for the current public relations industry, and what they've developed is still used extensively by the U.S. government. Bernays coined the terms 'engineering consent' and 'group mind,' terms still used today by the programmers. Hitler's propagandist Joseph Gobbles used Bernays and Lippman's propaganda blueprint, along with the United States Office of War Information.

The mainstream media is used to support the interests of the prison industrial complex. Network television is designed to direct your focus. TV programs focus on minority criminal groups and exploit minor threats to appear more dangerous than they really are. The media specializes in the art of dehumanization. The elitists can attack the population without fear of consequence (because so many are sleeping), so they use network television. Mind scientists working for the empire use sophisticated propaganda techniques to keep you in a state of fear. Scientific breakthroughs better explaining how the human mind learns, behaves, functions, and retains information are used by the ruling elite to keep you focused on fear. All of the major news (propaganda) networks use effective brainwashing techniques to diffuse revolution and keep humanoids in check. The music behind TV programs and the flashing glitzy graphics are designed to keep you from thinking with your own mind. Entertainment with the proper amount of glamour shuts your thinking mind off and catches the attention of your lower brain regions. Just cut the damn TV off!

Stop spending hours a day watching corporate media groupies. Most of what they tell you is a lie, but repetition tricks you into believing it. Notice the repetition behind the lies that the politicians and news reporters tell us. The TV news lies are ridiculous, but dark psychology deceives you into believing them. The brain doesn't know the difference between reality and trickery if one listens to a lie repeated often enough. Repeating lies is a technique used to allow merciless men and puppeteers to hypnotize billions of people. No mainstream media source is fair and balanced. They operate on the principle, "say it enough times and they'll believe it."

The media, entertainment, and economic industries monopolize on the imprisonment and enslaving of the population. The same people own everything, for the purpose of mass mind control. 97% of the media is controlled by six illuminati controlled corporations: General Electric, Disney, News Corp, Time Warner, Viacom, and CBS. The end is here, not near. The ruling establishment has used its media to pre-condition our minds to accept a police state society and economy. What you read in the newspapers, see praised on the news, hear on talk shows, and see in movies is designed to condition your mind with foolishness. Hollywood's job is to frighten you with violent films or support the shadow government's agenda. Globalists have released movies in support of the official story of 9/11 and made other movies glamorizing the War on IRAQ. The official versions of world events are always a lie.

The saviors of the earth have been crying out, warning humanity about what's really going on. Humanity won't listen because of network television's mix of disinformation with entertainment. The unseen rulers of planet earth have won the war for our minds. The majority are slaves to the system and have lost their minds due to the indoctrination programmed into them through network TV. As a whole, our minds are controlled on a massive scale psychologically. Our culture has been conditioned incriminatingly through newspapers, radio, TV, sports, music, and magazines. Deceived humans are given a fake world reality through radio waves, ink on papers, or lies on a screen. The world is controlled by liars and deceivers.

David L. Robb, author of 'Operation Hollywood,' said, "Hollywood and the Pentagon have a long history of making movies together. It's a tradition that stretches back to the early days of silent films, and extends right up until the present day. It's been a collaboration that works well for both sides. Hollywood producers get what they want – access to billions of dollars worth of military hardware and equipment – tanks, jet fighters, nuclear submarines and aircraft carriers – and the military gets what it wants – films that portray the military in a positive light; films that help the services in their recruiting efforts. The Pentagon is not merely a passive supporter of films, however. If the Pentagon doesn't like a script, it will usually suggest script changes that will allow the film to receive the military's support and approval. Sometimes these proposed changes are minor. But sometimes the changes are dramatic. Sometimes they change dialogue. Sometimes they change characters. Sometimes they even change history."

The Universe/God always makes sure that Wise Ones are in the earth to reveal the truth about everything. I've quoted many of them in this book. These are the true saviors of the world in our generation. Every generation has humans in it whose function is to reveal the truth. These are the gods of the earth; Light-workers for the Kingdom of Truth. Highly evolved human beings are in the earth right now, placed here by the Divine to assist humanity. The gods of the earth reveal information and knowledge to deliver humanity from deception and the Kingdom of darkness. Those from the dark side (network television, media programmers, the religious and education systems, and the status quo) have taken a lifetime to mold your reality for you and control your mind. The journey towards truth begins with a single step. It will take longer than a day to fully awaken. Get things moving in the right direction by receiving what's being presented here. In your journey towards the Light, stay informed and inform others. Spreading the truth is the only way to fight the illuminati.

Unadulterated violence is accepted in video games, movies, and on regular TV. Killing in the name of government is praised as long as assassins are fighting for the system. Violence that's committed in self-defense to protect someone from the government/system is rejected. Police departments, the military, and all associated with groups that control the masses are allowed to commit unadulterated violence if they are fighting for the system. This is why law enforcement can treat protesters against the system so badly.

Network television, the video game industry, and the entertainment world support homicide and injustice when it favors the elite. Violence is condoned and condemned when it's done to protect one's freedom, land, or family from government terrorists. The reality of the elite's view of violence is transferred to video games where the plot and task is to kill as many 'enemies' as the player can. The elite want to kill off a great portion of humanity, and represent their killing desires in video games. Violent video game selections are offered and played by 70% of young children. These games have a 'Mature' rating, with the common goal of killing as many insurgents as possible (to fulfill some mission). Children are being indoctrinated through violent video games, which are law enforcement programs designed to condition them to accept tomorrow's world's weapons of mass destruction.

All politicians work for the establishment, not the people. They talk like they're working for the people, but their hearts are with their controllers. House bills and senate bills are mostly further steps in dismantling the Constitution and free speech. Bills that have already passed have destroyed (PEG) cable access centers where the general public owns the airways. Local programming without commercial gain or censorship is good for humanity, which is why it's being dismantled. The corporate takeover of locally based programming is the centralizing of communication. The diversity and freedom of public owned airways has been destroyed to move the viewers to official and nationalistic programs promoting violence, slavery, and uniformity.

Network television is the problem. Locally based programs are creative and promote peace. Network TV uses repetitive programming to deceive and destroy you. Cable access featured free speech and perspectives ignored by mainstream television. It's being taken over to control the free flow of information. The new block of programming will be universally accepted network coverage designed to indoctrinate and brainwash on behalf of the owner's interests. Network television creates the hive mind as a result of the general public's massive brainwashing. This is why all habitual news-watchers share the same thoughts, false knowledge, goals, and misguided understanding.

Beware of what's universally accepted. Our hive mind society is a slave towards conformity and fights against diversity. Mainstream television, network programming, weather, news, and drama shows are designed to artificially create your reality and world. Most people live their lives through the television set because they're hypnotized through large amounts of sensationalism and entertainment. If you watch TV every day, you're having a love affair with your abuser.

If you fall asleep while watching television, you're sleeping with the enemy. Most anchors and actors are good looking people, which is why they were chosen for network programming. Research reveals that attractive people are perceived as truth worthy. These beautiful puppets ignore or alter the real news to sell you on the police state. The media is intentionally deceiving you. Applying the principles of problem-reaction-solution will cause you to come to the conclusion that the media is about mass mind control. The elite create a problem or allow it to happen, then use their media to present it to the population. They blast the radio, television, and newspapers with an artificial problem to solicit a reaction from the people. Terrorism, crime, molestation, or any topic that creates fear is used to draw in the people's attention; anything that they wouldn't support in their right mind. The plan is for the people to request more control to ensure their safety, which was already the pre-planned solution.

There is no difference between one network's coverage of the so-called news and another's. No real education or information is being dispersed, only propaganda. Everything is owned and controlled by the same media manipulators. All television and radio stations were bought out by big international media outlets, since the Telco act of 1996. The largest corporations in radio have centralized the distribution of information to eliminate a free society. The media serves its illuminati owners, and their interests don't benefit the general public. The media acts like it's operating in the public's best interest, when its owners are interested in the prison industry, defense contracting, oil business, and other financial endeavors. What's on TV isn't the real news.

The Administration and media monopoly participate in a dehumanization program to attack those who dissent the official version of events. The truth is hidden from the public most of the time. Any partial truth is misrepresented and distorted for manipulative purposes. Indoctrination through these mediums keeps the majority attacking views other than those presented by media manipulators. Mass mind control through network television makes anything other than the official version of events unimportant and to be condemned. The media works to get us to do things their way, serve their interests, and support government interest. Their goal is to implant into your subconscious, and you allow them to do so by watching network television uncontrollably. We must recognize the system in order to beat it. This oligarchy system has a concrete foundation in our world because viewers keep watching television and consumers keep putting their dollars into the system. Free yourself by refusing to watch today's mainstream corporate news programs. If you continue, you'll lose your mind to the system, and its thoughts become your thoughts. The TV is mass mind control.

The news feeds your fear and emotional side. The whole media presentation is to control your decisions. When you believe whatever the media tells you, you will support whatever decisions they promote. Glossy news anchors work to get you believing that the government needs more power over our lives. News reporters deceive the masses into believing that the government is working to free us from tyranny and make us safer. Real patriots and activists are painted with a negative brush on establishment programs. News-watchers will falsely believe that revolutionists are guilty of treason. So-called journalists are controlled by the large machine, which tells them what stories to report. Any reporter who paints the government in a dark light will be fired or murdered. Any anti-government propaganda that makes the news is part of the organized and controlled opposition. The real news will remain off the front page.

The end of the world as we know it has been in the works since the early 1900's. Network television is where the agenda is being sold. Modern Hollywood films and network cable news offer the same reoccurring themes in the backdrop. Everything on TV is disturbing, from the central ideas of investigative reports to features about potential threats over the horizon. Even those who don't watch the news are brainwashed by channels like the Discovery Channel and History Channel. Non-news channels discuss UFOs, asteroids, terrorism, serial killers, or earthquakes to craft a message that our world is unstable. Television programming, as a whole, is about an invisible and dangerous threat that only the government or military can fix. Films produced through the movie studios of Hollywood play on this theme. Everything is designed to condition and program you.

The elite have observed that we like to be terrified. The producers, owners, and editors know that fear sells. Local and network news focus programming on despair and fear to achieve the desired ratings. The masters of modern propaganda understand that the populace likes to be terrified. This is why there is great success in the suspense/action/terror genres; programs packaged by the elite for your consumption.

The editors in charge take advantage of every false-flag act of terrorism and use it to manipulate the public. They artificially raised the terror alert multiple times to scare people. When its effectiveness wore off, they raised the campaign of terror to the next level by using entertainment, Hollywood, and network television to sell the police state. Raised terror alerts and artificially-created nightmares brought to you by the mighty news are designed to get you to cry out to the government to rescue and protect you. TV news lies have been accepted by so many as truth because they watch mind-altering news programming every day. Current leaders are exalted by the media to promote the false belief that only through them will things get fixed. According to the media, we will only reach the gates of safety through our elected officials and their proposed legislation.

The daily news destroys one's mind. It makes people think that all of humanity's problems are by accident, hiding the fact that they're all by design. Related messages in the news scripts demonize those who stand for the truth and push the illuminati agenda. Reporters air the same false news stories repetitively to shape political opinion. The global elite use the networks to set the norms in society and control humanity through their TV sets. The media hides what it's stolen from us, which is our right to rebel and change the government by any means necessary. What's on TV is designed to keep us from changing our government through warfare or revolution.

American wealth has been transferred to other countries and the American dollar is falling, yet our nation's population doesn't know what's really going on because of the mainstream news media. However, brainwashed men can name the top football and basketball players. Those lost in the world's system believe that they're nothing if they're not in center stage, so they live their lives out through the stars. A lot of fans wish they were the celebrity on the stage, on the court, or the stars on the drag strip. People have a psychological need to root for something with other people, so their fantasies guide them to fixating on sports. Human nature naturally resists and fights what suppresses it, so multi-media sports are pushed to turn men to robots. Sociologists and psychologists in areas of influence know that spectator sports are just an escape from our own existence; no different than a drug or gambling addiction.

The decision of the network television owners (the ruling establishment) controls all editors, producers, and others involved in network programming, who can't present anything that doesn't fit the objective. The global elite control everything, including all politicians. Out of over 300 million Americans, the elite choose both candidates of both parties, who are both members of Skull and Bones or other secret societies. The elite choose the candidates and place them before you, while the daily news makes it look like the selected candidate is the best the country could come up with. In all mainstream political elections, both sides are controlled by the same people. Democrats, Republicans, and Independents in the spotlight are all a part of the same 3-headed dragon.

Numerous programs pretend to be entertainment, but are really brainwashing programs. Disc jockeys in radio today all work for the programming establishment. The mind-controllers saturate the airwaves with jokes and content centered on foolishness to keep us distracted from the real issues. The population is so lost in the structures of the world that general trash talk sells. The majority of young adults, children, and older audiences mimic what they see and hear on the radio, network television, and in the movies. The current 'norm' established by those behind network television is selling delusional behavior as cool. The conditioning is so intense that corruptive forms of content are considered the norm, and people stop thinking for themselves.

Anything other than what's promoted on network television is either uninteresting or bizarre to the average TV fanatic. The average American's attention span for truth decreases the more they watch network television. When your thoughts are no longer your own, due to network programming, the real news and issues will seem uninteresting. You may even fight to defend your favorite news anchor's position, not knowing what you're talking about.

Once you become a mass mind control victim, you'll be viewing things from a distorted perception. Any stories exposing government corruption at the highest levels will automatically be rejected by daily news-watchers. It's hard for a truth to be realized in the average TV viewer's brain because network television has already conditioned their minds to accept and reject certain information. Drastically cutting down television watching is one of many solutions to fighting this type of mind control and brainwashing. Eliminating the TV all together is your own awakening that will help you break outside of the manipulating box and mind control system. This unknown terrain is where you'll find your truth.

Reality exists outside of this controlled artificial system promoted by network television. The programming began decades ago and has become so advanced that few can recognize it. Over time, the messages are becoming increasingly deceptive, violent, and dishonest. Hollywood can make film makers believe anything, and because of the film industry, most believe they are free. Through the daily watching of the corporate mainstream news media, the world's populations have given their minds away to the official version of events, which are always 100% LIES. News programming makes the government the answer to everything, which is why the majority subliminally believes that the government is God.

The news makes it look like they're presenting different view points, but when it comes to controlled opposition, the prosecutor and the judge sit on the same side of the bench. When it comes to mainstream news programming, all the players are on the same team. Our collective free will has been hijacked through mass mind control to allow this nightmare called network television to take over our thoughts. Our collective free will can change it, but we'll have to let go of network television. After you win the battle in your heart and mind, extend knowledge outward from there by spreading information only to those open to it. Most people would rather remain in darkness and embrace network television. Living in the Light isn't very popular in this dispensation.

Choose to travel the road to the truth by examining the news behind the news and drawing from alternative news sources. Obstacles await the people of truth because they've been implanted into the mass mind control. Programming began at birth and will attack truth-seekers because that's exactly what it's designed to do. If you don't fall for the official version of events, you'll be criticized and condemned by your co-workers, friends, and family. These programmed attackers are fighting your attempt to get to the other side (truth). Not many make it to the other side of this life because wide is the road leading to deception. Those who live through independent thought and critical thinking are honoring their real selves. It will take faith to get off of the broad road leading to deception/destruction and follow your real self. Take the leap of faith to discover and live out your real self.

Mass Mind Control, Social Engineering, and Media Manipulation

The government and the media work together to control humanity. The corporate mainstream news media promotes the government's problem-reaction-solution deception. Alex Jones, '9-11 Descent Into Tyranny,' said, "The Hegelian dialectic of problem-reaction-solution. Attack yourself, blame your enemies, and tell the public you can protect them if they give up their freedoms." Paul Joseph Watson, 'Order Out of Chaos,' perfectly explained how the problem-reaction-solution trick works. He said, "It works like this – the manipulating body covertly creates a problem and then directs the media to incessantly focus on it without recourse. Remember, you only need to control the top of the pyramid – most media coverage is an exercise in regurgitating what the big newspapers and TV stations are reporting. ...The people that created the problem in the first place then come back in and offer the solution that the people demand. Remember – the people screaming for a solution do not know that the problem was artificially created in the first place. The solution to the problem is always a further curtailment of freedom and an advancement of one or more aspects of the New World Order agenda – whether that is geopolitical expansion, new laws or the implantation of new societal worldviews."

95% of the world's problems have been artificially created by the manipulating body for their own purposes. The media works to make you think that these global elite-created problems are natural. The people controlling the top of the pyramid control 98% of media coverage and use it to cover their created program. Big newspapers and TV stations are told what to report by the controllers. Anyone who watches the corporate mainstream news media every day is a PROGRAMMED fool! The power of the media creates the false perceptions living in 90% of Earthians. Big problems promoted by the media don't even exist; they were created to solicit the population to fall for the controller's pre-planned solution. Paul Joseph Watson said, "The problem could be anything—a war, a financial collapse, a rash of child abductions, or a terrorist attack. The power of the media can create the false perception that a big problem exists, even if it doesn't ... Once you have created this problem, you make sure that an individual, a group or an aspect of society is blamed. This then rallies the population behind the desperate lunge for a solution to the problem. 'Something must be done!' they cry in unison."

The only purpose of the media is to help the global elite incrementally implement their New World Order agenda. If you continue to watch the daily news against my warnings, never forget the problem-reaction-solution trickery. The ruling elite use the news programs watched by the masses to create a mass groupthink. When you trust the mass media, your thoughts are not your own. Media PROGRAMMING enables the ruling elite to further their agenda without opposition. Watching the news is nothing but BRAINWASHING! If you watch the news every day and believe what they present, you're the worst of fools!! There would be no police state or oppressed populations without the media. Abandon the manipulating body's media coverage in order to regain control of 'your own' thoughts.

Society is controlled, mainly by media deception. Most people won't believe something if it's not covered by the mainstream news media. I don't know why fools trust the media and believe that they're reliable. Media coverage controls the population for evil. If you watch the news every day, you're a victim of lies and manipulation. The elite create a problem designed to elicit a certain reaction out of the public, using the media to promote it. The deceived people (90% of the population) demand something be done about the fake problem. Because of the daily news, PROGRAMMED fools willingly accept the preplanned NWO solution. The solutions of the elite always involve legislation and actions that never would have passed/been accepted without media propaganda. Under normal circumstances, the people would never accept the loss of their freedoms. Since they didn't know anything about problem-reaction-solution, they fell by the wayside.

The German philosopher Hegal explained to humanity how the world works. According to Hegel, all historical, intellectual, and spiritual development progressed from the outcome of two opposing ideals, whether negative or positive. Synthesis is produced from the clash between thesis and antithesis. Resistance creates more muscles. They say what doesn't kill you makes you stronger. This is why there is good and evil, God and Satan, etc. (Satan is symbolic, not a real being.) Two opposing ideals produce the appointed synthesis. There would be no cute without ugly, no good without evil, and no light without darkness.

The news uses the modern day application of the Hegelian dialectic to pull the strings of humanity. The people controlling those at the top of the pyramid produce their pre-planned synthesis from the clash of thesis with antithesis. The ruling elite use the mainstream media to control the thesis, antithesis, and synthesis. They control and find all sides and fool news-watchers with their mass groupthink. Controlling all sides and their media presentations, the elite can further their agenda with no 'real' opposition. The world controllers in the past have played this game of controlling both sides to manufacture war. Paul Joseph Watson, 'Order Out of Chaos,' said, "Both the Bolsheviks and the Nazis were funded and supported by the global elite. These two forces were then made to clash in order to foment the chaos of World War Two. The widely used term amongst researchers today is 'Problem Reaction Solution' and the tactic is mainly used to oppress populations, advance the police state and further the geopolitical aims of the New World Order."

Be aware of the government's control over the media. The ruling elite control ALL government officials, and the government officials influence media content. The media get their largest amount of source material from controlled officials. The government protects media companies and provides them with subsidies. Officials censor or withhold true information from the masses by feeding garbage to journalists who are compliant. The government subsidies its media partners with public broadcasting subsidies, spectrum allocation, exclusives, and quotes. It's the government which allows the media to say, "According to official sources..." The manipulating news organizations depend on official 'government' sources for their raw materials. The Government decides the media's interpretations of events. When you watch the news, you're being fed government programming, not real stories.

The government has full control over the media and controls access to press releases, official meetings, press passes, and press conferences. The government determines who gets called on and who isn't invited back to the big news shows. The government has media control over the Army and all branches of the military. The government controls where they go, who they talk to, and what they say. Journalists are exploited with incentives to use their positions to advance government agenda. White House, Pentagon, and State department journalists are all controlled. The press is used as a weapon against opposition.

The President and Congress control all media sources, leaving no alternative for journalists to turn to. The President's administration has greater control over media sources of information than other branches of government. The President is the ultimate news source, and all media outlets express loyalty to the president.

Journalists get ahead in the business by getting inside information (from the controllers). Media owners are part of the elite; a fact that can be discovered by researching media ownership. The political elite own all the mainstream media firms. Since the media is controlled, it is used for extensive government advertising, censorship, intimidation, political favors, and threat of prosecution. Coercive actions designed to force compliance are promoted by the government's media. The government calls upon the media to keep a story out of the public eye or promote a fake story. Authoritarian governments influence the media through its control of resources used by the media. The media is all about DECEPTION.

Modern US Government propaganda was devised by Nazi

masterminds. 98% of what you see on the mainstream news media is nothing but propaganda to control your mind. The media does not communicate the facts about something, only false information to influence people's opinions or behaviors actively. The most obvious propaganda method is an appeal to one's emotion. This is why the news reporters talk how they talk and use the tone of voice and facial expressions that they employ. Volume is a common characteristic of propaganda, used to trick you into thinking that what's being discussed is important.

Propaganda is not used to present a true position, but garner either support or disapproval of a certain position. Propaganda works to try to convince people of something that's not true. Normal communication is not seen on the news, only insidious and subtle messages attempting to shape behavior or opinion. The propaganda on television watched daily by programmed and deceived humans functions as self-deception. News watchers think they know what's going on, but they've deceived themselves by watching news PROGRAMS every day.

Most humans don't think, which is why they always fall for these pre-planned fake wars. Propaganda is the most effective weapon during and leading up to fake wars. News PROGRAMS are used to dehumanize and create hatred toward a supposed internal or external enemy. Violence or the threat of violence is promoted by the media with artificial evidence. Media brainwashing techniques create false images in the news watcher's mind by using special words or special avoidance of words. The news tells lies to people by falsely claiming that the enemy is responsible for certain things 'the imaginary' enemy never did. All modern wars are no more than propaganda wars pushed by the corporate mainstream media. The news is used to PROGRAM the home population to falsely believe that the media-created enemy has inflicted an injustice. The injustice and enemy are both fictitious, but media PROGRAMMING tricks you into believing lies. The purpose of the news is to garner support from the population for wars that would normally never be supported by the people.

Propaganda is a part of psychological warfare and false flag operations. The U.S. mass media reports lies in the style, content, and language of their Nazi predecessors, modeling their program. The Nazi program and modern media propaganda wars both involved imperialistic armies slaughtering civilians, conquering countries, and destroying cities. Nazi Germany and contemporary U.S. are both basically the same. They both have used the mass media to brainwash the people into believing that the invading armies are "spreading democracy" and "liberating the country." In the U.S. and Nazi Germany, the media made the enemy foreigners or insurgents. In reality, the countries we invade despise the U.S. invaders and are opposed to the U.S. military.

The frontmen media reporters are puppets, and U.S. military operations overseas are puppet regimes. The U.S. media falsely labels those defending their country from U.S. imperial invaders as insurgents, when they're really a nationwide force of freedom fighters. The media lies and says that the foreign casualties are a result of sectarian violence and civil war. The people fighting for their country are actually attacking the puppet police units. You can't believe anything the media reports these days. Media reporters are ALL liars for the elite.

The major U.S. radio and TV networks report in the same manner as the Nazi media, telling the lie that they're "freeing the city of insurgents." The systematic murder of neighbors, friends, and relatives is justified by media propaganda. The media garners support for hundreds of missiles, jets, and helicopter gunships to terror bomb hospitals, homes, and religious buildings in the name of "securing the city for free elections." Washington and the mass media resort to these deceptive tactics to galvanize support with the U.S. population for human madness. The "war on terror" and other acts of human unconsciousness (madness) are promoted by the media to force inferior countries into submission while energy corporations steal their country's oil supply dry.

The original techniques were perfected by Goebbels in Germany, than practiced in the U.S. Today, lies and euphemisms are repeated to daily news-watchers until they become accepted 'truths.' The news repeats lies until they become embedded into every language. Goebbels created and perfected the propaganda for Nazi Germany. His methods are behind the propaganda for the U.S. media. Leonard W. Doob wrote 'Goebbels' Principles of Propaganda,' a book summarizing Goebbels' propaganda points. According to Leonard W. Doob's book, Goebbels' propaganda points state that: propagandist must have access to intelligence concerning public opinion and events. Propaganda must be planned and executed by only one authority (the ruling establishment). In the planning of an action, the propaganda consequences must be considered. In implementing a propaganda campaign, the propaganda must evoke the interest of the audience and be transmitted through an attention-grabbing communications medium.

If you aren't armed with the knowledge of how propaganda works, you're not as intelligent as you think you are. Those living in the Light can easily pick up the PROGRAMMING techniques being used upon the masses. Those who can figure out the PROGRAM will be surprised at how often the public is being attacked by mass programming. The news is 95% propaganda, so don't watch it. The news isn't credible, but the media gives themselves credibility. The real truth is always ignored or refuted by the mainstream media. Propaganda is utilized in government operations to help diminish a (fake) enemy's prestige or solicit support for the propagandist's own objective. Propaganda is designed to affect the (false) enemy's action and policy.

The controlled leaders under the rule of the global elite carefully time and facilitate propaganda. Media propaganda facilitates the displacement of aggression by pointing out who the targets for hatred should be. Propaganda is used to manifest an optimum anxiety level and reinforce anxiety concerning the consequences of not going along with the 'pre-planned' program. Media propaganda is also used to diminish anxiety when the elite believe it's too high and can't be reduced by the sheep (people) themselves. It's all designed to evoke desired responses and reach the audience ahead of competing propaganda. Through the government's media, events and people are labeled with distinctive slogans or phrases. Propaganda themes are repeated long enough to not diminish effectiveness. These lies are utilized again and again in appropriate situations as part of a propaganda campaign launched at the optimum moment. The majority of people are deceived because of government influence on the media.

The media is used to promote all false flag operations. What's going on in this generation is simply history repeating itself, but the media keeps people from noticing. An examination of history will shed light on what's going on now. Adolf Hitler burned down his own Reischstag building in 1933 and blamed it on his political enemies. The U.S. Government learned from Adolf Hitler when he declared that "Terrorism is the best political weapon, for nothing drives people harder than a fear of sudden death." Hitler's Luftwaffe Chief and Nazi Reich Marshall Hermann Goering is quoted as saying, "Naturally, the common people don't want war ... But, after all, it is the leaders of the country who determine the policy and it is always a simple matter to drag the people along, whether it is a democracy or a fascist dictatorship or a Parliament or Communist dictatorship. Voice or no voice, the people can always be brought to the bidding of the leaders. That is easy. All you have to do is tell them they are being attacked and denounce the pacifists for lack of patriotism and exposing the country to danger. It works the same way in any country."

False Flags, like the 9/11 terror attacks, are covert operations conducted by governments which are made to appear as though performed by some other enemy. The media is used to blame another entity. For example, Hitler burned his own Reichstag, then blamed the communists. The USS Maine was intentionally blown up to blame Spain/Cuba. The implementation of the Hegelian Dialectic is used for the common false flags in modern times. Hi Li Mencken said, "The whole aim of practical politics is to keep the populace alarmed and hence clamorous to be led to safety by menacing it with an endless series of hobgoblins, all of them imaginary."

History reveals what's happening now and is a model for modern-day false flags. In 1898, the explosion of the USS Maine was used to falsely justify the Spanish-American War. Entry into World War II was previously unpopular until the Japanese attack on Pearl Harbor, which was designed to justify entry into World War II. The White House used the Gulf of Tonkin incident of 1964 to justify the extension of the Vietnam War to North Vietnam. Media propaganda was used to portray Iraq as harboring an arsenal of weapons of mass destruction to justify a false war. To justify recourse to war, the media was used to brainwash people into thinking that Iraq was in defiance of international law and the United Nations.

The news programs the masses to behave with unquestioning acceptance. The only purpose of the media is to manipulate public beliefs. Society is lost because of the media. Most of the population sits in front of the television every day listening to liars. The real news isn't on TV, just like real history isn't in the sanctioned history books. Everything mainstream is manipulated. The corporate news media is the reason why habitual news-watchers are stupid. These idiots fall for every false flag operation because they're victims of media programming. Richard Falk, Forward-'The New Pearl Harbor,' said, "There is no excuse at this stage of American development for a posture of political innocence, including an unquestioning acceptance of the good faith of our government. After all, there has been a long history of manipulated public beliefs, especially in matters of war and peace. Historians are in increasing agreement that the facts were manipulated, ..."

Media manipulation controls the human race. The mainstream media is controlled by the manipulators, who place their thoughts in your head. Jim Marrs, 'Rule by Secrecy,' said, "Corporate ownership intermingled with secret society members, many of whom are employed in the media, may explain why Bilderberg, Trilateral, and CFR meetings are not reported by America's 'watchdog' media. In fact, the membership lists of these societies read like a Who's Who of the mass media."

All the media giants are headed by past and present members of the globalist secret societies CFR, Trilateral Commission, and Bilderberg. The global elite (illuminati) control: ABC, CBS, NBC, CNN, AP, PBS, Sesame Street (CTVW), Reuters, New York Times, New York Post, Washington Times, Washington Post, L.A. Times, Newsweek, Wall Street Journal, Fortune, Time, Reader's Digest, Life, World Review, Scientific American, U.S. News and World Report, McCall's, and all major news sources. If you get your news from any of these organizations, you're PROGRAMMED.

Almost all of the minor media publisher/newspapers are CFR owned. The ruling establishment, through the CFR, own the Arkansas Gazette, Louisville Courier, Denver Post, Houston Post, Minneapolis Star, Des Moines Register, Minneapolis Tribune, Guy Gannett Co., Des Moines Tribune, and many others. Any journalist writing for any of these organizations is a CONTROLLED puppet unable to reveal the unadulterated truth. Everything of influence is controlled and manipulated, which is why the CFR owns all major book publishers, including: Macmillan, Yale University Press, Harper and Row, Xerox Corp., Random House, Simon and Schuster, Harper Brothers, Viking Press, Little Brown and Co., McGraw Hill, and all publishers specializing in children's textbooks.

Secret society members sit on the boards of directors of the corporations which own ALL the media. All of the well known reporters, columnists, and anchors are members of the Trilateral Commission and/or CFR. Since the global elite own everything, there is a conspiracy of silence among media peers to hide the truth. The Rothschilds own the two largest news organizations in the world: the Associated Press and Reuters. Reuters is "the world's largest international multimedia news organization." The Associated Press says that it is "the backbone of the world's information system serving thousands of daily newspaper, radio, television and online customers with coverage in all media and news in all formats. It is the largest and oldest news organization in the world, serving as a source of news, photos, graphics, audio and video."

The power elite have full control over the internet, recording, publishing, and top cable companies via Newscorp, Viacom, Time Warner, Disney, and GE. All major companies are indirectly or directly owned by the Rothschilds, Morgans, Rockefellers, and Oppenheimers; all illuminati bloodlines. The boards of directors of all big companies of influence are the same as CFR rosters. David Icke, 'The Biggest Secret,' said, "Look at Ted Turner, the Council on Foreign Relations member who was supposed to be taking on the system with his Cable News Network (CNN). He sold out to Time Warner, one of the greatest Brotherhood operations on the planet, and CNN pounds out the official line hour after hour, day after day ... The three television networks in the United States, CBS, ABC, and NBC are controlled by members of the Round Table network and so are the Washington Post, Los Angeles Times, New York Times, Wall Street Journal, and a long, long list of others. The same goes for country after country." Gary Allen, 'The Rockefeller File,' said, "Instead of three competing television networks called NBC, CBS, and ABC, what we really have is the Rockefeller Broadcasting Company, the Rockefeller Broadcasting System, and the Rockefeller Broadcasting Consortium."

Members of the elite control and own everything. CBS has over 200 TV and over 255 radio affiliates nationwide, set up to control the flow of information. ABC has over 150 TV affiliates, all designed to control your thoughts. Time Inc. (which is really Skull and Bones and CFR) owns all major/ influential magazines, book publishers, newspapers, movie houses, and over 30 TV stations. The ruling establishment, operating through corporate giants, own ALL major names in media, and most of the minor ones also. Big corporations merge, monopolize, and purchase all competition to control what's fed to humanity. Five mega corporations own 90% of the media. Huge corporations are all Brotherhood controlled.

AOL Time Warner is the biggest U.S. media giant, and the holdings of this one company control publishing, television and movie companies, cable and satellite TV, magazines, and record labels. An AOL Time Warner spokesperson said, "We know in the not too distant future, a half dozen corporations are going to control the media. We took this step (merger) to ensure we were one of them."

Through AOL Time Warner, the global elite control all cable and television, including HBO, Cinemax, CNN, New York 1, Court TV, Comedy Central (shared ownership with Viacom), Time Warner Communications, etc. Television and movie companies are controlled by AOL Time Warner, including Warner Brothers, WB Television, WB studios, Hanna Barbera Cartoons, The Warner Channel, Warner Home Video, WB International Theaters in 12 countries, etc. AOL Time Warner owns almost all of the publishing industry, including Time Life International Books, Time Life Education, Time Life Music, Time Life Audio Books, Paperback Book Club, Money Book Club, History Book Club, One Spirit, Warner Books, etc. All major magazines are owned and controlled by AOL Time Warner, including Time, Fortune, Life, Money, People, Parenting, Entertainment Weekly, Sports Illustrated, Weight Watchers, 80 magazines in Britain, Health, Baby Talk, Food and Wine, etc. Almost all the major record labels are owned and controlled by AOL Time Warner, including Asylum, Warner Brothers, Warner Music, Atlantic Group, Warner Sunset, Warner Alliance, Warner Nashville, etc. Enlightened humans who know the truth have tried to warn humanity that everything is controlled, but the masses keep allowing the mainstream to brainwash them. The ruling establishment own everything, which is partly why 90% of the population is lost in outer darkness. It's also their own fault for allowing themselves to be deceived.

Be Not Deceived!

Rich men behind the scenes deceive the whole world through their ownership of the media. David Icke, 'Tales from the Time Loop,' said, "AOL Time Warner is followed in size by Disney, Viacom, Vivendi Universal and Rupert Murdoch's News Corporation. This network dominates television, movies and publishing. In 1997, the films produced by the four biggest motion picture companies, Disney, Warner Brothers, Paramount (Viacom) and Universal (Seagram) accounted for two-thirds of the total box office receipts for the year. By 2003, only 20% of American newspapers, even local ones were not owned by the media corporations and the same can be found across the world."

People who know the truth have spoken out, but many haven't listened. John Swinton, former editor of The New York Times, addressed an audience of journalists during a banquet speech. He shocked them by saying, "There is no such thing in America as an independent press. You know it and I know it ... The business of the Journalist is to destroy truth; To lie outright; To pervert; To vilify; To fawn at the feet of mammon, and to sell his county and his race for his daily bread. You know it and I know it, and what folly is this toasting an independent press? We are the tools and vassals for rich men behind the scenes. We are the jumping jacks, they pull the strings and we dance. Our talents, our possibilities, and our lives are all the property of other men. We are intellectual prostitutes." It is an undeniable fact that the media is the tool of the enemy. The people seeking to destroy you are brainwashing and controlling you through the television. David Cromwell said, "The mass media is itself part of the same power structure that plunders the planet and inflicts human rights abuses on a massive scale."

Illuminati men control and manipulate ALL media. Rupert Murdoch's NewsCorp has full control over the American, Asian, Middle Eastern, and British media markets. Murdoch's media empire reaches 3/4 of the world's population, which is 4.7 billion people. Murdoch owns the New York Post, The Times of London, and 175 other newspapers. Murdoch also owns Fox, 19 sports channels, and 100 cable TV channels. According to 'Rupert Murdoch: Outfoxed Documentary,' he also owns 40 regular and 9 satellite TV networks, a movie studio, and 40 publishing houses. His media empire, stretching across 5 continents, reaches a TV audience of 300 million in Asia and 280 million in America. All the magazines owned by Murdoch reach 28 million. With Murdoch's media empire and all outlets combined together, Murdoch controls the world. Ted Turner said, "Rupert Murdoch is the most dangerous man in the world."

All editors and newsmen on the staffs of the biggest magazines and newspapers, and all editors, commentators, and reporters at NBC, ABC, CBS take their editorial cues and news from the shadow government. Every chairman of the board is a member of the CFR, and all the people in high positions with the biggest media corporations are CFR members. The top editors and management personnel of all the newspapers and media outlets are members of the CFR. The owners and publishers of all the major news and media corporations are members of the CFR, Trilateral Commission, and Bilderberg Group. In his 1991 Trilateral Commission speech, David Rockefeller said, "We are grateful to The Washington Post, the New York Times, Time Magazine, and other great publications whose directors have attended our meetings and respected their promises of discretion for almost forty years. It would have been impossible for us to develop our plan for the world if we had been subject to the bright lights of publicity during those years. But, the work is now much more sophisticated and prepared to march towards a world government. The supranational sovereignty of an intellectual elite and world bankers is surely preferable to the national auto determination practiced in past centuries."

Thomas Jefferson knew about media deception. He said, "I really look with commiseration over the great body of my fellow citizens who, reading newspapers, live and die in the belief that they have known something of what has been passing in their times." News-watchers think they know what's going on, but don't know anything. They are victims of deception. Katharine Graham, a member of the CFR, Trilateral Commission, and Bilderberg Group, was the owner/publishers of the Washington Post from 1963-2001. She stated her view of democracy in a 1988 speech at CIA headquarters when she said, "We live in a dirty and dangerous world. There are some things the general public does not need to know and shouldn't. I can't believe democracy flourishes when the government can take legitimate steps to keep its secrets, and when the press can decide whether to print what it knows."

The news is designed to support the government and the agenda of the global elite. Gary Allen, 'The Rockefeller File,' said, "the only time the Post has ever opposed big governments when it has been used to investigate communism. When this has happened, the people at the Post frantically start waving the Constitution and babbling about 'freedom of speech,' something they regularly suppress when it involves opposition to fascism, socialism, or the Rockefellers." You're a fool if you trust media PROGRAMMING. If you watch the news every day, you're a stone-cold dummy. Ted Turner, CEO of AOL/Time Warner, said, "The United States has some of the dumbest people in the world. I want you to know that we know that." Richard Salant, former President of CBS News, said, "Our job is to give people not what they want, but what we decide they ought to have." Those who continue to fool with the media are destroying their minds. John Kricfalusi, creator of The Ren and Stimpy Show, said, "I think we are destroying the minds of America and that has been one of my lifelong ambitions."

The elite philosophy of classism and moral relativity justifies their lying and corruption because they claim mental superiority over the masses. During interviews, Ted Turner has called the majority of humans "useless eaters." Americans are dumb useless fools because they trust the ruling establishment's media and allow themselves to be programmed with lies. It's your own fault if you're manipulated because in a world of lies, all my books present the truth. 98% of Americans would rather sit in front of the TV and listen to a liar! If you believe and regurgitate what media liars say, you become a liar. Why listen to lies every day? Liar, liar, pants on fire! Christopher Mark, 'Grand Deception: The Theft of America and the World,' said, "The news is a farce. As is the case with the financial institutions, which are concentrated in the hands of the few, long ago the media was bought and paid for ... What you read and what you see on a daily basis is largely manufactured. You are being lied to each and every day."

The mainstream media lies and uses one-sided editorializing. The nightly news gives you incomplete and uneven coverage to cast dissenters in a negative light, lie by omission, and suppress dissent. Even if the media establishment accurately reports an event, it will not report on the real history of the situation. The quasi-informed populous are idiots falling for the official media explanations of pre-planned events. People watch each day's events on the television unaware of the conspiratorial control manipulating their minds daily. Programmed news-watchers feel informed when they're really brainwashed drones unable to piece together what's really going on. Those who trust in the news are FOOLS!

The illuminati bloodlines use their media propaganda machine to create false dichotomies and maintain the illusion of opposites. They control all sides to herd human thought, demolish lateral thinking, and dampen intuition. Dr. Stanley Monteith, 'Brotherhood of Darkness,' said, "J.P. Morgan and his associates financed the Republican Party, the Democratic Party, conservative groups, liberal organizations, communist groups, and anticommunist organizations." On the corporate news media, there are no opposites, and all groups are the same. All sides work for the same people. Carroll Quigley, 'Tragedy and Hope,' said, "The argument that the two parties should represent opposed ideals and policies, one, perhaps, of the Right and the other the Left, is a foolish idea acceptable only to the doctrinaire and academic thinkers. Instead, the two parties should be almost identical, so that the American people can 'throw the rascals out' at any election without leading to any profound or extreme shifts in policy."

All opposites are the same, unnoticed to victims of media manipulation. The unseen rulers of the world get their desired synthesis result by controlling or creating both the proper thesis and antithesis. False dichotomies promoted on television give the illusion of choice. There is no choice, and all sides are controlled. This is why freedom fighters say, "The revolution will not be televised." The political sphere, governed by illuminati bloodlines/societies, intentionally place members on both sides to CONTROL the spectrum. Everything political is the same. For example, the far right is fascism, and the far left is communism, BOTH representing dictatorial government control. The purpose of the media is to create a false thesis/antithesis to promote the synthesis, which is always another system of dictatorial government control. The perceived middle ground and socialist democracy promoted by the media is a sham to suppress dissent through omission. The media, as a whole, promotes both sides of the coin, but the elite own both sides!

The power elite own all the media, publishing, and entertainment companies to leave no place for non-establishment ideas. The 'owned' establishment creates false dichotomies to deceive the public into believing in polar opposites. Both parties (which are really the same) use the media to build the false perception of opposing positions on major issues. The purpose of these false conflicts is to build consensus on other non-debated issues critical to the new world order. The Congressional Record for 1917 reveals how things really go down in the world's system. U.S. Congressman Oscar Callawayx, in 1917, reported that "In March, 1915, the J.P. Morgan interests, the steel, shipbuilding, and power interest, and their subsidiary organizations, got together 12 men high up in the newspaper world and employed them to select the most influential newspapers in the United States and sufficient number of them to control generally the policy of the daily press ... They found it was only necessary to purchase the control of 25 of the greatest papers. An agreement was reached; the policy of the papers was bought, to be paid for by the month; an editor was furnished for each paper to properly supervise and edit information regarding the questions of preparedness, militarism, financial policies, and other things of national and international nature considered vital to the interests of the purchasers."

The crime accidents, and celebrities filling the newspapers and mainstream media are distractions designed to hide what's really going on. Jim Marrs, 'Alien Agenda,' said, "While the media obviously cannot dictate how we are to think, they certainly set the agenda on what we are to think about. Who has time for tedious stories of government conspiracies and financial manipulations when the newspapers and airwaves are filled with crime, accidents, and celebrities? Who bothers to notice when a primetime TV network 'news break' contains nothing but sports scores?" David Icke, 'The Biggest Secret,' says, "Every day on television stations all over the world, journalists and correspondents give their viewers the official version of the event they are reporting. 'White House sources say this ..., the Prime Minster says that ..., the FBI say the other ...' In all my time in journalism, I cannot recall a single conversation in a newsroom that didn't reflect the official version of life and the world. Most journalists are not manipulating, they are simply stunningly uninformed and often incredibility arrogant. They believe that if anything of magnitude was going on, they would know about it because they are the 'journalists'. In truth, they are the last to know."

The Western Goebells, Edward Bernays, was known as the nephew of Sigmund Freud. He died in 1995 at the age of 104. Edward Bernays worked with many corporations behind the scenes in his century to propagandize and advertise various groupthink patterns to the public. He worked with the government to brainwash the American public and take over their thoughts. Bernays was top advisor to the founder of CBS, William Paley. In his 1928 book 'Propaganda,' he wrote: "the conscious and intelligent manipulation of organized habits and opinions of the masses is an important element in a democratic society. Those who manipulate this unseen mechanism of society constitute an invisible government which is the true ruling power in our country ... We are governed, our mind's are molded, our tastes formed, our ideas suggested largely by men we have never heard of ... we are dominated by a relatively small number of persons who understand the mental processes and social patterns of the masses. It is they who pull the wires which control the public mind and who harness social forces and contrive new ways to bind and guide the world. ... It remains a fact in almost every act of our daily lives, whether in the sphere of politics or business in our social conduct or our ethical thinking, we are dominated by this relatively small number of persons ... As civilization has become more complex, and as the need for invisible government has been increasingly demonstrated, the technical means have been invented and developed by which opinion may be regimented."

The news is fake. Journalists write what they're told. The corporate news uses charismatic personalities to draw the charm of humanity. These string puppets are used to control the people and fill their minds with foolishness. The only purpose of the media is to control your mind. Hal Becker, Futures Group think-tank veteran, said, "I know the secret of making the average American believe anything I want him to. Just let me control television. Americans are wired into their television sets. Over the last 30 years, they have come to look at their television sets and the image on the screen as reality. You put something on television and it becomes reality. If the world outside the television set contradicts the images, people start changing the world to make it more like the images and sounds of their television. Because its influence is so great, so pervasive, it has become part of our lives. You lose your sense of what is being done to you, but your mind is being shaped and molded."

Students of spiritual history know the origin of the media. The word 'media' comes from an ancient place in the Middle

East near Libya called Media. The Medes lived in Media. The Medes were involved in the same activities practiced today by the corporate mainstream news media. The modern media got its blueprint from the ancient cult in Media. Scholars familiar with the Medes can see their influence all over modern television. Michael Tsarion, 'The Subversive Use of Sacred Symbolism in the Media' Lecture at Conspiracy Con, said, "In Media were the sorcerers and astrologers, not necessarily negative people, but a tribe, a very adept cult from the ancient world who specialized in the use of talismans, amulets, mantras and sorcery. And the kings of the world knew that if a battle hadn't worked, or if legal means hadn't worked to get rid of an enemy, or you didn't want it known that you were getting rid of your enemy, you simply called on the Medes. And you bring the representative of the Media into your court and he will take care of the problem because he is going to put the spell on your enemy, the hex, because they know how to do it. And that's where we get the word Mediterranean, Mediation, Meditation, and Medication, the Medics. Study this alone and a whole interesting subject will open itself up, because we still have the sorcerers and the voodoo and the witch doctor, we still have it today, only now it's the Techno Shamanism, it's the Silicon Sorcerers, it's the Ivory Tower and they're still very busy at what they're doing up at Madison Avenue and behind the other great corporate giants who are only too happy to tell you what to think."

Global media control is a form of sorcery to control humanity. The news is dangerous to one's mind. Seek the news behind the news, and you'll be able to maintain a sound mind (you're own mind). Masters of the human psyche are controlling your mind when you watch the daily news. Thoughts are implanted into your mind for the projection of lies into reality. Media masterminds work hard to get you into groupthink and subservience. If you watch media programming enough, they're thoughts will become your thoughts and their ways will become your ways without you knowing it. Wise Ones living on earth have tried to warn humanity how this type of sorcery works, but fools won't listen. They've watched the daily news for so long that they've lost their minds! Michael Tsarion, 'The Subversive Use of Sacred Symbolism in the Media' Lecture at Conspiracy Con 2003, said, "These individuals, they do go back a long way and they have understood completely your psyche, they've had generations, centuries to study it. Their type of sorcery involves different kinds of techniques but it's still the same effect: Tele Hyphosis, Metacontrast, Hemisync, Synaesthesia, Embedding, new names, new terms for a very old, well-known practice to get you into groupthink, into subservience, to get you to embody dialectical divisions of which there is no end in our society, to fasion your allegiances for you, to implant associations that your mind might not normally associate, to purvey escapism, rampant escapism and projection of fantasy into reality, to inflate false personas so you don't have to be you, you can live it out through the person on the screen, and the excessive eroticization especially of the female."

Median sorcerers in Media carried wands with them made out of holly wood. Medians and other wizards carried wooden staffs made from holly wood to cast their spells with. Magical wands and wooden staffs were always only made of just one specific kind of wood: holly. This is the origin of Hollywood. Jordan Maxwell, 'Matrix of Power,' said, "Merlin and the old magicians of Celtic England always used their magic wands and these magic wands were always made out of holly wood. And that's why today we still have Hollywood, working its 'magic' on us-showing us in movies how to view things, what we should think, or just offering us a big box office diversion." The name Hollywood subliminally reveals what holly wood is about. The movie business does nothing but cast programming spells on you. Michael Tsarion, 'Astrotheology and Sidereal Mythology,' said, "So we still find those magi in the movie business are putting their 'spells' on us. The makers of cinema know all about the libido, sexuality, desires and drives of the human beings that they are trying to pacify and control. The fact that 'programs' are called 'programs' is fascinating in itself.

Programs are what one puts in a computer. They see the human mind as a computer and have been putting in their programs every day for decades."

98% of Americans are controlled by programs and spells. If you believe in America, you're the victim of a program! No history book will reveal to you the truth about America and its history. William Cooper said, "The United States was founded by Freemasons, members of the illuminati for one purpose and one purpose only. It was an experiment in government to see if man could really rule himself or if he would have to be brought under control by those who can rule and in the process topple the Kings and Queens of Europe off their throne. Well, the experiment was successful in that it did topple the Kings and Queens off their thrones, but it has not been successful because man has abdicated his responsibility to rule himself, and the New World Order is going to put him in chains again."

William Cooper was killed by the global elite for revealing the truth. Truth is forbidden in our dispensation, and those who speak it will eventually be silenced. William Cooper said, "I've been threatened. I've been attacked. All kinds of things have happened to us, but that's not important to anybody out there. Anytime anyone stands up and fights for what is right, they're gonna come under attack." I've had my share of threats and attacks. I believe in what I'm doing and am willing to die for what I believe in. I've been ostracized by my fellow humans and have gone through hell to release my books. A traditional publisher dropped me for not being commercial enough, so I worked hard labor jobs to finance my first few books. I lived on the streets for several years with no help from family. No one believed in me, and MANY threatened to sue me for exposing them. I risked my life and freedom to release these books with no help. No family member believed in me, and they all left me in the streets when I was homeless. I bought a used car, lived in it, then allowed my dad to CON me out of it, leaving me with no car to this day. I could try to sacrifice to get another one, but I'd rather use any extra money to support my book business. My 6th book 'Sacred Scriptures of the Apocalyptic Oracle: The Gospel of the Kingdom' will probably be my last book because my message will be complete.

Only death can stop me. I'm ready and willing to die to remain a minister of truth. William Cooper said, "Don't be too concerned about my health or what happens to me because I really believe in what I'm doing number one. And number two, I believe that any man or woman on the face of this earth who does not have principles that they're ready and willing to die for at any given moment, in my estimation, are already dead and are of no use or consequence to anybody."

William Cooper was killed by the illuminati for speaking the truth. Therefore, we should listen more closely to what he died to reveal. The late William Cooper said, "Let me make one thing perfectly clear here. I'm not into mysterious things, or witchcraft, or disappearing ships, or anything like that. My only purpose, and the only reason I even began to do any of this is because that sometime in the near future we're all in danger of losing our personal freedoms and becoming somebody's slave in the New World Order, and that's the only thing I care about. That's the only thing I'm fighting, and that's the only reason I'm doing any of this." William Cooper warned about brainwashing and mind control. He talked about operational programs designed to control every human alive 24 hours a day. The masses don't listen to these types of messages and warnings because they're too busy being brainwashed by Hollywood. William Cooper said, "As I said before, if you begin to study the developments in operational programs of brainwashing and mind control, you'll find that what they can do is absolutely incredible, will blow your mind, and will teach you that right now, the possibility of total control over every human being on the face of this earth for every 24 hours of their lives is a distinct possibility in the very near future." Even now, 95% of the population are victims of the brainwashing and mass mind control of the corporate media establishment, organized religion, and network television.

The illuminati are a group of elite and powerful people who are rarely seen by the public. The 13 illuminati bloodlines are: Astor, Bundy, Collins, DuPont, Freeman, Kennedy, Li, Onassis, Reynolds, Rockefeller, Rothschild, Russell, and Van Duyn. The interconnected families are the Disney, Krupp, and McDonald bloodlines. The enemies are within our own government. Benjamin Disraeli said, "The world is governed by people far different from those imagined by the public." The illuminati own Hollywood, the film industry, and the few companies that own everything. This subject is a complex issue. I choose to believe William Cooper's interpretation of the unseen rulers of the world. The late William Cooper said, "Well, nobody's really a bad guy. You gotta understand these guys aren't doing this because they're evil or they think that they're bad. They're doing it because they actually believe that it's the best for all humanity. But their assumption is wrong. Anything that has to be manipulated, anything that has to be brought about by lies and deceit is inherently wrong in its premise to begin with. So, they're fooling themselves. They believe that the rest of us are so stupid that we're just like cattle, and that's what they call us, and that they're the only ones with truly mature minds, and that they've got to bring the rest of us under total and complete control so that they can run the world the way they want to, and they actually believe that there's going to be a Utopia because of what they bring about." The illuminati are a criminal super secret group who have been in control of the world for awhile. This is why the U.S. Presidential elections are ALWAYS rigged even before the first ballot is cast. The whole 'major election' voting system is rigged to keep control of the people in our so-called democratic societies.

Vaccines Kill, Steal, and Destroy

Longstanding CFR members run all the magazines and corporations of influence. Parenting magazine and all other subsidiaries of Time Inc. and Time Warner provide propaganda to trick you into yielding to deception. The presidents and editors in chief of the biggest companies are corporate members of the Council on Foreign Relations (CFR) and other illuminati groups. Parenting magazine and other mainstream disinformation sources use propaganda to push harmful vaccines. The truth about vaccines is hidden, along with the fact that we are being used as guinea pigs without knowing it. Dr. Leo Horowitz, 'Parenting with Deadly Timely Propaganda,' said, "One CFR published policy objective is substantial worldwide depopulation, including half of the current U.S. population being targeted. This population reduction program is largely funded by the Rockefeller Foundation and the Merck Fund, both financially and administratively linked to the Merck Pharmaceutical Company, the world's leading vaccine manufacturer.

The FDA's VAERS (Vaccine Adverse Effects Reporting System) receives over 1,000,000 reports of serious vaccination reactions each year. 97.5% of vaccine related disabilities and deaths ARE NOT reported to or by the FDA according to the NYIC (National Vaccine Information Center) investigation on VAERS reports. Based on this New York study, the number of annual American fatalities is over 1,000, and disabilities over 100,000. Of course, all the dangerous effects of vaccines are intentional and preplanned.

SIDS (Sudden Infant Death Syndrome) kills over 10,000 babies a year. These deaths mysteriously occur shortly after vaccinations and immunizations. Vaccines have intentionally been created to be dangerous. The entire vaccine supply has been contaminated on purpose, which is why DNA fragments, cancer viruses, and mercury have been found in vaccines. The government is behind the destruction caused by vaccines, which is why more and more injections on children are mandated. Many top scientists have presented overwhelming evidence that cancer viruses are in most vaccines. Alex Jones, '9-11 Descent Into Tyranny,' said, "A recent poll in the United Kingdom showed that over 80% of the population opposes the mandatory injection of the measles, mumps and rubella (mmr) vaccine. A news anchor has gone public with the fact that this vaccine has brain damaged his child. Autism is up over 2,000 percent and is rising in the industrial world proportionately with the increase of mandated vaccinations."

All vaccines create long-term adverse effects. The intentional side effects of vaccines have been documented and include ADD, dyslexia, cancer, autism, ADHD, allergies, and all chronic immunological and neurological disorders. Alan Philips, 'Dispelling Vaccination Myths,' said, "A German study found correlations between vaccinations and 22 neurological conditions, including attention deficit and epilepsy. The dilemma is that viral elements in vaccines may persist and mutate in the human body for years, with unknown consequences. Millions of children are partaking in an enormous, crude experiment; and no sincere, organized effort is being made by the medical community to track the negative side effects or to determine the long term consequences."

Medical doctors are also victims of the brainwashing propaganda that I've been talking about. They work for the great conspiracy, but aren't wholly to blame. Medical students have no reason to question the information taught, so they generally believe what they're told. Individual doctors are not presented with the information addressed in alternative reports against the system. The illuminati create the medical school curriculum, which is why most doctors are still blind. The field of medicine demands conformity, and the world's system doesn't tolerate opinions opposing the status quo. Doctors can't warn you about what they themselves don't know. They are kept busy to leave little time for truth. Doctors are legally bound to adhere to the world's legal mandates and are held captive by the system. Ultimately, doctors are working towards your destruction like all the other branches of the illuminati system.

Doctors are administering death by pushing poisonous vaccines. The thoughts of the system have become their own thoughts unknowingly. The system that pays medical doctors discourages them from acquiring information independently to form their own opinions opposing the status quo. Any doctor who questions the status quo will be ostracized and still commanded to adhere to legal mandates established by the ruling establishment. Doctors are all CONTROLLED, and you thought these PROGRAMMED intellectuals are highly intelligent! Dr. Guylaine Lanctot, author of 'medical Mafia,' said, "The medical authorities keep lying. Vaccination has been a disaster on the immune system. It actually causes a lot of illnesses. We are actually changing our genetic code through vaccination ... 10 years from now we will know that the biggest crime against humanity: vaccines." Dr. Viera Scheibner conducted an independent study of the medical literature on vaccination and concluded, "There is no evidence whatsoever of the ability of vaccines to prevent any diseases. To the contrary, there is a great wealth of evidence that they cause serious side effects."

Vaccines are intentionally designed for our destruction. Childhood immunizations are not in the best interest of the child. 12 of the 18 average vaccination doses to children are contaminated with evil. Childhood vaccines contain mercury, a toxic metal to man, and the chemical preservative Thimerosal. Before the age of two, children receive about 200 micrograms of mercury, which is 3,040 times the safe level for adults. We are all in danger, not just the children. Formaldehyde is a preservative found in almost all vaccines. Formaldehyde is very poisonous, and there is no safe or acceptable amount for the human body. One of the leading experts on mercury poisoning, Dr. Boyd Haley, said, "Thimerosal is one of the most toxic compounds I know of. I can't think of anything that I know of is more lethal." Dr. Boyd Haley was also the Chairman of the Chemistry Department at the University of Kentucky. Take heed to the warnings in this book.

Children diagnosed with autism is on the rise, and it's because of vaccines. Children who've been immunized have come down with autism. Some have had seizures or began mentally going downhill not too long after vaccinations. The wise Amish religiously oppose vaccinations, which is why they've never had a case of autism! Based on established statistics, the Amish should have a few autistic among their 200,000, but have none. The Amish remain unaffected while the ratio of autistic children rapidly increases. If possible, avoid all vaccines!

Autism in children is caused by Thimerosal and Formaldehyde in vaccines. Thimerosal and Formaldehyde also cause Alzheimer's in the elderly and multiple neurological diseases. Vaccines are used in the third world for depopulation purposes. In Africa and Asia, vaccines are used to sterilize women without their knowledge. Throughout the world, vaccines are used to spread a plethora of health problems, diseases, and manmade plagues. If you trust any vaccine, you're an idiot. In a speech before the Citizens Against Legal Loopholes Rally, the Capitol Mall, Dr. Ley Horowitz said, "Indeed, it was contaminated live viral vaccines that spread this disease [AIDS] and likely others, including chronic fatigue, certain leukemia's, and possibly Gulf War Syndrome as well, to vast populations. In fact, today's live viral vaccines, including the oral polio vaccine required by law be given to our children, are still littered with simiah (monkey) virus contaminants since they are developed in monkey kidney cells, and the U.S. Food and Drug Administration turns a blind eye to as many as 100 live monkey virus contaminants per vaccine dose, and is barred from telling health professionals and even health scientists this truth because of pharmaceutical industry dictated proprietary laws and nondisclosure agreements."

Dr. Robert Mendelsohn, M.D., said, "The greatest threat of childhood diseases lies in the dangerous and ineffectual efforts made to prevent them through mass immunization .... There is no convincing scientific evidence that mass inoculations can be credited with eliminating any childhood disease." Dr. Robert Mendelsohn is a Light worker speaking the truth about his profession. He said, "Modern Medicine would rather you die using its remedies than live by using what physicians call quackery." We all need to listen to what this good doctor is saying to us. Dr. Mendelsohn said, "There are significant risks associated with every immunization and numerous contradictions that may make it dangerous for the shots to be given your child .... There is growing suspicion that immunization against relatively harmless childhood diseases may be responsible for the dramatic increase in autoimmune diseases since mass inoculations were introduced. These are fearful diseases such as cancer, leukemia, rheumatoid arthritis, multiple sclerosis, Lou Gehrig's disease, lupus erthematosus, and the Guillain-Barre syndrome."

I don't go visit doctors. I know who they are, but Dr. Robert Mendelsohn confirmed it when he said, "Doctors turn out to be dishonest, corrupt, unethical, sick, poorly educated, and downright stupid more often than the rest of society. When I meet a doctor, I generally figure I'm meeting a person who is narrow minded, prejudiced, and fairly incapable of reasoning and deliberation. Few of the doctors I meet prove my prediction wrong." Don't fool around with modern medicine! Dr. Mendelsohn said, "What does a Catholic do when he decides that his priests are no good? Sometimes he directly challenges them, but very seldom. He just leaves the Church. And that's my answer. Leave the Church of Modern Medicine. I see a lot of people doing that today." Doctors are more dangerous than the symptoms you see them for. I'm not the only enlightened human advising people to avoid doctors if possible. Dr. Robert Mendelsohn, M.D., said, "I don't advise anyone who has symptoms to go to the doctor for a physical examination. For people with symptoms, it's not such a good idea, either. The entire diagnostic procedure l—from the moment you enter the office to the moment you leave clutching a prescription or a referral appointment – is a seldom useful ritual." The doctor's job is to find something wrong with you. The great Dr. Mendelsohn said, "the door to the doctor's office ought to bear a surgeon general's warning that routine physical examinations are dangerous to your health. Why? Because doctors do not see themselves as guardians of health, and they have learned precious little about how to assure it. Instead, they are latter-day Don Quixotes, battling sometimes real but too often imaginary diseases. The disastrous difference is that doctors are not tilting at windmills. Rather, it is people who are damaged by their insistent search for dubious diseases to conquer."

Alternative medicine is the only safe option in our times because modern medicine is designed to destroy us. In Wes Penre's article 'The Witch Hunt on Alternative Medicine,' published by Illuminati News, he says, "In the mid 1970's President James E. Carter signed a Rockefeller document called the 'Global 2000 Report.' The basic intention with this report was to reduce the American population to 10% the current level, and the CFR's [Council on Foreign Relations] insider newsletter has expressed its intents to help that process along in the USA to about 45% current population levels. The agenda is very much on its way through immune-whacking vaccines they injected in us when we were children."

The media tries to scare us with threats of World War III, but WW III is a silent war that has already begun. The mass mind control of network television tricks blind Americans into believing that WW III will be the ultimate war where a large part of the world population will be wiped out via nuclear weapons. A nuclear war is planned, but World War III is already happening through vaccinations. Our current Third World War is a devastating quiet war with no classic weapons, only doctors, vaccines, and medications. WW III is a silent mind control war involving epidemics, lethal diseases, and the implanting of viruses. Vaccines are used to poison the population, which is why additives designed to make us sick are intentionally placed in them.

AIDS was implanted upon humanity through vaccines. The illuminati call blacks and homosexuals useless eaters, and implanted AIDS in them through hepatitis and vaccines laced with live AIDS virus. The AIDS virus exploded from and was implanted by the UN's World Health Organization. AIDS is a manufactured virus that has been artificially created. The article 'AIDS/HIV: An artificially Created Virus,' published by Godlike Productions, says, "Robert Gallo has publicly published experiments in which he crossed two sarcoma retroviruses to yield a genetic relative of the AIDS virus, 15 years before the AIDS virus was discovered. This guy was creating AIDS-related retroviruses 15 years before AIDS was discovered, AND he coincidently received the award for being the first scientist to discover the AIDS virus in 1984. ...AIDS is now a pandemic. In 2007, it was estimated that 33.2 million people lived with the disease worldwide, and that AIDS had killed an estimated 2.1 million people, including 330,000 children. Over three-quarters of these deaths occurred in sub-Saharan Africa, retarding economic growth and destroying human capital."

The power elite defense establishment seeded the whole baby boom generation with cancer viruses through vaccines. The contamination of polio vaccines was the intentional genocide of millions of Americans. One out of 3 baby boomers gets cancer when age kicks in and their immune systems are no longer able to fight off laboratory-created viruses. All vaccines given to children are biological time bombs that activate later in life. This is the real reason for the cancer rate in older Americans.

The destruction taking place now has been planned for many years. Right after President Clinton took office, David Rockefeller ordered him to take over (socialize) the health care system. The Rockefeller's oligarchy monopolizes the economy and health care, which is why 97.5% of health care is actually disease care. It was designed this way. Disease care is a part of the program, which is why most things are designed to make you become seriously ill faster. Mass media control, food and drug advertisements, and chemical-laced food are population control; a silent war waged on the American public.

Even though the ruling establishment intends to kill us off, people in the developed world live longer than previous generations. Medicine keeps sick people alive so all the different parties having financial interests in the Silent War can profit. The illuminati own the pharmaceutical industry and bring in trillions of dollars a day treating what they've created. Sick people with good health insurance are their milking cow, so they are allowed to hang around for profit while those in the Third World are eliminated. The Third World is excluded from exclusive media care and medicine, so their food supplies and resources are stolen from them. Undeveloped countries could be self sufficient by themselves or with a little help, but the global elite stop them. Starvation is a scam because there is an abundance of food in the world. The elite cut the supply off because the people in the Third World are the ones appointed to be killed first. Sooner or later, you'll discover that the people who control America from behind the scenes are the planet's greatest terrorists.

Vaccines are one of many ways the members of the elite will reduce the population. Some will be killed in real and staged wars, many will die in staged terror attacks, and others will be killed by the medical/pharmaceutical industry. Those who oppose the New World agenda will be jailed, murdered, or sent to concentration camps. The remaining population not affected by the above mentioned will live the rest of their lives as obedient slaves under terror and oppression. Artificially created diseases, sicknesses, and vaccine-induced illnesses will help the pharmaceutical industry continue to make their trillions. The end is here my friends.

Tracing history will help us understand how we got to where we are now in the apocalypse. Rockefeller and Carnegie created a medical monopoly in the early 20th century by financing 1640 medical schools with pharmacology. The Rockefeller and Carnegie families owned and controlled the drug companies. They originated the drug pushing that's been in practice since they took over the pharmacology medical school programs. The legislation that destroyed the influence of naturopathy (herbs), homeopathy, and other natural cure modalities was financed by John D. Rockefeller. Members of the elite want to forbid alternative medicine and vitamins, which is the natural way of healing.

John D. Rockefeller had a cartel of monopolies in numerous fields. He controlled all oil, chemicals, communications, banking, and drugs. Rockefeller merged his monopolies with the IG Farben cartel of monopolies in Europe. IG Farben brought Hitler to power. All of these monopoly cartels were cover organizations for the ruling establishment. After the war, IG Farben split up into Bayer, Hoechst, and BASF. IG Farben was still working undercover through these cover organizations. From then until now, the illuminati work undercover through cover organizations.

John D. Rockefeller destroyed nature-based medicine in America (which is the only real medicine). He raised up Hitler to enforce his IG Farben cartel agreements throughout Europe while he secretly did what every human should do when a doctor is needed. John D. Rockefeller had a homeopathic and naturopathic doctor who kept him alive until the age of 98. Alternative and natural medicine is the way God intended us to heal ourselves. The world's system ridicules natural cures so that the pharmaceutical industries can profit. Wherever alternative and natural medicine shows up, it's legislated against to protect pharmaceutical profits. Earthians run to doctors and submit to vaccines because of programming. The only sane thing to do is seek out a naturopathic and homeopathic doctor.

In the dark ages, those who practiced alternative treatment were burnt at the stake. Female witches used herbs and old wisdom to heal. These so-called witches exist today as practitioners of alternative medicine, naturopaths, and homeopaths. They were hunted in the Dark Ages, and are hunted now by the world pharmaceutical organization. The real cures are found in natural areas and contain no side effects. This is why the practitioners of alternative medicine were Rockefeller's worst enemies. Homeopaths and naturopaths halted the genocide of the world population, so John D. Rockefeller fought to actively destroy nature based medicine. Naturopathic and homeopathic doctors decrease the income of the Drug Cartels, which are controlled by the global elite.

The illuminati control the medical field and use it for your destruction. The field of medicine doesn't operate in your best interest. Poisoned vaccines are given to you to make you sick and die early. All vaccines decrease your immune system and work against your overall health. When people get sick, they're programming and conditioning drives them to go to the doctor. The doctors are all programmed to give you chemical drugs from the Rockefeller-owned drug companies. Doctors hammer the last nail into the coffin by recommending you receive poisoned vaccines.

Stop believing that doctors are intelligent people! Dr. Robert Mendelsohn said, "The admission tests and policies of medical schools virtually guarantee that the students who get in will make poor doctors. The quantitative tests, the Medical College Admission Test, and the reliance on grade point averages funnel through a certain type of personality who is unable and unwilling to communicate with people. Medical school does its best to turn smart students stupid, honest students corrupt, and healthy students sick. It isn't very hard to turn a smart student into a stupid one. First of all, the admissions people make sure the professors will get weak-willed, authority-abiding students to work on. Then they give them a curriculum that is absolutely meaningless as far as healing or health are concerned." Stop believing in doctors and trusting everything they say. Only an honest doctor will tell you the truth about the medical industry. Dr. Mendelsohn said, "Greed plays a role in causing unnecessary surgery, although I don't think the economic motive alone is enough to explain it. There's no doubt that if you eliminated all unnecessary surgery, most surgeons would go out of business. They'd have to look for honest work, because the surgeon gets paid when he performs surgery on you, not when you're treated some other way. In pre-paid group practices where surgeons are paid a steady salary not tied to how many operations they perform, hysterectomies and tonsillectomies occur only about one-third as often as in fee-for-service situations."—Robert S. Mendelsohn, M.D. 'Confessions of a Medical Heretic by Dr. Robert Mendelsohn.' Chapter 3 ("Ritual Mutilations"), pp. 58-59.

Doctors are programmed by the illuminati. Doctors are indoctrinated at CME (Continuing Medical Education) seminars. Every 3 years they must attend 50 hours of accredited CME seminars for programming. An AMA panel made up of doctors representing pharmaceutical companies determines CME seminar accreditation. Pharmaceutical companies provide all of the speakers for these pharmaceutical-sponsored seminars. Visiting reps from the pharmaceutical industry are the doctors' core avenue of learning throughout their practice. It's designed for doctors to rarely hear about alternative effective treatments. Dr. John R. Lee, M.D., said, "Pharmaceutical companies are very clever in their advertisements to doctors. When confronted by difficult treatment problems, doctors tend to be overly optimistic and gullible about believing the advertisements ... Doctors tend to be very busy with ... problems in their practice, and have little time or energy to read all the literature themselves. They therefore rely on supposed authorities to tell them what to do. They like to believe in authorities because it saves the time from having to study to seek out the best treatment options."

WW III is not a traditional war, but a silent war. A real war with weapons will occur shortly, but for now, vaccinations and medical treatments are the weapons of this quiet war. Vaccinations are pushed on every child in the name of health. Radiation is causing a massive epidemic of cancers intentionally. The media depresses people with bad news, which deactivates the immune system. Everything going on is in agreement with the Global 2000 Report.

There are cures for everything, but we're not privy to it. The cure for cancer has been around since the 1930's. The elite don't get cancer (very often), and their bodies live long. The unseen rulers of the world are not prone to get sick like regular people. RIFE is the answer. The article 'The Witch Hunt on Alternative Medicine,' published by Illuminati News, written by Wes Penre, says, "In the 30's-40's, a Doctor named Rife in the U.S. developed a machine that can be tuned to kill any micro-organism with RF modulated sound ... the AMA and the pharmaceuticals in the US and the equivalent in Canada and Britain threw up a fit and forced laws against the technology. About 5000 of these machines were produced. Only 3 to 5 are known to be in existence today ... but the governments have the others ... Many doctors and owners of these machines turned up dead and the machines disappeared ... The technology was so simple and cheap it would have ended health care as they knew it then as we know it now ... in Less than 20 minutes a day for about 2 weeks ... without any intrusion into the body, this machine would eradicate all cancer cells ... RIFE was developing the machine to find the exact frequencies that encourage the good cells or immune system cells to grow also ... [Cancer Research-A Super Fraud, Chris Gupta, www. newmediaexplorer.org]. He determined that all disease are micro-organisms which the immune system had trouble rejecting and they could be killed by the correct sound frequency ...”

People donating to Cancer societies are fools trusting in the medical community. Two-time Nobel Prize winner Linus Pauling, Ph.D., said, “Everyone should know that most cancer research is largely a fraud and that the major cancer research organizations are derelict in their duties to the people who support them.” Cancer research is a fraud, which is why cancer continues to increase despite the billions of dollars spent on cancer research. The Cancer Establishment is a very costly fraud. The poisoning of the planet by the petrochemical industries is used to sustain highly profitable and toxic therapies. Rising cancer rates correspond to the rise of the petrochemical industry's massive pesticide use on food. Synthetic organic chemicals created by the illuminati are living in the soil that grows your food and in your tissues through eating food. Over 70% of the food sold in supermarkets is poisonous and genetically and artificially engineered. Most of what we eat is fake food designed to give us cancer and make us sick.

Fear of cancer in the public influences people to put their cash in false hopes. Money donated to groups like the American Cancer Society and the National Cancer Institute is money wasted. The American Cancer Society spends over $1,000,000 a day. Only 16% of their money goes directly into help for cancer patients. The cash reserves of the American Cancer Society is over one billion dollars. The majority of donations are used for expensive drug research and bureaucratic overhead. The Cancer Establishment's Board of Directors isn't concerned about true cancer dialogue. Many former board members have moved on to high-ranking positions in the processed food and pharmaceutical industries.

Katy Schiel, 'The War on Cancer Is A Fraud,' said, "Cancer therapy money has become the proverbial 'pot of gold' for the armies of research facilities, charities, pharmaceutical companies, and lobbyists. Treating the sick and dying is big business – the average American diagnosed with cancer spends upwards of US $25,000 of their savings attempting to save their lives. Sadly, these people are not getting much for their money. Claims of serious 'progress' in the fight against cancer are bogus. The Cancer Establishments' statistics include many people with benign diseases; people in remission for more than five years are declared 'cured'. Many of those 'cured' patients will die from treatments or cancer after five years. With more money pledged to Nixon's failed war, no end is in sight."

The medical and pharmaceutical industries don't exist for your best interest. Toxins and poisons are intentionally placed in medicine to harm and weaken you. All side effects are placed in so-called cures on purpose. The side effects of most prescriptions are part of the plan. Doctors criminally promote toxic cures to help and destroy you at the same time. It's all about pharmaceutical profits, NOT your health. The article 'The War on Cancer Is A Fraud,' written by Katy Schiel, says, "One example of the almost criminal promotion of toxic 'cures' is the breast cancer drug Tamoxifen, the most widely subscribed drug for prevention in 'at risk' women and treating the cancer. What isn't know is that Tamoxifen is highly carcinogenic itself, causing high incidences of uterine and liver cancer not only in already ill women, but also in healthy women who are urged to take it for "prevention." Contrast this with a little publicized wonder drug which is cheap, readily available, has no side effects, and has been shown in five separate studies to reduce breast cancer risk by 30%: aspirin. Unfortunately, the Cancer

Establishment chooses to promote Taxoxifen over aspirin, which is not patentable, nor profitable to promote."

When you go to a doctor and accept prescriptions, you're participating in experimental drug testing. Pharmaceutical companies make you well and sick. The prevalence of complications in live-virus vaccines is intentional. Pharmaceutical companies are nothing but big businesses destroying people's health. The prescribed toxic drugs are destruction disguised as a humanitarian effort. The pharmaceutical industry does nothing out of the goodness of their hearts, but for the avariciousness of their wallets.

Refuse to get yourself and your children vaccinated. The article 'The Sinister Vaccine Scam,' written by John Quinn at News Hawk, says, "...most, if not ALL, vaccines are a literal abomination; EXTREMELY toxic to our bodies; almost CERTAIN to promote or engender severe and sometimes terminal reactions from the victims they were administered to; and are many TIMES more damaging to infants and toddlers—to whom these terrible health threats are MOST OFTEN administered. ... in many areas, parents are actually coerced/threatened and forced by the New World Order Gestapo to vaccinate their children or have it forcibly done to their children. Then of course, resisting or uncooperative parents can look forward to the feds (often hiding behind county and state social services sub-Gestapo units) taking legal steps in the crap-hole courtrooms of the uncountable number of corrupt, paid-off and lunatic judges in this country to TAKE THEIR CHILDREN AWAY FROM THEM, and put the kids under the direct control of the Brave New World Order STATE." When it comes to fighting the New World Order in court over forced vaccination or anything else, know that the legal system is a sham. 90% of Judges are corrupt and paid off. The system that you're looking toward to save you is CONTROLLED; for the Judge and prosecutor sit on the same bench.

Vaccines intentionally cause autism. Current childhood vaccines are nothing but bad news. The incidence of autism increasing has a small number of good-hearted medical professionals questioning the FDA's vaccine safety tests. Adverse effects of all vaccines are part of the depopulation plan. We don't have the full conclusion of effects because of the illuminati's FDA. The lack of enough research to determine the harm of all vaccines is intentional. Dr. Harold Buttram said, "A small but growing minority of physicians and scientists are becoming aware that safety testing for the various vaccines has been woefully inadequate...The basic question, therefore, is whether the benefits of current childhood vaccines outweigh the harm, or whether the reverse is true."

The use of vaccines has caused a great increase in diseases of the mucous membranes, such as eczema and asthma. According to Dr. Harold Buttram, some experts believe that measles, mumps, rubella, chicken pox, and certain childhood illnesses are necessary and helpful in strengthening the immune system. Physicians and government officials are siding with evil through vaccines given by injection. The officials make childhood vaccines mandatory, and the medical professions administer the evil. In the article 'Vaccine linked to autism? New report points to dangers of MMR immunization,' written by Julie Foster, she said, "A new report by Dr. Harold Buttram, a practicing physician in Quakertown, PA, suggests the recent increase in the number of autistic children could be caused by the combination measles, mumps and rubella, or MMR, vaccine routinely given to children at age 8 months – a phenomenon the Centers for Disease Control and Prevention claim is highly unlikely. In a past study of autistic children, researchers found that 84 percent of the children had antibodies against a certain type of brain tissue, indicating that the immune system was destroying brain cells. The researchers also found the brain tissue antibody to be very similar to the antibody that's formed against the MMR vaccine. Additionally, MMR antibody was found in 59 percent of the autistic children compared to 10 percent in normal children."

Founder and director of the Autism Research Institute in San Diego, California, Dr. Bernard Rimland, told Discovery Health. com, "There are no data on the triple vaccines." According to

Rimland, many parents have mentioned that the diphteria, pertussin and tetanus, or DPT vaccine had an adverse effect on their children. The same harmful effects were reported about the MMR vaccine. According to the FDA, between 90 and 99 percent of vaccination adverse effects go unreported, even though doctors can report them through the Vaccine Adverse Effect Reporting System. Many doctors don't report adverse effects resulting from vaccinations because of the lack of a penalty. Rimland noted and pointed out that the triple vaccines put extra stress on the body. The immune system deals with one virus at a time, so combining the individual measles, mumps and rubella vaccines into one makes the vaccine like all others, DANGEROUS!

Government involvement in the medical field is not in your best interest. Dr. Bernard Rimland said, "When arbitrary decisions in the mandating of vaccines are made by government bureaucracies, which frequently work hand-in-glove with the pharmaceutical industry, with no recourse open to parents, we have all the potential ingredients for a tragedy of historic proportions." Physicians participating in the conspiracy are programmed. Dr. Rimland said, "The physician has been taught repeatedly that these vaccines are perfectly safe and that any event that is supposedly associated with them is just a coincidence." There is an autism – MMR vaccine link that hasn't been properly investigated. Executive director of the Association of American Physicians and Surgeons, Jane Orient, M.D., said, "I think that there has been a frightening increase in cases of autism that has not been explained. There are a number of anecdotal reports from parents that symptoms of autism have appeared close to the time of the vaccine. With each vaccine and each patient, there needs to be a risk-benefit analysis" to determine if the vaccine is worth the risk of developing autism.

Save the Children!

The psychiatric diagnosing and drugging of American children is the new child abuse. In societies throughout the world, the most vulnerable members are abused. Those who have been widely abused in every society are children, the elderly, women, the poor, the physically disabled, the mentally distressed, and those with unconventional lifestyles. These victims have been abused to varying degrees. Every society has its own methods of abusing ethic, racial, and religious minorities. Abuses will never be eliminated completely, and will only expand because of the world's distractions. The mass mind control of network television, entertainment, and celebrity gossip keep people from focusing on the real issues in societies throughout the world. Individual citizens justify or ignore abuses and fail to take a stand because they're distracted. The mainstream media keeps the real issues at hand wholly unacknowledged.

The mass unconsciousness in this world has turned earth into a hell realm for many. Rampant abuses on society's most vulnerable members have been justified on ethnic, religious, or patriotic grounds. The worst abuses are rationalized by the media, doctors, and the government. Destruction has attacked children, the elderly, and the psychologically distressed on scientific and medical grounds. The most devastating form of child abuse in our society has been rationalized and justified by science and medicine. Millions of children are victims of the new child abuse: the psychiatric drugging of our children. Many children are wrongly subdued by multiple psychiatric drugs. Perfectly normal children will at some time in the future be falsely diagnosed or drugged. The Psychopharmaceutical Complex, the pharmaceutical industry, organized medicine and psychiatry, insurance companies, and NIMH are responsible for the psychiatric diagnosing and drugging of innocent children.

Various groups supported by the drug companies prey on the most vulnerable children. The easy targets are nearly every child in foster care, special education classes, or on SSI/SSDI. Typical child and adolescent behavior has been falsely redefined as mental illness. Children who get bored or distracted easily, talk too much or too little, fidget, have mood swings, aren't obedient, or defy rules most likely will be tagged with Avoidant Personality Disorder, Attention Deficit Hyperactivity Disorder, Bipolar Disorder, Oppositional Defiant Disorder, or other fake ills. The psychiatric industry ensures that millions of children are branded with illusory mental disorders so that they can be prescribed stimulants to benefit the pharmaceutical industry.

Children who are normal fall victim to psychiatric drugs at the hands of educational authorities, child services, or psychiatric authorities. Parents are deceived, misled, and intimidated by various authorities coercing them to medicate their children against their personal judgment. The psychopharmaceutical Complex is behind the innumerable diagnoses slapped on normal children, including LD, OCD, ADHD, bipolar disorder, Asperger's spectrum disorders, oppositional defiant disorder, and autism. Children fall victim to tricky psychological tests designed to set them up. These traps allegedly identify frontal lobe dysfunctions based on flawed executive functions or inattention.

Many diagnoses have been intentionally created to open the door for every class of psychiatric medication to be administered to children. The abundance of psychiatric drugs forced upon children include stimulants, antipsychotic agents, tranquilizers, mood stabilizers, and antidepressants. The illuminati's FDA has given official approval for giving children Geodon, Risperdal, Seroquel, Zyprexa, and many other deadly anti-psychotics. Anti-hypertension drugs, anti-seizure drugs, and all psychiatric medications have a harmful impact and can sedate any child's growing brain. Psychiatrists and such routinely dispense dangerous drugs with callous disregard for their harmful effects. All psychiatric drugs have potentially lethal or horrible adverse effects. Antipsychotic agents cause chronic depression, growth stunting, severe obesity, shortened lifespan, diabetes, and disfiguring neurological disorders.

Research antipsychotic drugs or read 'Brain-Disabling Treatments in Psychiatry, Second Edition' by Dr. Peter Breggin.

Psychiatric diagnosis are flawed, and the chemical structures of the psychiatric drugs are dangerous. The world's system creates promotional strategies to promote the psychiatric diagnosing and drugging of children. The pharmaceutical industry, organized psychiatry, and the Psychopharmaceutical Complex are benefiting off of flawed philosophies. It is abusive to psychiatrically diagnose and drug children. Evil psychiatric and educational authorities have robbed children of their self-esteem and unlimited future by falsely convincing them that they have something wrong in their minds. Parents have been presented with the flawed philosophy of biochemical imbalances or genetically crossed wires. Children are convinced that they have a psychiatric diagnosis and treated as if something is wrong with them. Authorities in these children's lives teach them to rely on psychiatric drugs, while psychiatrists strive to make them lifelong mental patients.

Doctors, psychiatrists, and medical authorities give children psychiatric drugs while ignoring the known adverse effects. Scientific evidence proves that psychiatric treatment is based on the brain-disabling principle. Psychiatric drugs and all psychoactive substances don't improve the function of brain and mind, but compromise and reduce it. Some drugs are designed to artificially make you feel good, but partially disable your highest mental life. All psychoactive substances are poisonous to brain cells and negatively impact the mind. The brain and mind react to the brain-disabling chemicals crossing one's blood brain barrier, disrupting normal biochemical functions. Psychiatric drugging makes one more accustomed to his or her reduced mental acuity and more flattened emotions. Brains drenched in toxic substances are forever chemically altered and extremely polluted. To discover what's really going on here, read 'Medication Madness: The Role of Psychiatric Drugs in Cases of Violence, Suicide and Crimes,' 'Brain Disabling Treatments in Psychiatry' and 'Second Edition: Drugs, Electroshock and the Psychopharmaceutical Complex' by Dr. Peter Breggin.

The emotional and spiritual life of a child falsely diagnosed with a mental disorder and forced to take psychiatric drugs is ruined. Toxic intrusions keep children from becoming what they should become. When children are told that they're mentally impaired or different, it impacts them negatively. When expectations of parents and teachers are tailored to false limitations that are based in lies, the child suffers. It's not productive to tell a child that he or she is not normal and has a disorder. Just because mental health professionals working in the best interest of pharmaceutical companies say millions of children need psychiatric drugs doesn't really mean that they have to take a drug to make them normal. The psychiatric diagnosing and drugging of children is BIG BUSINESS. It's the new child abuse because children can't do anything about it. Children have an inherent desire to love, and want to appease adults. They've been penalized for wanting to play and have fun.

The rampant abuse of children via psychiatric drugging is supported by universities, medical and scientific authorities, and the government, who all misled the parents. The medical and pharmaceutical industry benefit from these abuses. Authority at the top of society justifies the psychiatric abuse of children and use their resources to allow these widespread abuses to persist. Children stigmatized and marginalized by psychiatric diagnoses feel bad, but those in authority could care less. Spiritual people will be emphatic toward these abused children and protest in their own way to make a difference. When you educate yourself to the world of education, science, and philosophy about children and childhood, you'll become motivated, angry, engaged, and energized. The world's system isn't offering children genuine inspiration, love, education, and service, which is why the conscious must work to protect children from psychiatric abuse.

Psychiatric drugs impair one's ability to perceive and evaluate the change caused by psychoactive substances. Psychiatric medication causes an emotional and cognitive disruption. The psychiatric drugging of children should cause alarm, but society is too busy being entertained, distracted, or programmed by network television. Children diagnosed and drugged for profit is pure tyranny. Thomas Jefferson said, "All tyranny needs to gain a foothold is for people of good conscience to remain silent." This is the purpose of the corporate mainstream news media. The main purpose of the media is to lie and deceive.

The psychiatric industry is the grand hoax. Over 20 million children worldwide are falsely diagnosed with mental disorders so that they can be drugged for profit. After criminals diagnose vulnerable children, they're placed on psychiatric drugs for years to life. Parents, children, and schools are deceived by insidious yet profitable misinformation campaigns designed by the ruling elite. Modern society is programmed to accept the psychiatric industry's madness. The article 'The Hidden Tyranny: Children Diagnosed and Drugged For Profit,' written by Monica G. Young says, "Kids who fidget, get distracted or bored easily, talk too much (or too little), defy rules, are not obedient as some adults may like or have mood swings, are liable to be tagged with Attention Deficit Hyperactivity Disorder, Oppositional Defiant Disorder, Bipolar Disorder, Avoidant Personality Disorder or other such ills. In short, what used to be known as typical child and adolescent behavior has been redefined as mental illness. ADHD is the disorder most commonly assigned to kids (over five million in the U.S.). Statistical studies in the U.S. and other nations show boys are far more likely than girls to be branded with ADHD and prescribed stimulants."

Boys are being medicated with Ritalin because psychiatrists have practically made boyhood itself a psychiatric disorder. Getting in a fight at school is enough for a child to be led at once to a referral for psychiatric treatment. The psychiatric industry is such a fraud that many children are evaluated, diagnosed, and prescribed in a manner of minutes. African-American males get the worst treatment. In many classrooms, 50 percent of the black male students are being referred for medication according to Umar R. Abdullah-Johnson, a psychologist and activist for the educational rights of black boys. He has traveled to schools across the country, and wrote the article 'Psycho-Slavery.' Umar R. Abdullah-Johnson said, "It has become a travesty of epic proportions; black boys are being sent in record numbers to the psychiatrist for mind-altering medications that come with a plethora of side effects. They claim to LEAVE NO CHILD BEHIND, but are totally content leaving our boys with side effects from these drugs years after they have graduated from school, if they ever graduate at all." The hidden tyranny at this moment is drugging a generation of black boys on substances. This child abuse leads to illegal drug use later in their lives.

The system is forcing the children into submissive conformity with a psychiatric standard of normality designed to trap most of them. Children are brainwashed into believing that they can't deal with school or life without psychiatric drugs. Massive propaganda asserts the validity of (so-called) disorders and efficacy of psychiatric medications to fool parents and others. There's inadequate evidence proving that drugs used to treat ADHD are safe or help school performance. No medical tests are used to diagnose children. Youths are diagnosed based on false opinions, then put on highly toxic drugs. Psychiatric drugs have been shown to cause sudden death, violence, suicide, heart attacks, hallucinations, psychosis, anxiety, stunted growth, and insomnia. Not only children, but toddlers are being falsely diagnosed with mental disorders and prescribed toxic drugs. Peter Breggin, M.D., stated in the Huffington Post, "Our society's particular form of child abuse is the psychiatric diagnosing and drugging of our children. All psychoactive substances from alcohol and marijuana to psychiatric drugs reduce and compromise the function of brain and mind, and none improve it."

A look at history reveals that society should leave all children alone. Let the children be, without psychiatric drugs. Mental illness is a myth. Children diagnosed and drugged for profit is an abomination. Jawara King loves the children! Thomas Edison was kicked out of school when his teacher got upset with his wandering mind and persistent questions. Where would we be if one of the world's most prolific inventor's creative spirit was destroyed by prescription drugs? The father of modern physics, Albert Einstein, didn't communicate with his peers as a child and was labeled a foolish day dreamer. He resented the school's learning methods. In modern times, he would've been medicated into conformity. The orator and statesman Winston Churchill was often in trouble as a youth. Today he would have been diagnosed as ODD (Oppositional Defiant Disorder) because of his independent and rebellious nature. Leader of the abolitionist movement, Frederick Douglass, defined the rules for blacks as a child. The list is never-ending of great individuals in history who would've been diagnosed and drugged if they were growing up in today's psychiatric standards.

Psychiatric drugging of children is all about money, and used to bring in BILLIONS of dollars a year. Labeling vulnerable children as mentally ill is a form of tyrannical social control. Drugging innocent children conditions them to be robots who won't deviate from the status quo. Over 84 percent of ADHD-labeled children are forced to take psychiatric medications. Children who are drugged with psychoactive drugs are more likely to develop serious substance abuse problems in the future. The psychiatric and pharmaceutical companies want to make children life-long psychiatric patients for profit. It's a grand conspiracy where psychiatrists classify out-of-the-box, divergent behavior as one of many (made-up) mental disorders that must be subdued with psychiatric medication (according to them).

Children diagnosed and drugged for profit is the hidden tyranny destroying the next generation. Parents are allowing it because they've been programmed, deceived, and conditioned. The pharmaceutical and psychiatric industries make BILLIONS while weak brainwashed parents allow their children to be destroyed psychologically, socially, and mentally. A former drug company sales rep named Gwen Olsen wrote a book called 'Confessions of an Rx Drug Rusher,' explaining what's really going on. Gwen

Olsen said, "Children are known to be compliant patients and that makes them a highly desirable market for drugs. Children are forced by school personnel to take their drugs, they are forced by their parents to take their drugs, and they are forced by their doctors to take their drugs. So children are the ideal patient-type because they represent refilled prescription compliance and 'longevity.' In other words, they will be lifelong patients and repeat customers for Pharma."

The world's sick social system has millions of children on Anti-Psychotics. Millions of individual children are prescribed Seroquel, Zyprexa, Risperdal, Abilify, Geodon, Invega, and other anti-psychotic drugs. Children shouldn't be drugged with stimulants and anti-depressants. These anti-psychotics steal from and work against the children. The world is insane, evidenced by the number of anti-psychotic prescriptions dispensed to children (0-17 years old). The children aren't insane, but their deceived parents, pharmaceutical companies, and the psychiatric industry. Insane psychiatrists have applied diagnoses to infants and toddlers (aged 0-2) such as: Residual Schizophrenia, Behavior Problems, Emotional Disturbances, Attention Deficit Disorder, and other illusory Mental/Behavior Problems. According to the mental health world, diagnosis are made on the basis of "odd beliefs and unusual perceptual experience." This sham is the new child abuse.

Our psychiatric civilization must be dealt with. The use of powerful anti-psychotics with privately insured U.S. children is cause for alarm. The widespread number of children being medicated with prescription psychiatric drugs is increasing every year. Drug companies are pushing and benefiting from this madness. The psychiatric and pharmaceutical industries want the children to be hooked on medications for life. Monica G. Young's article 'The hidden tyranny: children diagnosed and drugged for profit' says, "ADHD, ODD, Bipolar and the others were voted into existence by APA committees and made official by issuance in the Diagnostic Statistical Manual. A 2006 investigation by the University of Massachusetts and Tufts University disclosed that the majority of the committee members had financial ties to drug companies. The psychiatric and pharmaceutical industries admittedly do not cure anything, but only claim to manage symptoms with their psychoactive drugs. Vice President of drug giant Bristol-Myers Squibb recently announced FDA approval for an expanded use of their bipolar blockbuster. He states, "Because bipolar disorder is a lifelong and recurrent illness, this labeling update provides physicians with the option to prescribe Abilify as an add-on to either lithium or valproate as a long-term treatment to help manage symptoms of Bipolar I Disorder." Translation for bipolars: "You'll be hooked on our medications for life."

Record numbers of American children are being prescribed toxic psychiatric drugs for profit-making opportunities. The life of the parents affect the children. The corporate class exploits workers and pays them less than what their labor is worth. When many are laid off, the rest of the workers are commanded to work harder for much less. This exploitation and deprivation of a child's parent affects the child. Children who live with a distressed, overwhelmed, anxious, or angry parent will respond to parental distress with their own behaviors and symptoms. The parent's distress gives birth to the child's distress. The world's system doesn't invest in families, so the distressed children of distressed parents are being labeled with (phony) mental disorders. Children are drugged into submission instead of receiving help for the real issues at hand. Putting children on anti-psychotics robs them of their health and any real life improvement. The power of drug-company marketing has brainwashed parents into allowing their children to be drugged with powerful anti-psychotics. The effects of psychiatric drugs on children are unknown. In adults, the toxic compounds in anti-psychotics increase the risk of obesity, nervous-system damage, infection, suicide, diabetes, stroke, kidney failure, cardiovascular disease, seizures, and sudden death.

The lifestyle of the parents affect the child. There's nothing wrong with the millions of children on anti-psychotics. If someone would take the time to listen to and understand their stories, it would be discovered that the children are just being children. The parent and the child should be looked upon as a single entity. In the article 'One Million Kids on Anti-Psychotics,' published by Dissident Voice, Susan Rosenthal says, "A more accurate diagnosis for these children's symptoms and behaviors would be "Parental Distress due to Heartless Social Policies." A recent report from the Urban Institute found that 7 percent of all 9-month-old infants live with severely depressed mothers, and 41 percent of 9-month-old infants live with mothers who suffer some form of depression. These rates are higher among mothers living in poverty, who are more likely to suffer domestic violence."

Stay away from ALL psychiatric drug use! Normal occurrences have been mistaken for mental illness. Psychiatric drugs are prescribed to those going through a personal crisis (which is a natural part of life). Those who've had a series of traumatic events in their backgrounds have been placed on tranquilizers. Psychiatric diagnosis and drugs are used as a substitute for the real answer: counseling and encouragement. People who run into emotional difficulty and seek help from the wrong people (anyone involved with the Psychiatric industry) are prescribed anti-psychotics. Psychiatrist Peter Breggin wrote an article for the Huffington Post entitled 'Our Psychiatric Civilization.' In it, Dr. Peter Breggin said, "People email and call the office identifying themselves as "bipolar" or "clinically depressed." Or they describe their children in the same terms, as well as "ADHD." By the time they contact our office, their lives or those of their children have been deeply complicated, compromised and sometimes ruined by psychiatric drugs. They can no longer separate their original emotional problems from their complex array of drug side effects. They devote themselves to adjusting their diagnoses and their drugs instead of addressing their lives. ...The culture is so imbued with biological psychiatry – which is to say, modern psychiatry – that self-defined patients diagnose themselves, sometimes with the help of a one-minute TV ad. They visit their family doc, give him the diagnosis, "I think I have an anxiety disorder," and get the appropriate drug. If they arrive a few minutes early, or the doctor is a few minutes late, they'll get a chance to get educated by a flat screen TV in the waiting room which instructs them about the symptoms of the psychiatric diagnosis de jour as well as its treatment with a propriety drug."

The medicating of American children is medication madness. Mental health assessments, psychotherapy visits, and visiting with psychiatrists are designed to increase anti-psychotic drug use. Even without the service of these so-called mental health professionals, children are being drug-treated. The psychiatric drugging of American children is a trick because the medical, pharmaceutical, and psychiatric industries created a false evaluation structure designed to condemn over 70% of normal children. Through trickery, anti-psychotic treated children are falsely diagnosed as having disruptive behavior disorder, pervasive developmental disorder, attention deficit hyperactivity disorder, or other illusory labels. I said earlier that death is one of the many side effects of psychiatric medications. 4-year-old Rebecca Riley was killed by the psychiatric industry. Writer for the Portland Press Herald, Leigh Donaldson, wrote, "Highlighting the controversial nature of medicating American children is the recent death of Rebecca Riley, a 4-year-old Boston girl diagnosed with ADHD and pediatric bipolar disorder at 28 months of age. According to a medical examiner, she died from the effects of a combination of Clonidine, a blood pressure medication prescribed for ADHD, Depakote, an anti-seizure and mood stabilizer for her bipolar disorder, as well as a cough suppressant and an antihistamine."

If you or your children are on prescribed psychiatric drugs, cut back, then get off to avoid drug withdrawal. Without a slower taper of your current medication, you may have a withdrawal reaction. Save your mind and save your children by abandoning the psychiatric industry. No child should be on any kind of antipsychotics whatsoever! Anti-depressants, anti-psychotic substances, stimulants, and mood stabilizers threaten the normal development of the brains of growing children. Long-term use of psychiatric drugs hazardously effects the metabolic and cardiovascular systems. Vera Hassner Sharav, president of the Alliance for Human Research Protection, warned, "Anti-psychotics, which are being widely and irresponsibly prescribed for American children – mostly as chemical restraints – are shown to be causing irreparable harm." These drugs do nothing but harm and destroy. Dr. Peter Breggin said, "There is no drug that improves the function of the brain."

11 year old Stephanie Hall, 14 year old Matthew Smith, 10 year old Shaina Dunkle, and many other children have been killed by psychiatric drugs. Alternative therapies, homeopathy, and counseling are advised over what the psychiatric, pharmaceutical, and medical industries have to offer. Learn the truth about the drugs used to treat children diagnosed with ADD or ADHD. Due to lack of knowledge, parents allow their children to die or suffer side effects at the hands of the psychiatric and pharmaceutical industries. Find a holistic nutritionist and naturopath to help with your child's overall health and wellness. The mass psychotropic drugging of children with psychiatric drugs is the result of the methods used in the miss-diagnosing of millions of children. The labels of Attention Deficit Disorder and Attention hyperactivity disorder are slapped on children so that they can be drugged for profit. Parents allow this because they are not familiar with the dangers of psychotropic drugs. Countless children have died as a direct result of using psychotropic drugs, but no one cares. Suicides, dangers, deaths, and health risks are the direct result of administering psychiatric drugs to children. Stop believing in the validity of these fake disorders, which are ALL of an unscientific nature.

The large numbers of children's deaths linked to drugs used for 'psychiatric treatment' isn't advertised. Methylphenidate (Ritalin), used for Attention Deficit Hyperactivity Disorder, causes constriction of arteries and veins. Ritalin leads to damage to the heart because it causes the heart to work overtime. Parents aren't told of the unscientific nature of all so-called mental disorders, nor the risks of the treatments involving psychiatric drugs. Undiagnosed allergies, food sensitivities, and other things can manifest with the symptoms of psychiatry's ADHD.

Compare the unmedicated and medicated ADHD children to discover the dangers of psycho-stimulants. Any child alive can be described as suffering from ADHD based on the symptoms the system has set up. Children are only given a label to offer them a treatment, which benefits the drug companies. The symptoms which characterize ADD and ADHD (according to the system) may include: a short attention span, emotional liability, distractibility, impulsivity, hyperactivity, abnormal EEG, and minor neurological signs. Children are diagnosed to benefit the international drug industry, even though learning may or may not be impaired. Badly behaved children are given a pseudoscientific label. Once they are diagnosed as suffering from various types of brain hyperactivity, they will be forced to take psycho-stimulants. This is a scam in which vague diagnosis are used by teachers, parents, and social workers to excuse and explain unacceptable, undesirable, and uncontrollable behavior.

It's easy for teachers and social workers to define children who misbehave as suffering from MBD, ADHD, or some other false disorder. Any child who doesn't learn properly is given a convenient diagnosis. The treatment of badly behaved children has been reduced to toxic psychiatric drugging. Some of the side effects of Ritalin are nervousness, decreased appetite, insomnia, drowsiness, headache, dizziness, blurred vision, convulsions, dyskinesia, toxic psychosis, abdominal pain, nausea, visual and tactile hallucinations, vomiting, changes in blood pressure and heart rate, and palpitations. The pharmaceutical industry describes Ritalin as 'very safe,' but it also causes anaemia and minor retardation of growth during prolonged therapy in children. Ritalin aggravates the symptoms of tension, agitation, and marked anxiety. Prolonged therapy can result in growth retardation, causing a child to lose several inches in possible height. There is usually a growth spurt after so-called treatment is stopped. Drug withdrawal causes depression, renewed overactivity, and sometimes suicide. The answer is to avoid psychostimulants, regardless of what prescribers, teachers, doctors, and psychiatrists say. You're trusting the wrong people.

Parents who are too lazy to do their own research are victims of ignorance and misplaced trust, which is why their children are deteriorating. The world would be a healthier place without psychiatric drugs. Psychiatrists have blind parents believing in various behavioral disorders, causing the parents to sacrifice their children for the benefit of pharmaceutical drug companies. Doctors, programmed parents, and teachers may recommend psychiatric drugs, but they all cause permanent long-term damage. Even if some of the drugs work a little bit, the side effects do more damage than any 'perceived' good a drug might do.

Millions of children are taken advantage of by the pharmaceutical, psychiatric, and medical industries by being falsely diagnosed as suffering from ADHD, ADD, or MBD. None of these conditions, including hyperactivity, really exist. Children are falsely labeled so that they can be treated with powerful drugs for profit. The use of behavior modification drugs on children is against the Constitution of the Cosmos. The use of psychiatric drugs on children continues to rise inexorably because society is programmed by the big drug companies. The drugging of children by those whom they trust is authorized child abuse on a massive scale. Prescribing mind altering drugs is big business. Antidepressants and stimulants among toddlers aged between two and four is ridiculous. What's wrong with you parents? The period between birth and 4 years of age is when the brain is maturing and great change is happening in the human body. The effects of psychiatric drugs on tiny developing brains isn't worth the risk. Antidepressants, stimulants, Ritalin, and other powerful drugs are widely prescribed for toddlers simply for being restless and inattentive (the fake symptoms of alleged diseases). The world is insane, and drugging small children for profit is one of its characteristics.

Psychiatrists have attempted to study brain abnormalities or differences among people diagnosed with ADHD, which is a false study because post-traumatic stress disorder, victims of child abuse, and other factors cause smaller hippocampi and abnormal amygdala activation. Behavior, function, and experience can change or determine one's brain structure. Psychiatric researchers claim that total cerebral volume is approximately 3% smaller in children with ADHD, on an anatomic level. Psychiatric clinicians claim that ADHD children have smaller brains, when looking at ADHD and cerebral volume in children. What they need to be studying is the effects of psychotropic medication while conducting neuroimaging research with ADHD patients. ADHD is not a disorder, which is why the psychiatric community is trying to prove that biological correlates of abnormal behavior are the cause of brain basis of abnormal behavior. Neuroscience and the concept of the brain-behavior relationship with bi-directional causalities don't validate psychiatric research and psychiatric disorders. Brain differences (so-called abnormalities) are related to one's state of mind, rather than the trait of a symptom of psychiatry's behavior in question. The ADHD neuroimaging field is a fraud because the effects of medication exposure on brain volume remains unexamined. The conclusion of the matter is that psychiatry is not a medical science, mental illness as a biological entity is false, and the chemical imbalance premise for psychiatric drug medication is a myth.

Facts are withheld from parents to alter their life decisions in favor of the pharmaceutical and psychiatric industries. Every child labeled and drugged provides additional money from the state and federal government for the school. Schools that label and drug children receive a financial incentive, which explains the increase in the labeling and drugging within the school system. Parents on government welfare get more money for every child in their family that's labeled and drugged. Lower socio-economic parents in hard times are seduced into drugging their own children for financial incentives. The DSM is the unscientific billing scriptures for psychiatry, so you are labeling your child with a mental illness by labeling your child with ADHD. Children taking psycho-tropic, psycho-stimulant drugs after the age of 12 are ineligible for military service. The point is, keep your children away from psychiatric diagnosing and drugging!

The Drug Enforcement Administration, in their report on Methylphenidate, said, "However, contrary to popular belief, stimulants like methylphenidate will affect normal children and adults in the same manner that they affect ADHD children. Behavioral or attentional improvements with methylphenidate treatment therefore is not diagnostic of ADHD." (pill) This statement goes against what the 'professionals' are telling parents. Medical, psychiatric, and pharmaceutical people have a vested stake in the diagnosis itself. The DEA also states that: "Of particular concern is that most of the ADHD literature prepared for public consumption by CHADD and other groups and available to parents, does not address the abuse potential or actual abuse of methylphenidate. Instead, methylphenidate (usually referred to as Ritalin by these groups) is routinely portrayed as a benign, mild substance that is not associated with abuse or serious side effects. In reality, however, there is an abundance of scientific literature which indicates that methylphenidate shares the same abuse potential as other Schedule II stimulants." (p. 4)

CHADD and all the other groups available to parents are supported financially by pharmaceutical companies, proving that heavy brainwashing is going on. The Berkeley Study concludes that Ritalin and other stimulants raise the risk of drug use. Marilyn Chase wrote in the Wall Street Journal, "Nadine Lambert, a professor of education, followed almost 500 children for 26 years. She argues that exposure to Ritalin makes the brain more susceptible to the addictive power of cocaine and doubles the risk of abuse."

This information is hidden from parents because it doesn't support the theories of evil humans using false diagnosis to profit off of the children. Parents are given false research claiming that if their children go untreated and unmedicated, they will end up in a bad way. Biased and unproven research, such as the Beiderman study, infiltrates schools to program the unthinking with lies. Pharmaceutical companies, such as Novartis, distribute the false information, which is a conflict of interest concerning the health of children. Even after many more children die from psychiatric drugs, the horror won't end. People won't become outraged and act because they've been programmed by the psychiatric and pharmaceutical industries. Profit is more important than the safety and lives of children. The real information will remain suppressed and unexposed due to the enormous amount of money and profit at stake for the psychiatric, medical, and pharmaceutical industries. Over 20 million children worldwide have been diagnosed with mental disorders so that they can be placed on psychiatric drugs for years or life. This is the grand hoax; the most insidious and profitable misinformation campaigns in the history of mental health. Those who speak how I speak about this subject will be suppressed and quieted.

Hell On Earth

Read the (declassified) Kissinger Report – Global Depopulation Agenda – December 10, 1974. The National Security Study Memorandum, NSSM 200, Implications of Worldwide Population Growth for U.S. Security and Overseas Interests (The Kissinger Report), explains the drop in male fertility since the 1970's. The Global Depopulation Agenda explains a lot of things going on in the world. The world was introduced to AIDS on purpose. AIDS was intentionally given to Africa so that they'd adopt a contraceptive dependency, which would in turn bring down the population. The plan called for women in LDC to be paid to have abortions. Abortion is a form of income for these women, which is part of the plan. W.H.O. mandatory vaccines, artificially created illness, and the medical community have global sterilization potential. Read the Kissinger Report on Global Population Control and come to your own conclusions. All this 'hell on earth' was pre-planned.

There is a global Eugenics agenda going on that most are unaware of. The corporate insanity is the controlled demolition of the human race. Anabolic steroids, which weaken the immune system, are used to bulk up beef cattle. Oestrogen, which is demasculinises males, is used to increase the milk yield in dairy cattle. Mike Philbin's article 'Free Planet: The Kissinger Report – Global Depopulation Agenda,' says, "Evidently, there's a real pandemic of conflicting evidence out there. On the one hand you've got The Kissinger Report saying there's too many of us, and on the other hand, we've got attempts to INCREASE fertility, and a recent report suggests artificial sperm has been made in the laboratory. Maybe it's a simple question of numbers ... some statisticians have done some maths and arrived at a basic conclusion; any Global Government can't govern a population of more than 7 billion people." Everything is designed for our destruction. The things that appear to help us only exist for profits. We're participating in global chess games and corporate profit chasing. Behold, the end is here!

Water and our food supply are poisoned. Fluoride doesn't have any positive effect on holes in the teeth, according to an investigation of US school children. The good of fluoride supplies is a myth, scandal, and fraud. The aluminum industries originated the fluoride supplies in water, due to an excess of sodium fluoride, the residue from extraction of aluminum. The fluoride scam started decades ago in a town where citizens had good teeth. Researchers discovered that the drinking water in the town had a lot of calcium-fluoride in it. The aluminum industries have an excess of sodium-fluoride, which is a different kind of fluoride. Sodium-fluoride destroys metabolism and is toxic to humans. It's an ingredient in rat poison. The aluminum industries needed to get rid of their excess of sodium-fluoride, so they sell it for about 3 cents a kilo, which makes over $15,000,000 a year.

Sodium-fluoride has been purposely confused with calcium-fluoride to assist the global depopulation agenda. Nazi scientists during World War II knew that sodium-fluoride is toxic to humans. They also discovered that humans become easy to control and passive after given sodium-fluoride. Now, the ruling establishment puts sodium-fluoride in the drinking water and in all conventional tooth paste. The aluminum industry earns millions a year by providing sodium-fluoride to make people easier to control. Sodium-fluoride impairs the teeth and doesn't improve teeth health. Don't drink water if you discover that there's fluoride in it. Always use a water filter if possible. Don't believe the world's lies about sodium-fluoride. In truth, sodium-fluoride increases the number of Mongoloid children, and increases the number of people getting Alzheimer's disease.

The air, water, food, and seeds are poisoned to fulfill the Kissinger Report. Environmental factors are used to assist in your slow destruction. Mike Philbin's article 'Free Planet: The Kissinger Report – Global Depopulation Agenda,' says, "Chemicals known as zeno-oestrogens, or oestrogen mimics, became the number one suspect. Xeno-oestrogens were suspected because of their tendency to mimic the female hormone oestrogen, hence the alternative name. Found in shrink-wrap, pesticides, herbicides, solvents and some drugs, these substances were suspected because of the effects they had on animal reproductive systems. Source [Irish Health]."

Doctors are also a major part of the depopulation agenda. People put full trust in their doctors even though less than 5% are trustworthy. You'll never get 'real' information from doctors and health officials. Doctors kill more people than traffic accidents, war, and guns put together! Doctors and official health officials have been indoctrinated by the Medical Schools. They've been trained to treat symptoms instead of look for the causes. Doctors and those in the medical community have not been taught how to recover, maintain, or improve the human immune system, only treatment by the means of surgery or drugs. Doctors and health officials follow the guidelines of their Governmental Health Department like programmed drones. Governmental Health

Departments follow, support, and follow the guidelines of the World Health Organization, which is financed by tax money. The World Health Organization is influenced by pharmaceutical interests, playing the money game. The W.H.O. is behind all global vaccination programs because they are a front group for the ruling elite. The unseen rulers of the planet control the World Health Organization, which is why it is the fluoride propaganda machine poisoning the environment, children, and all of humanity.

The corporate-controlled media exists to program you with lies and foolishness. Journalist and publisher David Barsamian said, "One of the intentions of corporate-controlled media is to instill in people a sense of disempowerment, of immobilization and paralysis. Its outcome is to turn you into good, non-thinking consumers. It is to keep people isolated, to feel that there is no possibility for social change." All worldly structures follow the Global 2000 depopulation program, including the media, medical community, and food industry. The global goal is to eliminate at least 50% of the world population. Don't believe anything you hear from the mainstream establishment, which uses censorship to avoid other points of view. Become your own detective by looking into the real news behind the news. Cut off network television to avoid being another victim of mass mind control. Assume your own responsibility by following your intuition, NOT religious leaders, political officials, and media personalities. American linguist and US media and foreign policy critic Noam Chomsky said, "The smart way to keep people passive and obedient is to strictly limit the spectrum of acceptable opinion, but allow very lively debate within that spectrum – even encourage the more critical and dissident views. That gives people the sense that there's free thinking going on, while all the time the presuppositions of the system are being reinforced by the limits put on the range of the debate."

The World Health Organization is really the World Pharmaceutical Organization. The medical community is guilty of pharmacogenocide. In Robert Mendelsohn's book 'Confessions of a Medical Heretic,' he uncompromisingly placed the blame for pharmacogenocide on the members of his own profession: DOCTORS! Most humans have failed to discover the drug company/doctor marketing connection. Network television is used to solicit patients into badgering their doctors for drugs. The whole industry is full of corruption, and all Doctors know what's going on. Doctors have ethical superiority, so people put their trust in them. Doctors are committing harm because they indiscriminately prescribe harmful drugs, knowing their side effects and limitations. Many doctors prescribe drugs leading to the deaths of their patients. Death by pharmacogenocide? Drug-pushing doctors are responsible.

Doctors are part of the assault on humanity. Most information coming out of the medical community is world-wide brainwashing propaganda. Doctors are supposed to assist in healing but insist on treating their patients with toxic drugs. Pharmaceutical industries have taken over the planet. A full-scale truth-finding expedition will reveal that prescription drugs aren't given in one's best interest. The FDA approves highly toxic drugs while hiding the real purpose of the drugs. Don't be persuaded by the medical community, which pushes drugs with severe side effects in the name of staying healthy. The long-range effects of all toxic drugs are completely unknown, so you're putting yourself at risk by taking them. The pharmaceutical industry exists for your destruction, not your health. John Lauritsen's article 'HIV Voodoo From Burroughs-Wellcome,' published by New York Native, says, "Unscrupulous pharmaceutical companies, corrupt government officials, venal physicians, stupid and cowardly media people, incompetent and dishonest researchers – none of these things are new. ...The drug companies are in business to make money, and they do that by selling as much of their product as they can at as high a price as they can. And although the drug companies subvert the scientific process through which drugs are tested, certified, and made available to doctors, once the drugs are available, they do let doctors know – albeit subtly – just what these drugs can and cannot do."

AIDS fits into the poison by prescription and depopulation global agenda. It was artificially created to help destroy humanity. The Centre for Disease Control in Atlanta defined AIDS by listing 25 diseases. According to Peter Duesberg, there isn't one single viral cause, due to so many different diseases. Dr. Peter Duesberg said, "AIDS is a collection or syndrome of 25 old diseases, conventional diseases. Not one of them is new. They've all been known for centuries, or at least for decades. With the provision that you have to find antibody to HIV or you or virus or some other traces of that virus, when they are found then those who believe in the virus as the cause of AIDS, say, those 25 diseases, any one of them or combination of them, are caused by the virus. For example, if you have tuberculosis and you find HIV, they say HIV has done it. Eighty years ago, a hundred years ago Robert Koch used to say tuberculosis bacillus has done it." [The AIDS Catch (Meditel)]

AIDS and TB statistics in Africa have been wrongly reported. TB is caused by malnutrition, poverty, and lack of medicines, not AIDS. The article 'AIDS and Africa,' published by Meditel, says, "The rise in TB cases in Africa has led some scientists to speculate that the HIV virus is making some people more susceptible to the disease but it is hard to find any evidence for this. What IS documented is that flaws in the clinical case definition, that is the combination of symptoms used for diagnosing AIDS without an HIV test, have meant that many TB cases have mistakenly been called AIDS."

Many factors have been known to cause false positive HIV antibody test results. It's all designed to get people on the toxic drug AZT. The AIDS establishment has convinced people that ELISA, Western blot, IFA, and other HIV antibody tests are 95.5% accurate. Christine Johnson from HEAL Los Angeles listed conditions known to cause positive HIV test results, all documented in scientific literature. It's a documented fact that there are false-positives to every single HIV protein. Take heed that ye be not deceived!

Non-HIV antibodies can cause a false positive bands reaction representing the various proteins to HIV. The forbidden science is that there are 65 factors known to cause false positive HIV antibody test results. A few of the factors are: anti-carbohydrate antibodies, naturally-occurring antibodies, passive immunization, tuberculosis, vaccines against infection which contain antibodies, renal (kidney) failure, flu, flu vaccination, Herpes Simplex I, Herpes Simplex II, upper respiratory tract infection (cold or flu), recent viral infection or exposure to viral vaccines, high levels of circulating immune complexes, rheumatoid arthritis, Hepatitis B vaccination, Tetanus vaccination, anti-collagen antibodies found in Africans of both sexes, systemic lupus erythematosus, connective tissue disease, malignant neoplasms (cancers), antibodies with a high affinity for polystyrene (used in the test kits), lipemic serum (blood with high levels of fat or lipids), healthy individuals as a result of poorly-understood cross-reactions, normal human ribonucleoproteins, receptive anal sex, the test kit itself, and the proteins on the filter paper. For further reference on the factors known to cause false positive HIV antibody test results, study Christine Johnson's list of conditions documented in the scientific literature known to cause positives on HIV tests along with her references.

Medical doctors, nurses, and appointed health department officials promote the idea that the HIV virus is the sole cause of AIDS so that the infected person will start taking the AZT drug. They say that one's immune system will break down if he or she doesn't take the AZT drug to postpone death and prolong life. There isn't one single scientific document proving that HIV causes AIDS. It's just a false hypothesis designed to push toxic drugs. There are 65 false positive triggers for HIV tests that we know about. The AIDS establishment financed the lie that AIDS is caused by a virus. They created the problem using fear, then offered the preplanned solutions. The (deadly) HIV virus is the artificially created problem, and poisonous drugs like AZT are the solutions. This is another assault on humanity. All scientists, publishers, researchers, and truth seekers in the mainstream are censored, and all who expose medical lies will be ridiculed so that the global depopulation agenda can go forth.

The recommendation of AZT and other toxic drugs kills the healthy cells and endangers the life of the patient. The British Medical Research Council and its French equivalent conducted a study on HIV positive people and AZT. Their AZT studies exposed AZT mythology and the pressure from AZT's manufacturer. Celia Farber's article 'AZT Is Death' exposed AZT propaganda. Celia Farber talks about the British Medical Research Council's HIV/AZT study and said, "The team concluded that AZT-a highly toxic and carcinogenic drug – neither prolongs life nor staves off symptoms of AIDS in people who are HIV-antibody positive but still healthy. The blueprint for the Concorde "disappointment" has been in the literature for many years. As we reported in November 1989, the first objective study was completed in France in 1988 and was published with very little fanfare in the Lancet, a British medical journal. The study found that AZT was too toxic for most people to tolerate, had no lasting effect on HIV blood levels, and left the patients with fewer CD4 cells than they had started with."

You can test positive for antibodies to HIV and not have HIV. The goal is to get as many people on AZT as possible. The theory behind AZT (trade name Retrovir) is false because HIV doesn't cause AIDS. Molecular biologist at Berkeley, Professor Peter H. Duesberg refuted the hypothesis that HIV causes AIDS. According to Professor Peter H. Duesberg, AZT's alleged benefits aren't backed by credible evidence, its toxicities are severe, and the drug shouldn't be used. Professor Duesbert's interview with John Lauritsen of the New York Native revealed that: AZT is a poison and cytotoxic (lethal to body cells), the theories behind AZT are false, there's "no rationale for treating with AZT," prescribing AZT is "highly irresponsible," AZT is "guaranteed" to be harmful, and AZT hits all DNA that's made. Stop believing in the medical community!

The article 'AZT On Trial,' written by John Lauritsen, published by New York Native, says, "It is hell for the bone marrow, which is where the T and B cells and all those things are made. It's hell for that. It has a slight preference for viral DNA polymerase compared to cellular DNA polymerase, and that's based on in vitro studies only, but that's certainly not absolute. It kills normal cells quite, quite extensively. ...Doctors who prescribed AZT did so on the basis on very limited information, along with the assurances of the Public Health Service that AZT represented the "best hope"." Popular media and promotional films produced by Burroughs – Wellcome, AZT's manufacturer, were used to market AZT. AZT was granted government approval and approved by the FDA even though the AZT advisory label reads: "TOXIC. Toxic by inhalation, in contact with skin and if swallowed. Target organ (s): Blood bone morrow. If you feel unwell seek medical advice (show the label where possible). Wear suitable protective clothing." The label on an AZT bottle from the Stigma Co. indicates a deathly poison; the same goes for any medicine with side effects. If possible, stay away from all medication.

HIV is a virus believed to cause AIDS, but what's tested for is not HIV, but antibodies to HIV. Anyone who tests positive is urged by doctors to immediately start taking the AIDS drug AZT (marketed under the names Zidovudine or Retrovir. It's wisdom to stay beyond the reach of doctors, which is why some HIV-positive mothers have gone underground to avoid having their children treated with anti-AIDS drugs or taken away by child-protection agencies. US scientists have claimed that HIV is not the cause of AIDS, so one shouldn't take drugs designed to prevent the virus from becoming AIDS. The side effects of anti-viral drugs pose a greater risk than the virus due to the severe side effects. The FDA approved AZT for depopulation purposes. AZT was originally a failed cancer drug, formally known as Compound S. Celia Farber's article 'Sins of Omission – The AZT Scandal' says, "It had actually been developed a quarter of a century earlier as a cancer chemotherapy, but was shelved and forgotten because it was so toxic, very expensive to produce, and totally ineffective against cancer. Powerful, but unspecific, the drug was not selective in its cell destruction."

Poison by prescription is a big part of the depopulation agenda, which is why toxic drugs with no scientifically proven benefits are given to millions of healthy people. Corrupt government officials, network television, unscrupulous pharmaceutical companies, and incompetent researchers are all part of the grand conspiracy. Those who are aware of poison by prescription must do what they can. Anyone on AZT must get off of the drug if they want to live. Others must be told directly and forcefully about doctors indiscriminately prescribing toxic drugs to destroy them. AIDS experts are promoting lies and propaganda to poison you by prescription. The subtle corruption of the drug company/doctor marketing connection fits perfectly into the global depopulation agenda. The drug companies are intentionally harming and killing off humanity because the proper government agencies aren't policing their activities. Public health officials, the pharmaceutical industry, and representatives of AIDS organizations are not to be trusted. Prescription drugs are the genocide of humanity.

In the midst of hell on earth, unconscious humans may run to psychiatrists seeking help. The mental health community is part of the same system, and is not set up for your best interest. In trouble, the worst thing you can do is see a psychiatrist. Peter Breggin, M.D., said, "Going to a psychiatrist has become one of the most dangerous things a person can do." Psychiatrists only want to label you with a mental illness, then drug you. The psychiatric and pharmaceutical industries work together. Psychiatrists are so ruthless that they even drug 3 year olds! As soon as you visit them, they'll be looking for a label for you instead of helping you. Peter Breggin, M.D., said, "There is nothing worse that you can do to a human being in America today than give them a mental illness kind of label and tell them they need drugs, and these children are 3, 4, 5, 6, 7, 8, 9 year-old being treated in this manner."

Stop falling for the lies of psychiatrists. Mental illness has no biological existence. Peter Breggin said in his book Toxic

Psychiatry, "there is no evidence that any of the common psychological or psychiatric disorders have a genetic or biological component." The article 'Does Mental Illness Exist?,' published by www.antipsychiatry.org, says, "People are thought of as mentally ill only when their thinking, emotions, or behavior is contrary to what is considered acceptable, that is, when others (or the so-called patients themselves) dislike something about them. One way to show the absurdity of calling something an illness not because it is caused by a biological abnormality but only because we dislike it or disapprove of it is to look at how values differ from one culture to another and how values change over time."

Don't believe in the myth of mental illness, which is used to diagnose and drug you. Elliot S. Valenstien, author of 'Blaiming the Brain: The Truth About Drugs and Mental Health,' said, "Contrary to what is often claimed, no biochemical, anatomical, or functional signs have been found that reliably distinguish the brains of mental patients." A psychiatrist who resigned from the American Psychiatric Association, Loren R. Mosher, said, "... there are no external validating criteria for psychiatric diagnoses. There is neither a blood test nor specific anatomic lesions for any major psychiatric disorder." There is no scientific data confirming any mental illness. Psychiatrist Peter Breggin said, "...there is no evidence that these mental illnesses, such as ADHD, exist." There is no evidence that any psychiatric or psychological disorder is caused by a biochemical imbalance. Psychologist Bruce Levine, Ph.D., said, "Remember that no biochemical, neurological, or genetic markers have been found for attention deficit disorder, oppositional defiant disorder, depression, schizophrenia, anxiety, compulsive alcohol and drug abuse, overeating, gambling, or any other so-called mental illness, disease, or disorder."

Part 4: The True Word of God

- Soliloquy of Chaos

- Who Are the Fallen?

- Untold Truths Threaten Human Existence

- The Hidden Scrolls

- Religion Is Refusal of Enlightenment

- The Dilemma of Humanity

- The Great Awakening

- Run to the Light

- The Madness of Our Civilization

Soliloquy of Chaos

Slaves of Organized Religion are poisoning the Earth with groundless fear and confusion. Religion is mental illness! Good people who don't know any better can use their belief in a holy book for good. The same book (the Bible) inspires all types of people operating at opposite ends of the spectrum. Honest believers aspiring to saintliness use religious scriptures for good, while other sects carry out acts of inhuman cruelty. Religion is at variance with man's inherent nature, and the perceived Word of God is no more than fables constructed by men. No god wrote any religious holy book!

Religious followers are victims of fraud, and their religious leaders are guilty of perpetuating the deception. Trying to convert others, attending religious meetings, giving money to churches, and talking about hell are the symptoms of indoctrination and deception. The self-renunciation found in organized religion leads to spiritual poverty and other deficiencies. Those who limit God to what's written in a holy book suffer spiritual, mental, sexual, intellectual, and political deficiencies. Religious holy books are all based on pure fiction, fables, fairy tales, and myths. Only those with a determination to remain blind continue following fictitious religious belief structures. No god is behind religion.

Many humans fear death's inevitability and turn to religion to deal with their fear. Religious believers believe that they are immortal because they've committed to their holy book's god, and therefore will survive the carnage of Judgment Day. Religious leaders are profiteers profiting off of humanity's fear of death and judgment. Their teachings contaminate the universe with unnecessary fear and false hope. Life is hard. There are millions of religious clergy waiting to profit from human anguish. Religion helps people psychologically, which is why religionists are those who need a metaphysical crutch in order to bear their lot. Church-goers think they're going to church to bolster their faith, when the clergy is simply feeding them false material reinforcing their need for mental help. They're taught that they are unworthy without their holy book's god and will be condemned to hell for not following religious doctrine.

Organized religion is nothing but dreams and delirium. Those who leave rigid religious belief structures will experience restored mental health. Abandoning ALL religious holy books is a return to the spirit of Light. Structured religion is contempt for the sensual and materialism, but it's accepted because it's attributed to God. Enlightened living is living free of orthodox religion. Those living in the light soundly use their understanding, order their minds rationally, mobilize their intelligence, and implement their own critical will without religious gods.

All the gods found in religious holy books were manufactured by mortals. These false gods only exist to make daily life more bearable for troubled religionists. Every man-made god puts to death everything that stands up to 'him,' according to the writings of religious scripture. Believing that any holy book was written by God is the death of the critical mind, intelligence, and reason. The existence of the gods described by religious holy books are all fictions devised by men. The manufacturers of religious gods all created the same fantasized reality under different names (Yahweh, Adin, Baal, Allah, Zeus, Ra). All those who worship any holy book's god is worshiping a phantom of the imagination. This is the truth that will set you free.

What religionists call a nonbeliever is really a libertine or freethinker. Those who knew the real God will automatically doubt or deny religious dogma. Religious fundamentalism is destroying humanity and is the cause of unthinkable violence against freedom of thought. Christians are taught to reject all that deviates from the path of Christian dogma. Christian history documents abuse on the lives of independent philosophers. Those outside of religious enslavement were depicted as sodomites, gluttons, drunkards, heretics, fornicators, and other false labels in order to dissuade people from investigating their progressive works. Character assassination was used by religious authority to undermine the influence of freethinkers. Immoralists were all philosophers and free individuals who didn't think the Bible represents God's infallible and inspired word. Early Christian leaders who believed the Bible to be the ultimate truth controlled the official historiography of thought and condemned everything outside of their mainstream belief system. All who believe the Bible to be the Divine Word of God have put their faith in an unholy fraud. Organized religion is the biggest scam on earth.

Those who really know God will see God everywhere, like the pantheists. Those purported to be holy and know God have used religious holy books to justify intolerant violence. Religion is about an unending war against the godless, hence believers and unbelievers. The history of Christianity has denounced and stigmatized all who don't believe that God raised Jesus from the dead on the third day (as unbelievers). Those living in the light would never agree with nor believe in Christianity's official historiography.

Enlightened living implies an assertion of the nonexistence of the gods described in religious holy books. Socrates, Epicurus and his disciples, and other great spiritual philosophers are included in a history of free thought. Protagoras, the first Greek Sophist, wrote 'Concerning the Gods.' He talked about religious gods in his book and concluded nothing about them. As a wise man, Protagoras validated neither their existence nor their nonexistence. The writings of all the nonreligious intellectuals identified with skepticism, uncertainty, or a form of agnosticism. Either way, the God of the great philosophers was in conflict with the false God of Abraham, Jesus, and Muhammad. The God of Constantine and religious fundamentalists is based on obedience, revelation, and religious dogma. The God of the intellectual philosophers of the past proceeds from reason, argument, and intelligence; -- the REAL God!

Philosophical interpretations of God outside the dominant political Christian framework is reduced to heresy or false teachings. Churches and religious institutions are not about God and never

239

were. Church history proves that the early Christian leaders were of the Kingdom of Darkness. On February 19, 1619, in Toulouse, the Christian church cut out the tongue of Giulio Cesare Vanini, hanged him, then burned him alive in Jesus' name. Religious fundamentalists murdered him for writing 'Amphitheatre of the Eternal Divino – Magical, Christiano – Physical and Nonetheless Astrologico – Catholic Providence against the Philosophers, Atheists, Epicureans, Peripatetics, and Stoics' in 1615.

Epicureanism, atheism, and other pagan philosophical schools were condemned by the sanctioned church, and their practitioners were liable to the death penalty. Eclectic pantheists, free thinkers, and open-minded Christians were all heretics because what they believed was unorthodox. Spinoza and thousands of others of unequaled intelligence were silenced by the Christian church. Spinoza was a pantheist who was condemned for insufficiently rigid Jewish orthodoxy. On July 27, 1656, the Jewish authorities of Amsterdam falsely charged him with evil conduct, heresy, monstrous deeds, and having opinions against religious orthodoxy. Anyone who disagreed with the sanctioned religion or was against rigid religious orthodoxy was put to death.

Religionists in authority attempted to erase Spinoza's name from the surface of the planet to hide his teachings. The rabbis and theoretical supporters of religious orthodoxy excommunicated Spinoza and banned any verbal or written contact with the enlightened philosopher. Religious clergy with political power declared that society was forbidden to read his writings. When religious authority banned Spinoza's writings, he was only 23 and had not published anything yet. His book 'Ethics' was published posthumously 23 years later in 1677.

Spinoza didn't teach atheism; it was just that his writings weren't in 100% agreement with religious holy book scripture. Nowhere in any of his life's work can you find one sentence asserting the nonexistence of God. Spinoza denied the soul's immortality and used his writing gift to explain his disbelief in posthumous reward or punishment. I only agree with some of Spinoza's ideas.

He taught that the Bible is a man-made work created by diverse authors, not a work of 'revealed' facts. Like me, Spinoza refused to subscribe to the theory of a chosen people. God has no chosen people! This theory is explained in Spinoza's 'Tractatus Theologico – Politicus (A Theologico-Political Treatise).' Spinoza was a Jew who was not a denier of God. He discerned philosophical qualities in Jesus and thought for himself.

Judeo-Christian philosophy is about hatred of the world, the body, and the free self. The list of individuals put to death for disagreeing with 'the Word of God' is endless. Organized religion is the most destructive force in the history of the planet. All the false gods defined in religious holy books are evil entities. They demand you serve them or be condemned to an eternal hell. The god of Abraham and the god Allah both executed massive numbers of people who failed to profess their faith in the accepted religious norms. I'm not declaring that these gods are real, just demonstrating that they're not of the Kingdom of Light. My book 'Beneficial Instructions Before Leaving Earth: The Gospel According to Jawara King' explains who these false gods really were, where they came from, and who they are not. The mass murders of unbelievers found in religious holy books and religious history prove that the religious belief structures of organized religion are of the Kingdom of Darkness. My Gospel also explains the origin of government, taxes, and institutionalized religion.

Freethinkers allow themselves to have questions of thought and independent reflection that doesn't agree with traditional religious doctrine. The powers identifying themselves with monotheism killed millions of anonymous people who rebelled against traditional religious teachings of the book. Religious institutions condemn the thinking of all free people who are liberated from religious authority. Those who are free in God's eyes are described by religionists as god-deniers. These fundamentalists trying to live the holy life based on a religious holy book ARE NOT spiritual. Religion isn't from God, but an invention by men to control others, make money, and ensure power over their brethren.

Even unorthodox believers aren't allowed to have questions of thought and reflection. A Portuguese and former Jesuit named Cristovão Ferreira saw the Light and wrote a thirty page explosive book entitled 'The Deception Revealed.' He asserted that: the world had never been created, hell doesn't exist, Christianity was an invention, the resurrection was a hoax, confessions were nonsense, and Mary's virginity was a tale. Cristorão Ferreira was a spiritualist who abandoned the Christian religion and converted to Zen Buddhism. He never said, thought, asserted, or wrote that God didn't exist. He just believed that Christianity was an invention by men, not God. Ferreira was forced to renounce his ideas in 1614 under Japanese torture. He was just one of many who were forced to recant beliefs not in agreement with religious hierarchy.

Jean Meslier was a martyr, killed by the religious community. He was the parish priest of Etrépigny in the Ardennes. Meslier saw the Light, then wrote a voluminous testament attacking God, religion, the church, Jesus, and religious dogma. He violently denounced Christianity in his book 'Memoir of the Thoughts and Feelings of Jean Meslier: Clear and Evident Demonstrations of the Vanity and Falsity of All the Religions of the World.' Meslier spent most of his life working on his book, which wasn't published until 1729, after his death.

Dominant religious historiography hides the true way to God from our sight. Man made God everything he is not to trick us into believing in the Divinity of Biblical texts. Organized religion is against analytic examination. A comparative study of religions reveal the Christian Biblical texts as a lie. Morality, based on what's written in religious holy books, is a lie. Claude-Adrien Helvetius saw the Light and wrote a book called 'On the Mind.' This Light worker attacked all forms of morality based on institutionalized religion.

Men created God in their own inverted image as a way to deal with suffering. Ludwig Andreas Feuerbach gave his own explanation of what God is. He didn't deny God's existence, nor assert that God does not exist. Feuerbach asked the philosophical question, "Who is this god whom the majority of men believe?" He rightly concluded that the god described in religious holy books is a fiction, a fabrication, a creation by men. Human beings examined their limitness, morality, and suffering from the trials of life and invented a false god out of their desire for completeness.

Man made god in his image and endowed 'him' with the opposite characteristics of humanity to create a need for 'him.' Man is mortal, so created a god who is immortal. Man is finite, therefore created an infinite god. Man knows he is limited, therefore created a god who knows no limit. Man doesn't know everything, so he created a god who is omniscient. Man can't do everything, so he created a god who is omnipotent. Man is limited due to ubiquity, therefore his god is omnipresent. Man feels weak, therefore created a god who is Almighty. Man made god perfect because he is imperfect. God was designed to be everything, while we are nothing. We dwell on earth, therefore man created a god that's in heaven. Man manufactured false gods with characteristics to make religious believers prostate themselves at the feet of organized religion. The religious system is a fraud!

All history is false and fake. It's a proven fact that history is written by the dominant philosophy. Voltaire said, "History is the lie commonly agreed upon." When one group conquered another, they re-wrote their history. Christians in power placed Jesus in history and created all the Biblical tourist attractions to support the myth. There never was a city called Nazareth, and all the other Biblical locations were created like the props on a movie set. This religious falsification of history has been used to mislead religious believers into believing that the gospels were historical accounts. Jean Jacques Rousseau said, "The falsification of history has done more to mislead humans than any single thing known to mankind." Many scholars have known that religious and secular history is a lie. Michael Tsarion, author of 'Astrotheology and Sidereal Mythology,' said, "We may fairly agree that the subject of history, as commonly taught, is one of the most boring of all subjects. However, the study of how the subject of history has been manipulated is surely one of the most interesting of all subjects."

The doctrines taught in religious institutions/businesses are not from God, but designed to raise money for religious leaders. Jesus is big business! When you hear a religious leader praising Jesus in a service, he or she is just praising all the MONEY that marketing Jesus brings in! Jesus is a big money-maker, used to bring the religious hierarchy BILLIONS of dollars a year! Tithing and other church doctrines have nothing to do with God or spirituality. The tithe is just another lie designed to bring in hella MONEY. Tithing isn't even a Biblical doctrine. No one can prove that tithing was a New Covenant practice of the early church. You can't find one New Testament believer that paid a 10% tithe after the cross of Calvary. Every church leader who teaches tithing is a fraud. The tithing doctrine is a fraud because you can't find anywhere in the Old Testament law where tithes (as it applied to everyone) were paid in the form of money. There is not one person on the planet who can name JUST ONE New Testament saint in scripture from the resurrection of Jesus Christ who paid a 10% tithe.

The religious system doesn't allow religious followers to propose alternative hypotheses, which is why Islam and Christianity have severe penalties for leaving the faith. All the religions of the book promise hell to those who refuse to allow or leave the teachings of the book. Religion is about obedience to dogma and submission to religious law attributed to God. The submissive slaves who claim to be the elect believe that they must be obedient to what they perceive to be the Word of God. God didn't create their religious dogma nor write their holy books, and to believe so is a lack of intelligence. Intelligence is ailing in every mosque, synagogue, church, and temple.

As inhabitants of Earth, we must leave behind all our religious and secular hypotheses born of the monotheisms. Not siding with the Judeo-Christian and Muslim ideologies is a wise choice. Religious power calls upon every human being to choose sides in the religious war between Islam and Judeo-Christianity. Avoid choosing either side and opt instead for a position not based in religion. This silly religious war began with the Torah bidding the Jews to fight their enemies. God didn't sanction any of this, but other sources explained in my book 'The Gospel According to Jawara King.' This Biblical god of war is not the real God, but an artificially-made counterfeit god. The violence attributed to God in the Bible proves that the god described in the Torah is a false god. Bloody battle against others (enemies) is justified in the Torah and an important part of the Old Testament. The book of Numbers, chapter 21, verse 14, talks about the "book of the wars of the Lord." The Koran contains the same theme of slaughter of the enemy. The Bible and the Koran, neither written by God, are the reason for 25 centuries of calls by both sides to acts of religious war.

Nietzche was living in the Light and taught people the way to God. Nietzche didn't want people to follow him. According to his philosophy, he wanted people to obey him by following themselves. He taught people to follow no one else. One of his lessons was that we can choose not to choose. Therefore, those who are enlightened (free of organized religion) can make a decision not to side with Israel and the United States, the Bible and the Koran, or Muslims and the Christians.

Stay away from organized religion, which despises the intellectuals and philosophers who go against it. Religious thinking is based on folly, fable, myth, and fiction. Truth is birthed out of debate, deduction, and reason. The religious concept of believers and unbelievers is rooted in metaphysical placebos and fictions. Believing that you're a saved believer and strictly following religious dogma is self-induced insanity. Many of the Wise Ones of the past knew better. Feuerbach deconstructed god (the one written in religious holy books), Holbach dismantled Christianity, and Meslier denied all divinity. The search for the essential nature of reason reveals that organized religion is the borderline of insanity!

The church fathers started the Christian era and used

millenarian prophets to convert through fear. The universal teaching of institutionalized religion is that God will destroy the world, and only religious believers will be saved. Those who don't submit to religious dogma are condemned to an eternal hell full of endless suffering. God didn't create these false religious teachings and has nothing to do with religious holy books. As we abandon all religions of the book, the world will change for the better. It's time for change. First was a pagan era, then a Christian era, now time for a post-Christian phase. Religion is anchored in tradition, not God. Soon people will realize that Moses, Muhammad, Jesus, and their religions of the book are religious frauds. Great men of philosophical formulae, like Friedrich Nietzche, Baron d' Holbach, and Ludwig Feuerbach were able to deconstruct the false fables and myths of institutionalized religion. Without the radical deconstruction of religious ideologies attributed to god, one is lost.

<u>Who Are the Fallen?</u>

The fallen are those who've taken refuge in organized religion. Earthians who've turned to religious holy books and their artificial gods have fallen by the way side. Slaves of organized religion characterize the worst and most negative aspects of contemporary life as products of living life without their god. Their god is an imaginary projection of the human mind. Religious texts alone prove 'him' to be a fraud. Biblical texts reveal a quarrelsome, violent, intolerant, and jealous god. Instead of bringing peace to the earth, the false god of the Bible generated more brutality, bloodshed, deaths, and hate on the planet.

Those who believe and put their trust in the false gods of religious holy books are the fallen. Religious madness dominates the earth because billions of Earthians attribute their religious dogma to God. The Bible promotes the Jewish fantasy of a chosen people, which has caused animosity between peoples and hatred. The authoritarian and armed theocracy of religion has justified the French Religious Wars, the Crusades, the Saint Bartholomew's Day massacre of Paris' Protestants, and the Inquisition. The Pauline Jesus came bearing a sword, and the Christian image of the Temple moneylenders has Jesus committing a violent act. The 'holy' violence of the scriptures has been used to justify slavery, colonialism, support for fascist movements, and North American ethnocides.

Religion is bad news. The Koran exhorts Muslims to destroy unbelievers, along with Jews and Christians. All the religions of the book have caused misery and destruction on the earth in the name of what religious fundamentalists believe to be a merciful God. The most powerful religions have subdued other religions through war, slavery, and power. The political and financial power of organized religion has dominated other groups by taking over their civilization and culture. The real God exists independently of the Jewish, Muslim, and Christian versions. The existence of the false gods described in religious holy books has done NOTHING for humanity but create more hatred, holy lies, embezzlement, violence, perjury, depravity, false witness, perversion, infanticide, and contempt. Those who follow these false gods are the fallen.

The existence of false man-made gods has historically generated more massacres, wars, battles, and conflicts than anything else. God, as described in all religions of the book, does not promote serenity, tolerance, peace, and love amongst humanity. Instead of excelling in the practice of virtue, religious characters like Paul, Moses, and Muhammad excelled in torture, division, and murder. The biographies to witness prove that organized religion doesn't have anything to do with the theme of loving one's neighbor. Without religious belief structures, there would be no such thing as believers and unbelievers. No one has all the answers, but it's quite certain that those outside of religion are far less blind than the fallen.

The history of the human race unquestionably teaches that humans as a whole are insane. Religion just makes society worse by playing on the fear of death and promoting self-torture.

Religionists use metaphysical contortions to justify evil in the world and convince others that their god is the true god. They blame all evil on the devil and claim that serving their god is the only way to protect yourself from spending eternity with 'him.' This religious folly is full of divinities manufactured from one crises to the next. Anything bad that happens is attributed to Satan, while everything good is attributed to the blessings of God, as if religion is running the universe! Good and bad are part of Life (God), and the history of humanity reveals the disappointments of virtue and the rewards of vice. There is no immanent or transcendent justice, only spiritual law which says 'you reap what you sow/say.' No god has ever made anyone pay for despising, insulting, crossing, or neglecting him. This man-made god, based on the writings of religious texts, was created by the human mind and is a counterfeit god.

Humanity will only survive spiritually, intellectually, and philosophically in a post-Christian era free of religious dogma. The end of the official church monopoly over religious, political, and social issues will liberate humanity and bring peace on Earth. Judeo-Christian forces are a major source of evil on Earth due to their mental, spiritual, ideological, and conceptual control over Earthians. The epistemology of Judeo-Christianity controls most mental and symbolic exchanges between humans, due to its effective rule. Early Christian conquerors subdued the minds, bodies, flesh, and souls of the majority through religious Biblical texts, and their influence remains today. After two centuries of ideological domination, even non-religious humans remain manufactured, submissive, and formatted due to Judeo-Christian epistemology. Even atheists unconsciously have a world vision, an ethic, or way of thinking in agreement with traditional religious thought, due to living in a world saturated in Judeo-Christianity. God isn't behind Christianity.

Religion thrives on the fear of death and the unknown. The world is not all there is. A power, force, and energy exists outside of all explanatory apparatus. What happens after death cannot be explained and escapes the logical sequence. All explanations of life after death or what happens at the time of death are simply a philosophy or hypothesis. Religion created false answers to all the questions of humanity, creating a mental and conceptual empire pervading every component of culture, the body, law, and civilization. Thousands of years of Christian discourse have fasioned medicine, theology, anatomy, physiology, aesthetics, our bodies, and our customs. Even the irreligious seek religious ministers for funerals, evidenced by the tiny number of registered civil funerals. The positions of the majority are formulated by the church, even in those who don't follow organized religion, which is the problem.

For our civilization to advance, there must be a philosophical and secular reevaluation of the Bible's values. To produce a post-Christian ethic, the Bible must be revealed as a fraud; for God didn't write or inspire it. Biblical fables rule our world today, which is why pharmacology, psychiatry, emergency medicine, palliative treatments, oncology, and thanatology all obey Judeo-Christian law. The ethos of bioethics is Judeo-Christian, and even secular ethical committees independent of religious authority follow it. Most people, even atheists, are generally unaware that they think, act, and behave in the way they have been trained, which is usually based on the Judeo-Christian tradition. The believer and unbeliever's subconscious emerge from one and the same metaphysical bath; God. It's just that the religious believer mistakes the true God for the fables taught in Biblical texts. The religionist uses 'answer to prayer' and other experiences to validate the existence of their false god when it was really the power of the subconscious that came through for them. The workings of magical thinking change one's life, not religious texts.

The way of life of humanity as a whole proceeds from Judeo-Christian epistemology. Even those who call themselves secular think and believe in agreement with Christian thought, especially if they believe marriage to be ordained by God. Marriage is a man-made structure set up by men, not God. An analysis of politics, aesthetics, philosophy, and global teachings reveal that all these areas are influenced by Biblical religious doctrine. Almost all secular practices have Judeo-Christian roots unnoticed by the individuals concerned.

80% of the world is openly inspired by one of the three holy books. The world being dominated by religious thought is attributable to ignorance of Judeo-Christian teachings. Religious believers and churchgoers are usually undereducated because of only being informed by the information fed by religious clergy. The worship centers of monotheist religions aren't places of analysis and reflection. The repetition and recycling of fables doesn't promote the spread and exchange of knowledge. Religion thrives amongst ignorance and a lack of education, which is why no learning occurs in religious services. Religious rituals exercise memory, not intelligence. Listening to a clergyman read a scripture for the umpteenth time solicits not intelligence, but memory. Parrot-like repetition of unholy lies keeps one blind and enslaved to rigid religious belief structures.

Christian believers celebrate Christmas on December 25, proving that they have no knowledge. The church picked 12/25 to coincide with the winter solstice. December 25 was not Jesus' birthday, but a date when pagans honored Sol Invictus, the Unconquered Sun.

Christians are culturally blind, celebrating their salvation through the crucifixion. First of all, death by stoning was the standard punishment for Jesus' charged crime, not crucifixion. Christians are blind, and it was designed that way from Christianity's inception. On behalf of Christianity, Tertullian manipulated history to support the ideological agenda of Christianity. The Bible exposes itself in the ancient lessons from Genesis. The moral of the story is 'man is forbidden to seek awareness.' The Book of Genesis teaches us that we should be content to believe and obey, choosing blind faith over real knowledge.

The religions of the book suppress all interest in science, and demand obedience and submission. The Torah militates against reason by presenting laws regulating all the details of daily life. Religion is in favor of submission, which is why the religionist is a slave to organized religion. Muslim means submissive toward God, making Muslims slaves of the religious system. All the major religions teach defective information and the reliance on obedience rather than intelligence. Those who turn their minds over to religious dogma are the fallen. The official model of Pauline Christianity despises women and decries the pleasures of the flesh. If you follow these man-made ideas attributed to God, you are the fallen.

Koranic law is religious insanity expressing hated of Jews and non-Muslims. The pages of the Koran are filled with contradictory texts. To convince the fallen that the Koran is a holy book attributed to God, ayatollahs and mullahs give coherence to the contradictory texts by juggling verses, suras, and thousands of hadith. They fine-tune abrogatory and abrogated verses to give the illusion that the Koran is the one and only true word of God. All the religious texts are frauds working against humanity, hence the Pauline hatred of the body. Desires, passions, drives, and pleasures are denied in the religions of the book, and without them there would be no such thing as sexual immorality.

Even atheists are practicing Christian atheism, because they are denying god (one of the gods of the book), yet asserting the excellence of Christian values. Even people who don't want to have anything to do with Judeo-Christianity, at the same time unconsciously assert the virtue of evangelic morality. The Christian believer and the Christian atheist are the same because their values are identical. All the 'so-called' unbelievers and people who don't want to have anything to do with religion all operate on common ground with religionists if they ascribe to Judeo-Christian ideas.

The world will be free when it realizes that man made God. A deconstruction of the three monotheisms will reveal that man created false gods in his image to control humanity. An analyzation of the three monotheisms will demonstrate that they are alike with the same fundamentals. All three monotheisms reveal a hatred of intelligence, a hatred of life, a hatred of women, a hatred of the corruptible body, and an obsession with death. Monotheists reject true knowledge in favor of obedience and submission. Men not God created the condemnation of liberated sexuality. God didn't say that sex for pleasure is wrong, only religious holy books attributed to God. God didn't write any holy books and didn't create all these rigid religious belief structures promoted by the fallen.

All three monotheisms condemn the joy of life and the basic human drives as sin. Collective hysteria caused the growth of Christianity. The fears and volatile emotional state of humanity have allowed religion to dominate 80% of humanity. The fear of death and the promise of eternal life with God has caused the fallen to accept religious foolishness rooted in fallacious principles. Religious believers are following lies, myths, and fiction in the name of God, who didn't even create their religion! The World's System supports organized religion and conferred upon it the stamp of authenticity. Church and other religious institutions solidify religious lies in the hearts of the fallen as a result of the repetition of a sum of errors. From the Garden of Eden until today, in religious circles, humans are still forbidden to taste the fruit of the Tree of Knowledge.

A deconstruction of Christianity pinpoints that Jesus was forged. Jesus is not a historical character, but a conceptual character whose image was constructed over a hundred years after his purported death. Paul of Tarsus, believing that he had a mandate from God, promoted the life, death, and message of Jesus. Paul had psychological problems AFTER his conversion, hence his hatred of the world.

Christian history reveals how the gospel myth was fabricated. Emperor Constantine's conversion to Christianity was out of political opportunism and expanded the empire. Under Constantine, Christians became a persecuting majority and established a totalitarian regime. Constantine proclaimed himself the thirteenth apostle and enacted torturous laws against non-

Christians. Emperor Constantine attempted to systematically eradicate the ancient cultures via book burnings, architectural recycling, library burnings, physical persecution, demolition of pagan buildings, forced exiles, desecration of objects of worship, and assassinations. Ancient temples of non-Christian spiritual groups were turned into Christian churches. If they were destroyed, the Christians used their rubble to build roads and such.

Under several centuries of Christianity's unchecked power, the spiritual became confused with religion. An analyzation of Christianity is needed for the deconstruction of theocracies. Governments exert a political claim to power that religionists believe emanates from God. In the religious system, god does not speak, but priests, clergy and other religious leaders speak for 'him.' The leaders of the fallen purport to be bearers of God's word and convince religious slaves of their ability to speak in 'his' name. Only they can speak 'his' mind and interpret what 'he' thinks. Slaves of organized religion believe that their religious leaders represent God on Earth, speak God's word, or know the true path to God.

The supposed dominance of God is really the dominance of organized religion and those claiming to speak in 'his' name. God, as taught in the religions of the book, is a fraud/hoax. Centuries of history attest that the three monotheisms have caused nothing but division and bloodshed. Those operating in the name of God have caused wars, murders, massacres, and colonialism. Today's global terrorism is the result of those who praise the god of any of the three monotheisms. Religionists in political power are responsible for the elimination of entire cultures. The real God didn't cause all the inquisitions, genocides, division, and crusades, but a false god created by men.

Atheology must deconstruct theocracy and the monotheisms. One will only know the truth by demythologizing Islam and Judeo-Christianity. We must create a true post-Christian morality by formulating a new ethic independent of the religions of the book. Our interpersonal relationships should not be under the gaze of gods or religious holy books. With that behind us, we can honor our minds and our inherent natures.

The morality promoted by Judeo-Christianity is a false morality making the body a punishment, pleasure a sin, and intelligence a curse. The earth becomes a vale of tears to the fallen because physical pleasure and sex with women or men (outside of the man-made structure of marriage) becomes a passport to hell. There is only one law of morality, and that is to treat others how you want to be treated, or, do unto others as you would have done unto you. Sexual immorality is a religious myth, based on the religions of the book. Nothing sexually is wrong, provided that both adults are consenting. Sexual morality based on the three monotheisms is deception because no god wrote their holy books. God didn't create this religious foolishness that men and women subject themselves to.

Animals are much wiser than humans, but humans are too unwise to realize it. Animals are uncontaminated by false gods and are excused from religion. They don't follow religious leaders, build temples or cathedrals, nor pray to fictions like humans. Religious services are psychological treatment for the fallen. Believing in one of the gods of the book helps the fallen psychologically. The reasoning of Spinoza says that if animals created a god for themselves, it would be in their own image. The god of the donkeys would also have long ears, the god of the bees would sting, and the god of the elephants would have a trunk. Men have done the same thing when they took it into their heads to give birth to the false gods of the three monotheisms (Yahweh, Allah, and god the father of Jesus).

Only men invent false gods, weave fables, abase themselves, and humble and prostate themselves to religious folly. Humans believe unquestioningly in the religious tales they have concocted in order to raise money, fulfill psychological needs, and profit off of the fear of death. Only the fallen extract from this fiction and believe in dangerous nonsense as a way out. The fallen passionately lay their lives down for one of the three monotheisms in the hope of dealing with their fear of death. Those afraid of death turn to religion so that when the hour of death strikes, it will seem less difficult. The death instinct motivates the fallen to follow religion, which proceeds from the death wish.

The dying process starts after being born. Religion uses hell teachings to scare people into religious enslavement. The religionist's fixation with death generates self-destructive conduct and enslaving behavior in submission to religious dogma. The fallen have turned against themselves by supporting religion that discredits intelligence and self-hatred, the detriment of the body, and the despising of the flesh. The three monotheisms profit off of humanity's death drive. Most religious believers only submit to religious teachings because they were told that they would go to hell if they reject god. Not the true God, but the false god that says, "Believe in me or burn in hell." The fallen only serve this false god because they believe they'll go to hell if they don't. This is why religious fundamentalists (the fallen) are no more than religious slaves.

History confirms the misery and blood shed caused in the name of man-made gods. The three monotheisms share a hatred of reason, pleasure, freedom, sexuality, the body, normal drives, natural desires, the feminine, and intelligence. The obedience and submission demanded in Judaism, Islam, and Christianity isn't real faith and belief. The praise of virginity or monogamous love isn't real spirituality, but a religious concept created by man. Religion isn't about God, and is nothing more than a life crucified. Monotheism loathes intelligence, which is why followers of the three monotheisms are living in darkness. Those who follow the religions of the book are lost souls needing salvation, which is why they are the fallen.

Intelligence is an explanation based on reason. Therefore, one who is intelligent will reject every manufactured fiction. Intelligence sees right through fairy tales and myths. The all-seeing, all-knowing god found in religious holy books is a HOAX! Rationally directed intelligence wards off the illusory salvation message and redemption of the soul. Religion is a ban on intelligence, which is why Adam and Eve could do anything in the garden except become intelligent. They were forbidden to eat from the Tree of Knowledge. Eve is an example for humanity because she opted for intelligence at risk of death. Religionists won't be free until they're liberated from their state of ignorance.

Knowledge and intelligence is losing the illusion of religious faith and rejecting the fables of religion. The monotheist religions live exclusively by constraints that didn't come from god! Religious holy books tell the fallen what they can and can't do, think, and say. The religious texts are full of behavioral and existential codifications attributed to God. The fallen have renounced intelligence and submitted to the ideas of men pretending to speak for God. Religious slaves must always obey, conform, and do as their false religion demands. The god of the Bible ordered Adam and Eve not to eat the fruit of the tree of knowledge, revealing that religion doesn't want the scales to be removed from our eyes. Genesis 3:6 banned humans from a tree to be desired to make one wise.

Untold Truths Threaten Human Existence

The death fixation has plunged humanity into the grips of organized religion. Hell teachings feed on one's fear of death. So many people are filled with horror about what follows death that religion provides consoling fables and fictions to dominate the fearful. The denial, hatred, and contempt for the here and now found in religionists is the result of them trying to be found worthy of an afterlife with God. Out of their fear of hell, the fallen deny reason, unbiblical spiritual books, intelligence, culture, and science for religious dogma. Life in all its forms and the things that enhance our existence in this world are denied by organized religion. Once rigid religious belief structures dominate you, you will be trained by the religious system to hate the body, sex, love, the flesh, women, passion, desires, and natural drives. Therefore, victims of the religious system are suffering from serious mental illness.

All the religions of the book form a cult of death because they are based on the afterlife. If you follow the religious laws outlined in your holy book, you're going to Heaven. If you reject the teachings of your holy book, you'll spend eternity in hell. To avoid hell, the religionist abandons reason for religious foolishness. The religious mind expresses all contempt for women, yet esteems mothers, virgins, and wives.

Christianity is based on the blood of Jesus. All these false religions are based on the scapegoat, ritual murder, and sacrificial blood. Every false religion thirsts for blood, slaughtering unbelievers and innocent victims (men, women, and children). Blood blesses and sanctifies the monotheist cause, from the Jewish extermination of the Canaanites to the Christian crucifixion of the Messiah. The Muslim jihad of the Prophet shed hella blood for Allah. The followers of Muhammad and Muhammad himself regularly slaughtered people. In 623, an unarmed merchant of Nakhla Saudi Arabia was killed. Muhammad habitually practiced killing until he died on June 8, 632.

Religion is bloodthirsty and didn't come from God. Examining the history of the religions of the book proves that the real God isn't involved. Muslim warriors have participated in more wars, raids, battles, sieges, and attacks than can be numbered. 350 Muslims from Medina defeated 900 men who were commanded by Abu Jahl. Amir ibn Hisham was one of the polytheist leaders in Mecca, who was killed at the battle of Badr. He killed an old woman named Sumayyah, who was the first Muslim martyr. Islam is an ocean of blood because almost 250 of the 6,234 verses of the Koran legitimize and justify holy war. Some of the Muslim battles were Uhud (March 625), East Medina (626 & 627), the battle of the Trench (627), the conquest of the Khaybar oasis (May-June 628), and the raid on Mu'ta (September 629).

Just like the children of the Covenant, the Muslim community proclaimed themselves the chosen people. Muslims believe themselves to be set above all others by Allah and preferred by him (9:19 & 3:110). The elite status with God is claimed by both the Jews and Muslims. The religious madness believes that others are of inferior race. Believing in the concept of unbelievers is acknowledging that sub-humans exist and that god established a hierarchy among humans based on submission to religious texts. This is a lie because the real God doesn't distinguish a small designated community from the rest of humanity; for we are all ONE. The hatred of the Hebrews for the Canaanites of yesterday has evolved into today's hatred of the Palestinians for the Jews. When one group believes itself to be summoned by God to dominate others, it sees itself as empowered to exterminate them. This is all religious madness!

Religion based on religious holy books is about domination and deception. Men dominated women in the Bible, and through what's perceived to be the word of god, religious leaders dominate the slaves of organized religion. Believers attempt to dominate unbelievers by condemning them to hell for not believing in their religion of the book. The original primitive and tribal models of male supremacy, gerontocracy, and theocracy have remained unchanged since institutionalized religion was introduced to humanity. The religions of the book divide the world in two: believers and unbelievers, or those serving god and those condemned to hell for not believing. The brothers in Islam separate themselves from all the rest of humanity, while the Christians believe that they're the only ones going to heaven. All of this division caused by religion is part of the religious insanity that is destroying our planet.

Religion is illogical. Those who believe that their religious holy book was written by God are religious fools. Muslims put their complete faith in a book dating from the early 630s. Their revealed holy book was theoretically dictated to an illiterate camel herdsman, according to tradition. Just like the other religious holy books, the Quran regulates all the details of the daily lives of billions of people around the world. Those who have fallen for the religions of the book are the fallen. In the era of worldwide information networks, information is readily available to prove the religions of the book to be frauds dictated by men, not God.

The religious lifestyle is psychological insanity. Every action is judged based on its degree of conformity to Koranic, Muslim, or Biblical rules. People of the book (Jews and Christians) need to realize that their holy book's logic of inclusion and exclusion isn't from God. Religious believers don't see non-believers as equal. The Muslims had a pact of surrender between non-Muslims and their Muslim conquerors called dhimma. Over time, dhimmi referred to a non-Muslim citizen of a country governed by sharia (Islamic) law. In a land dominated by Muslims, dhimma was a contract to protect dhimmis and guarantee their personal safety. Dhimmis were allowed to retain their religion and the security of their property for a fee. In order to live in Islamic territory, the Christian, Jew, or Zoroastrian had to pay an extra tax imposed by dhimma. Islamists were guilty of financial extortion for forcing non-Muslims to pay for protection and normal rights. Non-Muslim believers paid the tax and allowed the Muslim community to have them live as sub-humans. At the end of the First World War, the Ottoman Empire abandoned the practice. The abolition of dhimmitude dates around 1839.

Religious believers don't treat unbelievers equally. Only the believer is going to heaven, while the non-believer is condemned to hell. The believer knows God, while the wrong-believer is a lost soul. The religious believers living by the edicts of a holy book are the real lost souls needing salvation. All the religions of the book are fixated on the immobility of death. Theocracy thrives on death and the irrational. Through the fear of death, organized religion rules the planet. Once one is convinced by the religious community to fear hell, he or she will reject the living forces of communication, negotiation, the use of reason, and dialogue among those who believe otherwise. Christian fundamentalists will use the writings of Paul to justify not having discussions with those who don't believe the Bible is God's word. Titus 3:9 says, "But avoid foolish controversies and genealogies and arguments and quarrels about the law, because these are unprofitable and useless." 2 Timothy 2:14 says to the religionist, "Keep reminding them of these things. Warn them before God against quarreling about words; it is of no value, and only ruins those who listen." I Timothy 6:4 tells the religious slave, "he is conceited and understands nothing. He has an unhealthy interest in controversies and quarrels about words that result in envy, strife, malicious talk, evil suspicious ..." I Timothy 1:4 says to religious leaders, "nor to devote themselves to myths and endless genealogies. These promote controversies rather than God's work – which is by faith." The New International Version of 2 Timothy 2:23 tells religious fundamentalists, "Don't have anything to do with foolish and stupid arguments, because you know they produce quarrels." These verses are why the fallen will not listen to spiritual truth or that which they perceive to be against the word of God. The religionist has been trained to cut off anything that threatens his or her false rigid religious belief structure. Following the writings of the Apostle Paul will cause one to die a religious slave, never discovering that the Bible never was the infallible word of God.

The microphysics of power states that religionists in power will theorize their holy book's intention within their sphere of influence. Politicians in government will quietly work to create a political testament based on their institutionalized religion. The people of the book are the most dangerous people to have in power because they will work to enforce the religious laws in their religious holy books. A Muslim leader will work for the Koran and Islam, and create a government inspired by the Sharia, Islamic law. Islamic government is based on knowledge of the Hadith and the Koran, the two sources of Sharia law.

Muslim theocracy has been in the works since the Koran was 'revealed.' Ayatollah Khomeini outlined the theory of Islamic government. He left a 'Politico-Spiritual Testament' after his death. The Shiite dignitary created the political program of an Islamic republic and wrote about using Muslim principles of the Hadith and the Koran to govern on the basis of Sharia. The fascist briviary of Islamic theocracy didn't just begin with the writings of Ayatollah Khomeini, for Islamic totalitarianism was the goal from the beginning. Everything is controlled by the dominant ideology, which is why a political religionist will try to get his or her jurisdiction to serve a Christian or Islamic ideal.

All the religions of the book are structurally archaic, yet the fallen still believe that God is involved. There is no logical reason for humanity to legitimize the immanent and totalitarian use of any religious holy book. Each of the three monotheisms claim to possess the only legitimate holy book reading. The religions of the book promote an incoherent logic. In the early days of religious enslavement, the people of the book contradicted the European Enlightenment or the philosophy of the Enlightenment, which rejected intolerance, condemned superstition, abolished censorship, and opposed absolutism. The Koran clearly rejected the aspiration toward the universal reign of reason sura by sura. The holy Bible rejected resistance to tyranny. It commands religious believers to submit to authority because all power comes from God. Equal rights between believers and unbelievers isn't found in any of the religions of the book. Biblical scriptures have always been opposed to the extension of freedom of expression and thought.

Islam is about fascist thematics. The imam in Islam is supposedly divinely inspired, and his word is law. The imam is the leader of mosque worship in Sunni Islam and determines the correct interpretation of the Koran. In Shiite Islam, the imam's authority comes from Muhammad, and he has a monopoly on Islamism. The imam is a spiritual and political leader in Islam who uses passages from the Koran to support total theocracy. He has the attribute of infallibility and a monopoly on the proper interpretation of the Quran. In reality, the fallen have made their religious leaders God by giving them all their power.

The religions of the book make their holy book and God equal to promote a transcendental logic which says that God (the holy book) is the solver of contradictions. Since a religious holy book is supposed to have all the answers, believing that God wrote it is the embodiment of the end of reason. Religion is serious mental illness because religious believers believe their holy book to be the supreme source, the holy text. The fallen people of the book find everything in the Torah, Koran, or the Bible and believe that it answers all the imaginable and possible questions of humanity. Everything appears to be in a religious text attributed to God with nothing missing, yet God didn't write it. Just because a holy book discuses money, the law, education, justice, sovereignty, family, divorce, women, culture, and diet doesn't mean that God dictated it.

Religious believers in Western governments find policy guidelines in their religious holy book, which is why religionists in power are dangerous. They'll work to influence politics with their organized religion, creating a permanent political indoctrination. The theory and practice of religiously-influenced government will create laws and justice based on each leader's religious beliefs. The world has been corrupted by political Islam or Christianity, which has worked to promote religious thought over true democracy. Political Christianity has worked for the promotion of the Judeo-Christian ethic, not what's best for humanity. Judeo-Christian morality is reflected in the laws of the land because those governed by Christian thought work to Christianize the world. This is why everything at the level of institutions, forms, public life, powers, and everything essential is mostly Judeo-Christian.

All the gods of religious holy books require the ethical purification of the religionist, which is why religious slaves are programmed to hate the body, natural desires, free sexuality, and the flesh. The moral order of the religions of the book condemns homosexuality, common sense, and free thought. The Islamic ayatollah promotes the condemnation of luxury, gambling, alcohol, drugs, cinema, perfume, lotteries, prostitution, and other vices. The religions of the book are responsible for the total religious mobilization of the world's system. Religion has a strong influence on all institutions, press, educational systems, journalism, and judicial bodies. Humanity will evolve spiritually when it makes an effort to de-Christianize the ethic, politics, and everything else. The fight for a post-Christian secularism may remain weak because there are too many humans afraid of hell.

Religion is the suppression of all individual freedom. The religious system is designed to dominate the body and soul. Monotheist religions are human insanity attributed to God. Religionists have waged a religious holy war, with Muslims and Saracens on one side, and Christians and Jews on the other. Muslims, Jews, and Christians are each a part of the same 3-headed dragon. For humanity to survive, it must launch a campaign against theocracy on behalf of intellectual democracy. Reason can enter human consciences once the religions of the book are discovered to be frauds. Free thinkers have deconstructed Christian fables with the help of the real God to advance the cause of modernity, but the fallen won't listen because they fear hell.

Christian thought is an enemy of humanity possessing full powers over the souls, bodies, and consciences of the deceived. The people of the book have poisoned the planet with their commandeering of all the controls of political, civil, and military society. The Judeo-Christian ethic and morality rules the planet, impregnating the bodies, consciences, and souls of those convinced by religious authority that hell is real. Once one fears hell, he or she will adopt religion's mistrust of the flesh, hatred of the body, and denial of natural passions to be found worthy on the day of judgment. Christendom doesn't have to worry about revolution because 'submission to political authority' is part of religious programming. Biblical monotheism and the religion of Christ have formatted society to the point that even unbelievers speak, live, think, and conceive as Judeo-Christians. Those who live in the Light do not choose between Western Judeo-Christianity and its Islamic adversary, but reject both the Bible and the Koran. The people of the book have 'fallen' for theological hocus-pocus.

Secularism is the way of enlightenment because unlike organized religion, it allows everyone to think as they wish and believe in their own god. Secularism is only holy if secularists don't make their belief systems a matter for the community. It's wrong to try to force everyone to believe exactly as you believe, though it's not wrong to share your ideas. The secular are the true righteous because they assert the equality of the Christian, Muslim, Jew, Buddhist, polytheist, Shintoist, atheist, animist, and all other groups in the contemporary Western state. True holy people make everything and everyone equal, while religionists cause division with their believer/unbeliever concept. Those who reject all religions are actually holier than religious believers who fail to decree the equality of all forms of spirituality.

Scientific thinking, national thought, and reasoned argument are the true ways of God. Religionists afraid of hell have abandoned God-given logic and common sense for myths and fables. Real thinkers examine beliefs, while religionists accept myths without exploring the creation of religious fables. The Jews have convinced themselves and others that God has made them 'his' chosen people. The Christians, after being threatened with hell, are convinced that Jesus was born of a virgin, crucified under Pontius Pilate, and raised from the dead on the third day by God. To be saved from hell, the Christian must believe this to escape hell-fire. If fear of an eternal hell didn't shut off reason and logic, the Christian would discover that there is no Devil and there is no hell!

Fear of hell keeps the religious community enslaved to organized religion. The promise of heaven keeps them inspired and dedicated to religious foolishness. Religion's promotion of an afterlife with God while the unbeliever burns in hell deprives 'the fallen' of the benefits and enjoyment of this life. Believing that God wrote or dictated some religious holy book is truly a sin, if you choose to believe in sin. I explained the origin of sin in my book 'The Gospel According to Jawara King.' Sin is a false doctrine.

Following religious dogma doesn't save you from hell and promise you a mansion in heaven. The religions of the book created religious laws, not God. Following man-made edicts doesn't make you holy and righteous. A life of holiness, according to rigid religious belief structures, is a sham. The people of the book are convinced that not living in agreement with their religious holy book disqualifies them from entering heaven. These afterlife fables didn't come from God, but are man-made fantasies designed to control people and benefit the religious system. Radical Muslims are convinced that the assassination of unbelievers will throw open the gates of paradise for them. All the religions of the book are spiritually and physically destroying the planet with all these false religious ideologies.

The people of the book are filling the earth with darkness. If they didn't believe that their holy books were written by God and their religious figures were exalted by God above all others, they would be somewhat sane. The holy books and the characters therein are no different than any other book or person. Moses is no greater than Descartes, and Muhammad is no greater than Nietzsche. Jesus and Kant are equal, though Kant was a real historical person. Scientific thinking knows that God didn't write or dictate these man-made holy books. The Wise Ones know that the Torah is no greater than Descartes' Discourse on Method. The Koran is no greater than the 'Genealogy of Morality.' The New Testament wasn't written by God and is actually inferior to the 'Critique of Pure Reason.' Your God-given freedom comes from discovering that the religions of the book are man-made, not God's word. God didn't write any holy books.

Organized religion has problems with logic. The roster of contradictions found in holy books proves that God didn't write them. The Torah, Koran, and New Testament are filled with contradictions and have been used for evil deeds. All the holy books are frauds because they were created by borrowing from sacred texts written thousands of years earlier. Holy books attributed to God are all full of inconsistencies and mixed messages. All three monotheistic books are nothing more than a collection of lies, fables, and myths.

The Muslims believe that they have the one and only true holy book. Sura 4:82 declares that the Koran was issued directly from Allah. The absence of contradictions is supposed to be proof that the Koran is the divine book. Irreligious scholars can conclude that every page is full of contradictions. The first line of the first Sura says, "In the name of Allah, the Beneficent, the Merciful," yet Islamic practice and Muslim theory aren't examples of compassion. Multiple verses of the Koran are contradictory and prove that Islam isn't about peace and submission to God. The Koran says to kill unbelievers (8:39) and polytheists (9:5). (9:6) praises those who offer them asylum, and Allah advises to "pardon them and turn away" (5:13). Sura 7:199 talks about "forgiveness and turning aside," yet 4:56, 4:91, and 2:191-94 authorize mass slaughter. Allah obviously has contrary qualities because he is referred to as beneficent and merciful, yet the Koran says he excelled in battle tactics, killing, and punishment (8:30). No God is behind any of these false religions!

All three monotheistic religious holy books abound in contradictory statements. The roster of contradictions proves that God didn't write them. These false holy books spread by the sword and terrorized humanity with slaughter, burning, and torturing. In antiquity, institutionalized religion was advanced by force. In the present, it's promoted by FEAR (of hell). If you don't accept Jesus Christ as you lord and savior, believe that God raised him from the dead, and live by the man-made edicts of the Bible, you're going to hell forever. The people of the book tell other Earthians that God is keeping records of their wrongs to condemn them on Judgment Day. This is another contradictory religious lie based on contradictory scriptures. Revelation 20:12 says that God keeps a record of wrongs. However, 1 John 4:8 says that God is Love. By rightly dividing the scriptures, you'll see that God keeps no record of wrongs. God is Love, and Love keeps no record of wrongs according to I Corinthians 13:5. Another Biblical contradiction, yet I choose to believe that God is love.

The Hidden Scrolls

The Koran doesn't honor women (43:17) and talks about a father being told that he's giving birth to a daughter: "his face becomes black and he is full of rage." Women are not inferior or superior to men, it's just that religionists use various verses to serve their own interests. If religious slaves only discovered that God didn't write their holy books, they would abandon religion. Muslim enthusiasts, Christian fundamentalists, and orthodox Jews have been brainwashed into believing that their holy book is inspired, scared, divine, revealed and dictated by God. The three religions of the book did not come from God, and to believe so is religious mental illness. Those believing in holy books need a savior.

Humanity has a death fixation, and religion plays on it by threatening unbelievers with eternal hell-fire. Preachers scare individuals by asking questions such as, "if you were to die right now, where would you spend eternity?" Then, people convert out of fear of hell. Without hell and eternal judgment in the lake of fire, the religious system collapses. Hell is needed by the religions of the book to scare people into religious enslavement and keep them there. If the religious community knew that there was no hell, they wouldn't fool with organized religion. Fear of hell is the only reason why the average religionist won't consider the ideas in this book. When you believe in hell, you become a slave to organized religion. All unbelievers go to hell while religious believers go to heaven, tricking people into believing for fear of hell.

All three religious holy books serve a death instinct and take advantage of the majority's fear of death. The three religions of the book are built on fear and violence. Religious groups have slaughtered, colonized, and deported entire populations in the name of the god of their religious holy books. Religious slaves are the cause of most of the madness on planet earth. Those suffering from the mental illness of organized religion have caused all sorts of religious madness individually and collectively in the name of their religion. From the bloody sword of the Israelites slaughtering

the Canaanites to present-day Muslims killing Christians and
infidels, the religions of the book are a DARK FORCE in the
earth. Evil is done in the name of God, and holy crimes are carried
out by religionists claiming to act in God's name. Religion is
destroying the earth and causing division between believers and
unbelievers. The religious fundamentalists causing the majority of
the world's problems will probably die as religious slaves because
they fear hell. The fear of hell enslaves the religionist.

Verses from the Torah, suras from the Koran, and passages
from the Gospels legitimize and justify division through the
believer/unbeliever concept. Monotheism is fixed on death, so
potential religionists are threatened with hell (after death) if they
refuse to believe. Once you're convinced that you'll go to hell for
refusing to believe, the religious community will convince you
that some religious text is God's word. The theory is that you
will not attack the utterance of God or the revealed word because
you'll be questioning God. All a religious leader has to do is give
his opinion backed by scripture and you'll fall for it if you believe
in the divinity of some holy text. It's dangerous to think that God
wrote, dictated, or inspired a religious text because then, you've
substituted the real God for a man-made book. The religious text
becomes an idol, placed above the real God, who has no children
or religious holy books. Opposing scriptures quoted from one
of the three holy books is equivalent to rejecting God in person,
according to institutionalized religion.

According to the subliminal message of the Holy Bible, God
only speaks through Jewish people. Without Jews, God does
not speak. The Jews made themselves the chosen people and
invented the holy war. The Jews are responsible for the creation
of monotheism and all the horrors that go along with it. Yahweh,
the god of the Jews, blessed and waged war. The god of the Old
Testament led, supervised, and sanctified combat. How can you
believe that the god of the Old Testament is the real God when
'he' sanctioned murders, assassination, and crimes, and gave
'his' blessing to the killing of innocent people? Exodus 12:12

authorized the killing of everything that moved, including the aged, children, livestock, and women. The wholesale slaughter of populations, book burnings, and non-Christian spiritual teachers being scorched alive were side-effects of religion. The god of the Bible split the sea in half to drown a whole army and stopped the Sun to give the Hebrews time to annihilate their enemies (Joshua 10:12-14).

In Genesis 17:8, god promised 'his' people a promised land to be theirs "for an everlasting possession." Yahweh made the Jews, singled out from among all others, the elect and the chosen. In Exodus 19:5, god says of the Jews that they a "peculiar treasure unto me." The real God shows no favoritism, nor exalts one group above another. The god of the Old Testament is an exterminator and declared of the Canaanites in Exodus 23:23, "and I will cut them off." All groups other than the Hebrews were of little importance. God promised total destruction to the indigenous population of Palestine, even though they were already well-established in the land before the Hebrews arrived. The false god of the Old Testament is the root cause and originator of the holy war (Joshua 6:21).

The pages of your favorite holy books are rooted in fable. It's highly dangerous to believe that God wrote your holy book because you'll be putting your faith and trust in fictions and nonsense. The fallen are humans living on this planet who live, think, act, and conceive of the world based on what's written in religious texts. All the religions of the book encourage racism, murder, division, and the lack of peace. Religionists study religious holy book passages and enslave themselves with religious laws that God didn't come up with. The god of the religious fundamentalist living by the tenets of a holy book is a false god created by man in the image of man. They were scared into religious enslavement through hell-fire teachings (threatenings). When you don't believe in hell, you're already in Heaven. Foolish religionists believe things to be sin that aren't sin at all. Sex outside of marriage isn't a sin;

for marriage is human law, not a divine source. Learn to love God without religion! God is love.

Throughout the history of Christianity, Christians have enrolled God in their misdeeds. The Jews made themselves the chosen people to falsely solidify their destiny as history's favorites. In the Old Testament, Yahweh gives 'his' chosen people divine justification for the annihilation of other groups of people. The Gospels present the humiliation of Jesus, which never happened. Jesus is a myth, yet real humiliations were carried out in his name. History bears witness to millions of dead in the name of the religions of the book. In the name of holy book gods, millions of innocent people in every century on all continents have been slayed. Christian zealots carrying the Bible in one hand and a sword in the other have terrorized the earth, killing for their god in the Inquisition, the Crusades, and massacres of unbelievers. The religions of the book are responsible for torture, exterminations, hangings, the African slave trade, genocides, exploitation, and exterminations. During Constantine's reign, in the fourth century of their era, bonfires were lit to burn all books that were a threat to exposing the Bible as a lie.

The Bible was created by men with the selective borrowing from other texts. The Bible is not God's word, but is used to control others in the name of God. For example, Matthew 22:21 says to "Render therefore unto Caesar the things which are Caesar's, and unto God the things which are God's." Convincing people that God wanted money rendered unto Caesar justified the payment of taxes as a means of pleasing God. The Bible's role in ancient society was to trick people into supporting the army of occupation, submitting to the laws of the empire, and financially supporting the imperial forces in the name of God. The early Christians weren't serving God, but Paulinism. The promised land of the Old Testament was stolen from the Canaanites. The New Testament wanted the world to follow Christ. Nothing good has been done by ancient religionists from the Old to the New Testament.

The Epistle to the Romans states that "There is no power but of

God" (13:1). According to the New Testament, all officials are given their power by God and are God's ministers. Paulinism was used to solicit approval of submission to Roman authority. Paul's writings would have you believe that disobeying anyone in authority is an offense to God. Once Saul became Paul, he dismantled Judaism and promoted Christian anti-Semitism. He convinced people that Jesus was the Messiah foretold in the Old Testament, and that he fulfilled the prophecy, abolishing Judaism. Through Paul, Jews became adversaries and enemies for not believing that Jesus is the Son of God who died on the cross to save humankind. The whole gospel story is an unverifiable fairytale.

The Christian version of the death of Jesus doesn't make the Romans responsible, but the Jews. The writings of Paul make Pontius Pilate neither responsible nor guilty for the death of Jesus. In Thessalonians 2:15, Paul was speaking of the Jews who "killed the Lord Jesus." Not only in the Epistles of Paul, but the Gospels are full of openly anti-Semitic passages. Jesus described the Jews as being "of your father, the devil" (John 8:44). According to Daniel Goldhagen, there are 140 anti-Semitic passages in the Acts of the Apostles, 40 in Mark, 130 in John, and 80 in Matthew.

There was an active collaboration between Nazism and the Vatican. Both Adolf Hitler and Pius XII loathed the Jews and shared the same points of view. No historian can ignore the relationship between the Catholic Church and Nazism. The Vatican's archives on the subject are practically sealed. Ignoring the teachings of peace and love of one's neighbor, the evil Catholic Church supported the rearmament of Germany in the 1930's. When Adolf Hitler took office in 1933, the Catholic Church signed a concordat with the chancellor. The Catholic Church gave the Nazis genealogical records to expose the non-Jewish from the Christian. The names of the Jews married to Christians or converted to Christ's religion weren't revealed. This is the real history of the Catholic Church which they've remained silent over. The leaders of the Catholic Church also know that Jesus is a myth, but remain equally silent over this fact. Jesus is nothing but a big money-maker these days.

The pro-Nazi Ustachi regime of Ante Pavelic in Croatia was aided and supported by the Catholic Church. The Vinchy regime in 1940, France's collaborationist, was given absolution by the Catholic Church. The policy of extermination set up in 1942 wasn't condemned by the Catholic Church. Not one Catholic bishop or priest condemned the criminal regime, nor did anything to defeat it. Cardinal Bertram of the Catholic Church, in memory of Adolf Hitler, ordered a requiem Mass. When the masses discovered the death camps, gas chambers, and mass graves, the Catholic Church expressed no disapproval whatsoever. The Catholic Church set up an underground network to smuggle war criminals out of Europe. The Catholic Church delivered papers to fugitive Nazis stamped with its visas and set up European monasteries to hide dignitaries of the ruined Reich. Important leaders of the Hitler regime were promoted into the hierarchy of the Catholic Church. The Catholic Church will acknowledge none of this, nor apologize.

The first Vatican Council in 1869-70 established the doctrine of papal infallibility. The pontiff is supreme and speaks as the representative of God on earth, according to Catholics. None of these men were constantly inspired by the Holy Spirit as claimed, and brought more hell to the earth. For example, Pius IX and Pius X condemned human rights as contrary to the word of god and church teachings. Pius XII excommunicated every communist in the world in 1949 to promote National Socialism. Those who've practiced anti-Semitism, operated gas chambers, or preached racism were never excluded from the Catholic Church. Adolf Hitler was honored and supported for his views and never excommunicated. Hitler's book Mein Kampf appeared in 1924, and the Catholic Church refused to put it in the Index. The Index Librorum Prohibitorium was written after 1924, and included books written by Henri Bergson, Jean-Paul Satre, Simone de Beauvoir, André Gide, and many other enlightened teachers. Hitler's writings (Mein Kampf) never appeared on it.

During Hitler's interviews, he expressed his admiration for Christianity. His published conversations with Albert Speer unambiguously express his admiration for the Vatican. The Catholic Church supported the very antithesis of Christian. Under Hitler, the words 'Gott mit uns' were stamped on the Reich's soldiers' belt buckles. The phrase came from Deuteronomy of the Torah, meaning, "For the Lord thy God is he that goeth with you" (Deuteronomy 20:4). Yahweh said this to Jews fighting their Egyptian enemies. In Deuteronomy 20:13, God held out his unspecified extermination promise. Hitler was labeled as a Christian because he ordered all school children in the National Socialist Reich to pray to Jesus in the beginning of their day. Hitler and Pius XII were compatible as a merger between National Socialism and Christianity. Hitler and the Vatican admired each other, establishing the partnership of Nazism and Christianity. Christianity wasn't created by God and has nothing to do with real spirituality.

The goal of the early Christians was not to spread the Gospel, but eradicate everything redolent of paganism. Paul recommended book burnings. The evil Christians destroyed temples and altars, and persecuted all who opposed Christianity. The theocratic evolution of Christianity was admired by Hitler (Mein Kampf, volume 2, chapter 5, page 454). On page 459 of Mein Kampf, Hitler praised the church's determination to stand firm in the face of science and all that contradicted its dogma and positions. Hitler talked about his version of 'true Christianity' (volume 1, chapter 11, page 307), and told his readers to "take lessons from the Catholic Church" (page 459, but also pages 114 and 20).

Hitler was impressed by the angry Jesus who used a whip to drive all the moneylenders from the Temple. He mentioned this passage from John's Gospel to support his argument. Critical thinkers will realize that the Christian whip that Hitler so greatly admired served to drive out Jews, validating the complicity between Reich and Vatican. The Christian whip of John's Gospel (2:14) drove out money-changers, unbelievers, merchants, non-

Christians, and vendors, making Hitler's anti-Semitism possible. Many New Testament passages consigned the Jews to hellfire, making it easier for Hitler to use religion to do his business. Hitler claimed that the Jews were the enemies of humanity and created Bolshevism. The gas chambers were operated in the name of Saint John. Hitler said, "to the political leader, the religious ideas and institutions of his people must remain inviolable" (page 116). You see, no one acts inappropriately according to his or her view of the world.

Religion is a serious mental illness contaminating the entire world. The writings of Paul of Tarsus justified the sword and fire. Augustine used the scriptures to justify capital punishment, war, slavery, and massacres. Augustine, Bishop of Hippo, sanctioned 'just persecutions' in a letter (185), with the church's blessing. The church wanted to convert the world to Christianity by any means. Universal Christianity made every continent a battlefield, and triumphed with unjust persecution. Hundreds of unbelievers have died at the hands of religious believers, who've committed innumerable crimes in the name of God. Muslims alone have killed over 270 million unbelievers. Christians started colonial wars to evangelize all continents. 90% or more of modern Christians don't know anything about the Crusades against the Saracens, holy wars against unbelievers, and the Inquisition against real spiritual teachers (who were called heretics). Learn the real history of Christianity. In 363, Saint Bernard of Clairvanx wrote in a letter, "the best solution is to kill them" and "a pagan's death is a Christian's glory." By studying the true history of organized religion, you'll discover that institutionalized religion didn't come from God.

Members of the church have been behind all the evil acts of humanity. Father George Zabelka blessed the crew of the Enola Gay, which dropped an atomic bomb on 8/6/1945 on Hiroshima. The deadly mission killed more than 100,000 people. The nuclear explosion, first blessed by Father George Zabelka, killed the old, the sick, women, children, and innocent people for the crime of being Japanese. Just because the Bible teaches that 'all power comes from God' doesn't mean that religionists were acting on God's behalf while terrorizing the world. Religion isn't godliness, but a man-made creation from the Kingdom of Darkness.

Genesis 9:25-27 defends slavery and was used by ruthless slave masters to justify their actions. In the Torah, the members of the Covenant were treated favorably, while the non-Jews had no rights. Leviticus 25:39-55 commanded the Jew to not use his own kind as a slave. As a rental agreement, a Jew could work as an indentured servant for 6 years, then restored to freedom. Non-Jews could remain slaves until death. The real God wasn't behind this division and placing one group favorably above another. The real God is not a respecter of persons and has no Chosen people.

Augustine encouraged slaves to work in a way that's pleasing to God. Worker–slaves of today are also told by religious leaders to work with a zeal pleasing to God. When are humans going to get tired of being worker–slaves, workers, and slaves of others? Slavery is the model of humanity. In the 8th century, the monastery of Saint-Germain des Pres had over 8,000 slaves. Pope Gregory I banned slaves from the priesthood in the 6th century. Constantine didn't allow Jews to keep slaves in their homes. In the Middle Ages, the supreme pontiff had thousands of slaves laboring hard in the agricultural domains. The Muslims practiced slavery and thought it was right because the Koran didn't suppress slavery.

Islam invented the slave trade. There was a constant exchange of millions of slaves between Kenya and China in the year 1,000. The sale of Muslims was banned by Muslim law, but non-believers could be sold. The trans-Saharan slave traffic began 9 centuries before the transatlantic trade. The faithful of Allah deported over ten million men in the name of slavery over 1200 years. Since religious texts support the justification of slavery, religionists used physical force and armed constraint to enslave those who worshipped any god other than their own.

The three monotheisms followed religious rules of slavery. Muslims and Jews forbade members of their own communities from being slaves. The Christians prohibited Jews from owning domestic slaves. Slaves were forbidden from entering holy orders to keep them from serving the word of God. The New Testament, Torah, and Koran justified enslaving their enemies because all non-believers were believed to have a subhuman nature. Those who worshiped other gods were reduced to the concept of 'unbelievers,' making it easier for the religionist to humiliate, kill, torture, or enslave. The religious community used their holy scriptures to legitimize slave raids and oppress unbelievers (wrong believers). Booty-hunting raids in the name of God advanced the religionist with stolen loot in animals, silver, women, gold, and men to be slaves. All the colonialism, ethnocide, genocide, and other religious madness done in the name of God is not the work of God, but religious foolishness. Those worshiping a god of the book are serving a false god. The real God isn't in the religions of the book.

Christianity and Islam want to have mastery of the whole planet. The three monotheisms are equally evil, so if you follow any of them, you're serving the same 3-headed dragon. The Apostolic, Catholic, and Roman Church destroyed civilizations and are responsible for the spiritual extinction of cultures. The year 1492 symbolizes the destruction of other worlds, not the discovery of the New World. Christian Europe destroyed all the Amerindian civilizations. After the religionists completed their ethnic cleansing, the priests decorated the stolen land with crucifixes, altars, and ciboria. Christendom took over America with its preaching of hatred of women, sexuality, and the body. Original sin, guilt, and forgiveness of sins was taught by religious leaders, shaping the nation to be a country full of religious slaves afraid of hell.

The church is about destruction and has nothing to do with God. The church and Nazism formed a partnership to exterminate a race. Gypsies, Communists, homosexuals, antifascists, laymen, Jehovah's Witnesses, Freemasons, left-wingers, and all others viewed as not being Christian enough were deported and murdered. Christian history is full of mass extermination. The Catholic establishment supported and covered up for the genocide of Tutsis by the Hutu of Rwanda. The supreme pontiff defended the Hutu of Rwanda and ensured that genocide war criminals and other Catholic community members escaped firing squad judgment. The pope requested a stay of execution for guilty Hutus, and offered no words of compassion to the Tutsi community.

The Catholic Church hid Christians from justice and smuggled criminals out of European countries. Christian organizations bought air tickets to protect bishops implicated in the genocide. The church maintained public attitudes of denial while shipping guilty priests to French and Belgium parishes. The church was silent after the genocide of Tutsis by the Hutu of Rwanda, which were executed with the blessings of French president Francois Mitterrand. One million died in 3 months between April and June 1994, and the church was no where to be found during the massacres. Pope John Paul II wrote a letter to the president of Rwanda on April 23, 1998 to request a stay of execution for the Hutus guilty of genocide. The Pope didn't express compassion for the victims, didn't repent or express regret, nor washed his hands of their actions. The Catholic establishment has always supported brutality.

Religion is Refusal of Enlightenment

In the early days of Christianity, Christians in power changed the law in favor of organized religion. Justinian set up Christian legislation in an attempt to destroy the lives of the unorthodox. Justinian's law forbade non-Christians from receiving wealth, testifying in court against Christian believers, drawing up legal deeds, and owning Christian slaves. Freedom of conscience was forbidden by Christian legislation; for all were forced to follow the holy Bible.

In 529, Justinian used all his power to destroy unbelievers for the sake of the Gospel. He forced pagans to take instruction in the Christian religion and made baptism mandatory. Anyone who refused to follow Christian legislation was threatened with exile or the confiscation of their goods. Justinian even dominated the Christian community with laws to keep them enslaved to the Gospel. He forbade all Christian converts from returning to paganism. For the first thousand years of Christianity, philosophizing became dangerous because of Constantine, Justinian, and others. Every succeeding period has also experienced the negative affects of theocracy. Even today, with less physical religious violence, the Wise Ones are experiencing more mental, spiritual, and social persecution.

Religious fundamentalists know nothing about the selective exploitation of religious texts or else they wouldn't believe their holy book to be the word of God. The whole world knows of the existence of the three books of monotheism, but most don't know the information I've discussed in this book. Religious believers have ALL been deceived because they don't know the dates or origin or the real authors of the three texts. Believers are unburdened of intelligence and reason, which is why they believe the three religious texts to be the final and immutable word of God. Believers of the Torah, Koran, and holy Bible claim their texts to be issued by Almighty God. Religionists will most likely spend the rest of their lives as slaves of religious dogma to please 'him.'

Monotheism's three books emerged from history with unverifiable claims, yet humanity was fooled into believing that these frauds were issued from God alone. God didn't write any holy books, and anyone can discover this truth by thoroughly investigating the three texts. Even scholars studying in libraries specializing in the history of religions can't find the exact dates of the texts forming the holy books. No one can be certain of the dates of the origin of the body of religious texts. Their dates of composition are uncertain. Men of reason, historians, and religious scholars are indifferent to how and when the texts were composed.

This knowledge is essential to our understanding of whether or not God, or men inspired by God, wrote the texts.

God didn't write any religious texts nor inspired them. As you examine each book of the Bible, you can discover where it really came from. The book of Genesis is contemporaneous with earlier books written by other authors, not God. The creators of Genesis used the Iliad, the Epic of Gilgamesh, the Upanishads, Hesiod's Theogony (origin of the Gods), and Confucius' Analects to put the book together. Religious fools believe that Genesis and the other books of the Bible have no human author. The religious community (the fallen) treat the Bible as if it fell from heaven by a miracle as was dictated by God Almightly to an inspired man. In the early days, many people questioned the historical veracity of the holy Bible, so Christian clerics banned direct reading of the biblical texts. The clerics banned the Bible from the public for centuries because they knew direct contact with and an intelligent reading of the texts would expose the Bible's incoherence. Common sense would reveal the Bible as a fake holy text because extraordinary claims require extraordinary evidence. There's no extraordinary evidence proving the Bible to be the word of God. The Bible is a lie full of religious madness! Abandon institutionalized religion and run to the Light. If not, you're refusing enlightenment. God isn't in the religious system.

After centuries of unreliable oral transmission, many people started writing religious texts. Stories covering a long historical span were eventually written down centuries later, then copied thousands of times by a considerable number of writers. The Bible we have now is 27 centuries in the making, with no god anywhere to be found. The scribes who copied religious texts thousands of times were outright forgers trying to create the perfect biblical text. The Bible is a fraud, which is why historians struggle with the task of political, sociological, and philosophical contextualization. Even today, religious scholars can't get the dates right. They only guess and assume. The Bible isn't God's word!

Joseph Trinquet and Emile Osty produced the French edition

of the Bible. They claimed it was composed over a ten-century time frame between the 12th and 2nd centuries B.C. The creation of the Bible came after the Egyptian books of wisdom. The royal scribe Ani of Thebes had more wisdom than the Bible, which was created by scribes borrowing from earlier spiritual texts. Some historians have the time frame of the completion of the biblical texts between the 3rd and 2nd centuries BCE. Some date the composition of the Bible between Socrates and Lucretius. Jean Soler's estimate is between the 5th and 1st centuries BCE. Be like the skeptic philosopher Carneades and not fall for this Word of God foolishness.

Those who believe that the Bible is a divine source are putting their trust in mythical fabrications. Christians accept the Bible as the infallible word of God, totally ignoring the vagueness surrounding the origins of the New Testament texts. The New Testament is unreliable because the first Gospel didn't come on the scene until a half century after Jesus' supposed existence. Jesus never existed, which is why the first texts about him didn't appear until many years after his purported lifetime. The oldest estimates date from 50 to hundreds of years after Jesus because none of the four evangelists ever knew Christ personally (in the flesh). Those who wrote of Jesus didn't do so from a personal relationship in physical form, but through accounts transmitted orally.

Mythological and fabulous accounts of Jesus were written down between the fifties of the common era. Paul's epistles are set at the end of the first century. If you choose to continue believing the holy Bible to be the Word of God, then view it as a history book (maybe). If you take the New Testament literally, the Apocalypse was the end of the first century! Revelation 1:1 says, "the revelation of Jesus Christ, which God gave unto him, to shew unto his servants things which must shortly come to pass;..." Matthew 16:27-28 says, "...Verily, I say unto you, there be some standing here, which shall not taste of death, till they see the Son of man coming in his Kingdom." So, Revelation said that all that was written therein would shortly come to pass, and Jesus said that some who were standing with him would not die until they saw his second coming. Therefore in context, the end of the 1st century was the Apocalypse. For a more detailed explanation, read my book World Transformation.

None of the Gospel writers knew Jesus personally. There was not one copy of the Gospels in existence before the end of the second century. There was still no copy during the beginning of the third! Mark, Luke, Matthew, and John are frauds based on the dates of the texts. The oldest document revealing Christ is a late arrival, exposed as a lie based on the given period of its inception. The decades of the second century of our era was the period of the forging of Christianity. True Christian history won't be discussed in any churches or theological seminaries. All the religions of the book are frauds!

The Bible as we know it was put together at the Council of Trent in 1546. Saint Jerome, a man with no intellectual honesty, translated the Hebrew text in the 4th and 5th centuries. Men have had their hands in this holy book thing from the very beginning! The Jews built their definitive corpus over a long span of time, forming their man-made creation attributed to the authorship of God. Certain texts of the Torah were made to date from the 12th century B.C. This is another lie because the rabbis didn't settle the details of the Hebrew Bible until AFTER the destruction of the Temple in Jerusalem around 70 CE. This is the same period when real spirituality and spiritual teachers abounded. Their writings were stolen to be used by the Christians or burned. During this time, Epictetus lived in imperial Rome as an emblematic Stoic. The Wise Ones living during this time period didn't fall for Christianity.

Religion is a man-made creation that is destroying planet Earth out of fear, division, and deception. All of the religions of the book were put together by men secretly playing the role of God. The Jewish oral laws (the Mishna) were codified and compiled in the 3rd century by religious scribes. These religious laws were created to supplement the laws in the Torah. Christian scribes stole the work of real philosophers and used it to make their religious texts spiritually profound. At the same time that the Mishna was compiled, Diogenes Laërtius was writing 'Lives, Teachings, and Sayings of Famous Philosophers.' A commentary on the Mishna called the Babylonian Talmud was created around 500 by rabbis from Palestine. This purported holy text was put together at the same time Boetius was in prison writing 'Consolation of Philosophy.' Men alone, not God, put these holy texts together, which is why the definitive text of the Hebrew Bible wasn't established until after the year 1,000. At the same time, Avicenna was working towards reconciling philosophy and Islam.

During the time that the definitive text of the Hebrew Bible was established, other holy books were being put together. The Muslims established their version of the Koran from a handful of Korans. The Koran is a forgery like all the other religious books because men put it together, then attributed its authorship to God. The definitive version of the Koran was chosen from other texts to form a textual and ideological calibration. To avoid incoherence, the Koran handlers compared the dialect of several texts, standardized the spelling, and used a handful of Korans to put together the final establishment of the definitive Koran. The forgers took all the Korans and separated abrogating and abrogated verses in order to avoid contradictions in the official Koran. Men did this, not God.

The most ancient Old Testament texts are dated 12th century BCE. The New Testament corpus was put together by Christians in power at the Council of Trent during the 16th century. Religionists put together the construction sites of the monotheism to support organized religion. Man was constantly at work for twenty centuries putting together the religions of the book and inserting their holy book characters into history. Serious archaeological spadework would prove that Jesus and other religious figures were non-historical and inserted into history many years after their purported existence. Religious holy books have been promoted as directly dictated by God to 'his' people, but numberless acts of human intervention expose them as man-made creations.

There is no official date of birth for worship of one God because it took time for organized religion to create an official god. Before institutionalized religion, people followed whatever they resonated with, which is how it should be. Christians are only Christians because they fear hell and believe that they'll go to hell if they reject Christianity. Some guess that the official date of worship of one sanctioned god began around the 13th century BCE. Jean Soler says that worship of the one (man-invented) god began very late, somewhere around the fourth and third century BCE. Once Earthians discover how these books were put together, they'll abandon all religions of the book.

The Jews used information from the Egyptian solar cult to invent their texts. As a small group of threatened people, the Jews used spiritual texts from other groups to create their own to ensure the cohesion and coherence of their own people. They used multiple texts borrowed from other writings to create the mythology of a bloodthirsty and aggressive warrior god who chose them to be the chosen people. The chosen people ideology is a myth because the real God doesn't favor one group over another.

Holy books are inventions of men, designed to appear as the real word of God. There is no word of God, and no God endorsed any holy book. Today, we have several thousand pages of canonical text that survived. Before they were put together over the course of more than twenty centuries, they had no worldwide influence. All of the religions of the book promote phony religious texts as the word of God. The Old Testament is 3,500 pages, and the New Testament is 900; mostly religious madness! The Koran is 750 pages, and like the other holy books, people only follow it because they believe it was inspired or dictated by God. The combined total of over 5,000 holy book pages is supposed to contain everything God wants said with nothing else ever needed to be written. These three founding texts are each supposed to be the final authority from God, but God isn't involved! Every illusory fact articulated in holy texts (like original sin) is immediately confronted with its opposite when you look outside of the religious system. Religion is a mind-control program having nothing to do with God. The contradictions abounding in religious texts prove that they weren't dictated by Almighty God.

The religions of the book may appear to be different, but they are all part of the same 3-headed Beast. The Christian, Muslim, and Jew are able to find material in the Koran, the Torah, and the Gospels to justify division, religious enslavement, and the inferiority of women. War leaders throughout history have used all 3 holy books to justify their actions. Quoting scriptures means nothing because anyone can find an unbelievable number of verses to choose from to justify his or her actions. Peacemakers and war mongers can both brandish words, quotations, and sentences from the holy books to defend opposite points of view. Religious leaders lift the maxims they need from religious texts to accomplish their purpose, which most of the time is to solicit MONEY.

The three holy books are all lies, yet have built nations, empires, history, and states over more than 2,000 years. Humanity is going in the wrong direction because billions of Earthians believe that God wrote or inspired these man-made religious holy books. Anyone who really studies the origin and history of institutionalized religion will know that no God is behind these 3 books. The three so-called holy books are not uniform or unequivocal, and had too many middlemen, scribes, and copyists involved in their creation to be from God. The holy books don't have a single source of inspiration and are just a bunch of pages written by anonymous people with too many sources. They contain too many pages with too many second thoughts, probably because they were written over too many years. If these holy books were really dictated by or inspired from God, they would be nothing but absolute, perfect, and definitive. If the holy Bible is true, each fragment would also be true and the entirety of it would reflect its perfection.

The religious community uses the so-called sacred texts for its own purposes. Religious leaders justify talking you out of your money by using biblical quotations taken out of context. Hitler used biblical scriptures to defend his measures and invoked Jesus driving the moneylenders from the Temple to do his own driving out. Martin Luther King quoted from the Gospels to justify his nonviolence campaign. Israel uses what's written in the Torah to justify its colonization of Palestine. The Palestinians quote the Koran to justify their fighting to eliminate Israel. Islamist extremists use the Koran to legitimize the murder of innocents. Those who lay their lives down for the religions of the book are suffering from serious mental illness!

Yahweh says in Deuteronomy 5:17 that "Thou shalt not kill." Believers in the Bible ignored this ban on committing murder and shamelessly practiced violence against non-believers for centuries. The history of Christianity is a blatant logical contradiction to the Ten Commandments. In the name of their holy book, Christians caused the Crusades, battles, the Inquisition, and holy wars against non-Christians.

The Bible is a lie full of contradictions. Deuteronomy 5:17 says, "Thou shalt not kill," yet in Deuteronomy 7:1, the same Yahweh allows the Jews to exterminate certain peoples. Since the Jews were the chosen people singled out by god according to Deuteronomy 7:6, exalted above all others, Yahweh authorized violence and destruction against other tribes. Monuments and altars were demolished, and the writings of other groups were destroyed in legitimized book burnings. Mixed marriages with other tribes were forbidden, and the Jews were banned from entering into contracts with them. Through his word, Yahweh authorized racism and division, and this same 'word of god' is causing separation today with the believer/unbeliever concept.

All of the holy book gods are evil and justify the extermination of people (mostly unbelievers). In the Torah, Yahweh justified the extermination of the Hittites from Asia Minor, Perizzites, Jebusites, Girgashites, and Amorites, Hivites, Canaanites, and most of the people of Palestine. The injunction not to kill, laid out in Deuteronomy 5:17, is ignored in the rest of Deuteronomy. Yahweh justifies ruthless slaughter in the vocabulary of Deuteronomy. The holy texts faithfully record the killing of men, beasts, donkeys, ox, bulls, women, sheep, and children. Common words in the Torah representing the repertory of war are: perish, dispossess, smite, destroy, kill, and burn. Joshua 6:21 lists all who perished by the sword. The taking of Jericho came at the price of killing innocent life. Joshua 6:21 says, "And they utterly destroyed all that was in the city, both man and woman, young and old, an ox, and sheep, and ass, with the edge of the sword." The city of Jericho was burned, and the gold and silver were spared. The conquest of the land of Canaan and the destruction of Jericho killed innocent women and children, yet the gold and silver were kept and dedicated to Yahweh.

Yahweh had no concern for other races and only dealt with his chosen people. Racism and the ontological and ethical inequality of races originated in the Torah. The image of a peaceable Christ is invalidated by the Christian scriptures, which promote division through the believer/unbeliever doctrine, and you know the fate of each. The parable of the other cheek is found in Matthew 5:39 and Luke 6:29. All the stories in the current Bible are those validated by the church authorities and approved to be in the canon. In John 2:15, Jesus drove the Temple moneylenders out with a whip. The violent ejecting of the moneylenders and vendors out of the Temple displays Christ's fury and is inconsistent with the message of tolerance, gentleness, and peace. They were selling oxen, doves, and sheep in the Temple then. Now, the church is about nothing but changing money in the Temple! Church is NOTHING but big business.

Passages from the New Testament reveal the true character of the Gospel Jesus. In Luke 11:42-52, he uttered 7 curses against the scribes and Pharisees. In Luke 10:15 and Luke 12:10, Jesus consigns all who do not believe in him to hellfire! This is the only reason why Christians are Christians; they're afraid that Jesus will send them to hell for not believing in him. 'Believe or burn in hell for all eternity' is the Christian doctrine. Once Christians believe in and fear hell, they shut their minds off from reason and common sense. Religion is loss of intelligence.

For their failure to repent, Jesus heaped abuse on the cities north of Lake Genesareth in Mark 13. Jesus predicted the 'destruction' of the Temple and the 'ruin' of Jerusalem in Mark 13. Jesus promoted division by declaring in Luke 11:23 that whoever is not for him is against him. In Matthew 10:34, Jesus tells people that he has not come in peace, but bearing the sword. How can one deny the dual message of the Bible, when it declares that the majority of humanity will spend eternity in hell? Exodus 21:23-25 calls for the exchange of an eye for an eye, bruise for bruise, hand for hand, wound for wound, a tooth for a tooth, burn for burn, and foot for foot. Christianity and other religions of the book are about violence, in the past, present, and future of unbelievers.

The Vatican supported Nazism. Adolf Hitler was inspired by the Gospel according to John and used the story of the Temple moneylenders as motivation. Hitler praised the Apostolic, Catholic, and Roman Church, and never renounced his Christian faith. In Hitler's book 'Mein Kampf,' he talked about Jesus' actions in the Temple and explicitly referred to the whip (scourge). He enjoyed the detail provided only by Saint John and admired this violent form of Christianity, (volume 1, chapter 11, page 307) and (volume 2, chapter 5, page 454).

The Muslim god Allah has problems with logic. Hitler admired the warlike, militant, and conquering essence of the Muslim religion. Religious holy books can be used for good and evil, but the point is: God DIDN'T WRITE THEM! None of the religions of the book were inspired or dictated by God. An intellectual examination of the New Testament, Torah, and Koran exposes innumerable contradictions and evidence of selective borrowing from sacred texts written earlier. The books haven't brought heaven to earth, but have been used as a pretext for evil deeds. The Old Testament prohibits killing, yet allows the annihilation of the enemies of the Jews. Not only does the Bible sanction violence, but the violence is dictated by God's anger!

Muslims insist that the Koran is the real word of God, but it is also full of inconsistencies. Mixed messages are found in all three monotheistic books, which is why they have been used for good and evil. Evil men have justified their actions using religious texts, leading to monstrous consequences in the name of god. The Muslims believe they have the truth because sura (4:82) declares that the Koran is issued directly from Allah. Their proof is the absence of contradictions in the Koran. However, almost every page of their divine book contains contradictions, proving that God didn't write it. The evident self-satisfaction of the Koran is found in (6:114) which says that it's "intelligently exposed." These are the same words by Spinoza. (22:16) says that the Koran is "coherently narrated," the same proposition by Descartes. The Koran says it has "no hint of tortuousness" (22:16), the same as found in a page out of Bergson. The book is full of contradictory statements and was written by scribes using previous writings. No God involved.

The Koran contains 140 chapters or suras. Except sura 9, all the chapters begin with 'In the name of Allah, the Beneficent, the Merciful.' Allah shows mercy by avenging, killing, and harming. Those actions are justified on almost all the pages of the Koran. Islamic tradition says that God has 99 names, and the 100th name will be revealed in a future life. This is one of the few things about God that Muslims have right, that God has 99 names. There is some truth in the 99 names of God because God can't be defined by one term. Though the 99 names for God that the Muslims came up with aren't totally right, we must know that God isn't defined in one word. For example, God is: nature, love, spiritual law, science, the creative principle, the laws of physics, all that is, that which is scientifically verifiable, the life underneath all forms of life, the universe, the breath of life, the force who is the source of all things, etc. There is no one definition for God. Actually, there are more than 99 names for God! God is the Force who is the Source; one God called by many names.

The 99 names of God according to Islamic tradition are mostly variations of the compassion and mercy theme. The translations of some of these names are: the Most Merciful, Lord of Majesty and Generosity, Source of Goodness, the Eraser of Sins, Most Kind and Gentle, the Most Compassionate, the Absolver, the All-Forgiving, Most Serene, the Gracious Benefactor, etc. Among the 99 names of Allah are negative titles such as: the Humiliator, Bringer of Dishonor and Disgrace, the Degrader, the Creator of Death, the Taker of Life, the Inflictor of Retribution, the Punisher, the Avenger, and the Bringer of Harm to Those Who Offend Him.

The 99 names of Allah are a roster of contradictions. The real attributes of Allah are revealed in the Koran, which promotes putting to the sword, slaughter, pillage, torturing, burning, and all things opposite of the love of one's neighbor. Muslims talk about mercy and compassion, but it's not a part of real Islamic practice and Muslim theory. The Muhammad of Medina participated in tribal wars and sent his friends out to commit extraordinary violence. He was about fighting and happily slaughtering Jews.

The gods of religious holy books are all frauds, and one can discover this by examining each god's character. The Koran says that Allah excelled in punishment, battle tactics, and killing (8:30). According to the Koran, Allah decided on questions of life and death (3:156), punished doubters (4:102), annihilated evildoers (3:141), punished those who held a false idea about him (48), and was the Master of vengeance (5:95 and 3:4). The Koran's injunction to kill unbelievers (8:39) and polytheists (9:5) proves that it isn't a religion of peace. The holy Koran authorizes mass slaughter (4:56, 4:91, and 2:191-94). The Koran allows for the hunting down of the impious, those who've strayed from God (4:91). The Koran talks about infidels with chains on their necks in verse 13:5. The Koran endorses lex talionis (2:178) and cutting thieves' hands off (5:38). Prayers to Allah for the extermination of Jews and Christians are found in sura (9:30). If you read these religious holy books with reason and common sense, you'll come to the conclusion that their origins are NOT divine, but human.

The Dilemma of Humanity

In antiquity, scientific minds troubled the church with scientific questions. The liegemen of the one god turned to Pythagoras and Plato to help them deal with the questions coming from thinking intellectuals opposed to church doctrine. Pythagoras was shaped by Eastern religious thought. Plato had creative ideas to help invent the Christian afterlife. Pythagoras and Plato created the biblical version of heaven. They built their city of the spirit with eternal and immortal ideas similar to the Judeo-Christian god. This heavenly place was created as a clone of the false holy book god: inaccessible to time, resistant to all corporeal conceptualization, and immune to decomposition.

Like the Judeo-Christian god, the place where 'his' believers go after death has the same characteristics as 'him.' Yahweh, the gospel god, and Allah are false gods created by men. Man made god and created 'his' image. These gods require nothing but themselves to exist, persevere, and endure in their being. Creative writers of the monotheisms built castles and thrones in the air to exalt their god and invented glorious afterlives to solicit a lifetime of faithfulness to 'him.' Since our planet is imperfect, religious scribes created a heaven that promises utopia, atopia, and uchronia. Religious believers go to an ideal society that's free of war, poverty, and conflict. Time has no beginning and no end where believers go, while the unbelievers are sentenced to eternity in hell.

Satan means "the accuser, the adversary." Anyone accusing you of something or functioning as an adversary in your life is Satan (for you). The Devil or Satan of the Bible is a fairytale created by men, though represents negativity in one's life. The Devil symbolizes the negative energy in the universe, most of which is created by rigid religious belief structures. The Christian Devil is actually more in tune with the real God because he frees humanity from control and supervision. People who live their lives freely, independent of religious authority, attract the hatred of the monotheisms. What Christians consider evil, Satan, represents the restoration of men to their power over the world and themselves. Usually, what the monotheisms call good is bad, and bad is good. Just because religion calls something evil doesn't mean that it's so. The 'holy life' is an illusion, because it's based on religious dogma. The spiritual life has nothing to do with religious holy books.

All the monotheisms are part of the same 3-headed monster. The Garden of Paradise is affirmed in Genesis, the Koran, and the Pentateuch. The Muslims offer the most detailed description of its conceived geography. The monotheisms follow the same rigorous logic, falsely determining the pure and impure, and the licit and illicit. The holy vs. unholy division of things by the religious community is man-made nonsense attributed to God. The content of religious holy books is the opposite of the real.

Muslims respect their rites as if God came up with them. In paradise, Muslims are free of prayers, obligations, and rites. Everything forbidden in religious law is now for the taking at the heavenly banquet. Muslims will sing and wear gold (18:31), drink wine (47:15 and 83:25), and eat pork (52:22). They believe that they will caress beautiful youths (56:17), fondle houris (44:54), and enjoy eternally virginal women (55:70). What's forbidden here below, Muslims will enjoy above. They will eat and drink from plates and cups of precious metal and wear silk. Unrestrained consumption in the Islamic version of the Celestial Kingdom is abundant, for intoxication is unknown (37:47). This is all man-made philosophy, having nothing to do with God.

The logic of paradise works to make the real world and undesirable religious dogma more tolerable. If you don't follow the religious rules and rituals outlined in your holy book, you don't make it in. The Christian Bible has the majority of the world going to hell for not following its plan of salvation. The Muslim and Christian holy books claim that there's only one way to God; their doctrine. The dilemma of humanity is that most of the world believes that the three monotheisms have something to do with God. The real God didn't write any holy books and doesn't have religious dogma for men to follow. Those laying their lives down for the gods of the three monotheisms are sacrificing the full human experience for an illusion. Religionists suffer from serious mental illness!

The monotheisms created an afterlife full of man-made fantasies to make the real world, made intolerable by religious laws, more bearable. For Islam, paradise is an eternal springtime with eternal light. There will be no sun or moon, and no more day and night. Organized religion makes the body a troublesome partner on earth. Humans only submit to religious domination because of what's promised to them in the afterlife. Unbelievers burn in hell forever for not believing in religious doctrine, while believers spend eternity in a fantasy land created by Pythagoras and Plato. Millions of Muslims have been lured into religious foolishness by the promise of a celestial dream vocation full of wine (83:25) and (47:15). These promised fantasies caused men to leave happily for battle, from the Prophet's first raid at Nakhla to what's happening in the present day.

Organized religion involves blood sacrifice, from Jesus sacrificing himself for the world to Islamic suicide bombers unleashing death on unbelievers. Yahweh demanded Abraham sacrifice his son Isaac, because the monotheism are about blood. Islamic radicals detonate powerful bombs on their enemies (unbelievers) to shed blood. Man-made gods are bloodthirsty men with no wives or daughters; 100% created by the human mind. How could humanity fall for a male god or a male god with a son? This angry man, bloodthirsty false god with no wife or daughter is a false god. God is genderless and formless, doesn't have children, and doesn't require blood sacrifices. Humanity believes that God had a son because they were told that they would go to hell if they refused to believe that God raised Jesus from the dead. The Muslim god Allah, Yahweh, and the Judeo-Christian god: all men! Believing in and serving them is deception and religious slavery.

Humanity will never be free until they abandon the gods of the three monotheisms. All of the religions of the book serve imaginary man-made gods that have nothing to do with true spirituality. Anyone bound by institutionalized religion is serving a counterfeit god. The real God didn't write any holy books, has no religious doctrine, and doesn't require a blood sacrifice of 'his' son for sin. The origin of sin is in my 'Gospel According to Jawara King' book. The Bible version of sin is a lie based on religious dogma that God didn't come up with. Any religion based on a book is false.

Judaism, Islam, and Christianity display a hatred for women and a hatred for intelligence. According to the holy books, a woman is responsible for the dysfunction of humanity and bringing evil into the world. Eve's decision is the root of original sin and error according to religious history. Her desire for knowledge condemned her, while Adam was content to submit and obey. In the Bible, the serpent addresses Eve and starts a dialogue with her. The tempter is called Shaitan or Iblis in the Koran. Inquisitive women were labeled as 'daughters of Eve' by most dictionaries. Original sin was perpetuated through Eve and transmitted during conception, according to Saint Augustine. The passing of sin from the father's sperm to the mother's womb is the sexualization of sin; another holy lie!

The religions of the book only esteem wives and mothers. These false religions detest women and surround them with consubstantial negativity. The feminine within is denied. Women are only good for marrying a man and then having his children. According to the religions of the book, women exist to ensure the male's piece of mind and care for their husbands. Women aren't important in religious holy books and are blamed for original sin. Judeo-Christianity teaches that Eve was created secondarily from Adam's rib as an afterthought (Genesis 2:22). Adam and his wife are also in the Koran (Sura 2:35), but her name isn't even worthy to be revealed. These stories overlap because all the religions of the book are part of the same 3-headed beast.

In the religious system, the male comes first, and the woman must serve her husband. The female was made from a crumb; a man's leftover fragment, according to religion. Religious holy books declare that a menstruating female is impure, according to religious law attributed to the authorship of God. The unfertilized egg symbolizes the feminine and is a sign of womanhood. Religion believes it negates the maternal, is a sign of empty womanhood, and symbolizes a woman divorced from motherhood. Sex divorced from marriage, or sex alone as an expression of pure sexuality, is absolute evil according to the religions of the book. Sexuality should be practiced for its own sake, dissociated from the fear of the false gods of religious books.

The three monotheisms hate all homosexuals and condemn them to death (Leviticus 20:13). The sexuality of the free individual isn't allowed because religious law must dominate all areas of one's life. The Talmud says that the bachelor is incomplete without his female partner and is only half a person. Single men are commanded by the Koran to marry (Sura 24:32). Paul of Tarsus endorsed marriage and only saw the perils of adultery and lust in the solitary male. The three religions are against free sexuality and condemn the free individual to hell. The truth is: marriage is a man-made institution, and there is nothing wrong with free sexuality.

The religions of the book are responsible for the serious mental illness on planet earth. If humans would realize that God has nothing to do with religious laws, religious belief structures, and religious holy books, humanity would be free. Religious slaves submit themselves to religious madness as if the real god requires them to. Orthodox Jewish men recite their daily morning prayer, according to (Talmud, Menahot 436), saying, "Praised be God that he has not created me a gentile. Praised Be God that he has not created me a slave ... Praised be God that he has not created me a woman." The church's prejudice against women is an undeniable fact, yet women give the church BILLIONS of dollars a year to continue spreading this false gospel.

The pre-Islamic tribal tradition ascribed shame to a man who fathered a daughter. The Koran allows him to decide whether to keep the baby girl or 'bury it beneath the dust' (16:58). All the monotheisms are a part of the same 3-headed bandit, I keep telling everyone! In 585, delegates to the Council of Mâcon discussed a book by Alcidalus Valeus called 'Paradoxical Dissertation in Which We Attempt to Prove that Women are not Human Creatures.' The Christian hierarchy was sympathetic of Alcidalus Valeus' point of view, and he won over many readers. The countless misogynistic pronouncements of Paul of Tarsus is the same religious madness. The Religious fool Origen took the eunuch discussion of Matthew 19:12 literally and sliced off his genitals with a blade. Origen decided to become self-mutilated in honor of the Kingdom of God. Those who wait until marriage to have sex have done the same, even though they haven't sliced off her genitals with a sword. Anything other than free sexuality is religious bondage created by men, not God.

Religious doctrine is the celebration of castration. Religious teachings about fidelity, marriage, family, and monogamy are all variations on the theme of castration. Monotheism convinces religious slaves to submit to a life of marriage with fidelity to the spouse. Jews and Muslims are convinced by their religious holy books to believe that all sexuality should be focused on procreation. Men, not God, came up with the doctrine of no sexual relations outside of marriage. Leviticus and Numbers give rules on Jewish sexual intersubjectivity. The illegality of marriage to a non-Jew is discussed, and sexual relations outside of marriage is forbidden. Women are prohibited to study the Torah, yet it's mandatory for men. Women are allowed to own financial assets, but only the husband is permitted to administer and manage them. Women are nothing in religion, which is why religion teaches that God made man in his own image, not the woman's.

The Koran has an obvious kinship with the other religions of the book. Islam believes in the superiority of males over females and teaches that God prefers men to women (4:34). Islam's hatred for women is found in its series of diktats. The Koran prohibits exposing the hair out of doors – the veil (24:30). The Koran teaches against women exposing bare arms and legs. Sexuality outside of legitimate relations with a Muslim man is forbidden, yet that man can have several spouses (4:3). Polyandry for women is prohibited, and chastity is praised (17:32 and 33:35). Muslims are prohibited from marrying a non-Muslim (3:28). In the Islamic religion, women are prohibited from wearing men's clothing. At the mosque, the mingling of the sexes isn't allowed, and a woman isn't allowed to shake hands with a man unless she's wearing gloves. In the Islamic world, there is no tolerance for celibacy, and marriage is mandatory (24:32).

Morality laws practiced in the name of religion is religious madness. Billions of people are trying to live up to the standards laid out by the religions of the book, which is the dilemma of humanity. Idiotic religious laws practiced by religious fundamentalists afraid of hell are not from god. An intellectual examination of the guidelines laid out in religious holy books proves that no god demands that humans follow them. Man-made edicts followed in the name of religion are no more than religious bondage. In the Koran, love and passion in marriage is advised against; only the interests of family is celebrated (4:25). The wife must submit to all the sexual desires of her husband, who "plows his wife whenever he likes, for she is his tillage" (2:223). The Muslim man can seek permission to beat his wife on nothing but suspicion (4:34). The woman has an existential minor status with legal inferiority (2:228). In Islam, a woman's courtroom testimony is worth half of a man's. A barren woman and a woman deflowered before marriage have no value at all. In man-made religion, women are nothing.

Christianity and the decisions arrived at by Paul are religious insanity. Religion is about the stripping of the body of all sins rooted in carnal desire. Nothing is wrong with carnal desire; it's only man-made religion that's against the totality of the body. Sins resulting from carnal desire are a religious phenomenon having nothing to do with God. What religious holy books call sin is not really sin. As long as you cause no harm to others and follow all state and federal laws, you've done no wrong. Judging right or wrong based on religious laws in holy books is delusion. These false holy books have nothing to do with spirituality.

The imitation of Christ required by Christian fundamentalism involves the daily asceticism of life. The believer must separate himself or herself from his or her flesh instead of filling its desires. The flesh must be brought under subjection to religious dogma as if God demands it. Religionists call it 'holiness' or living the 'holy life.' Humanity only accepts religious enslavement because they were told that they will burn in hell for rejecting god's word. Religion and the advent of Christianity is the cause of the death fixation, which has poisoned the whole planet. Religion uses hell teachings to scare people into religious bondage. Religionists only serve holy book gods to avoid hell. Ask any religionist why they believe, and eventually they'll tell you about hell. Organized religion works to convince you that hell is a real place and then uses your fear of hell to keep you imprisoned to religious insanity. Religionist, you're afraid of hell, which is why you've replaced logic and intellect with religious folly. Get saved!

The existence of Jesus is a HOAX that has never been historically established. Nothing certain exists today to attest to the truth of the historicity of Jesus of Nazareth. Nazareth never existed either. Students of intellectual honesty know that there never was a city called Nazareth during the purported lifetime of Jesus. There never was a flesh-and-blood Jesus who lived at a precise time and in an identifiable place. Outside of religious scriptures, we don't know him. So why do people believe in him? Whitney Houston said, "Everybody's searching for a hero. People need someone to look up to."

Believing in Jesus is based in blind faith alone, though some use personal experiences to validate his existence, even though there is no concrete, undeniable, verifiable, historical evidence for the certainty of his historicity. There is no contemporary documentation of the events described in the gospels. Just because the New Testament presents a nativity story doesn't mean it's true; there is no archaeological proof. The birth, burial, resurrection, and ascension of Jesus was created by the religious hierarchy, for there is no shroud, no tomb, and no archives proving so. The questionable aspects of Christianity are required to be believed in order to be saved from hell. This protects the fallacy from intellectual and logical questioning. If you don't believe that Jesus died for your sins and rose from the dead, you're condemned to hell for all eternity.

All the evidence supporting an historical Jesus is fraudulent. In 325, the mother of Constantine, Saint Helena, invented a sepulcher. She was artistically gifted and therefore used her supreme gifts to support the myth of Christ. She supposedly discovered Golgotha and the titulus, the wooden fragment listing the charges against Jesus. Religionists may also attempt to use the piece of cloth from Turin to validate Jesus' existence, but carbon–14 dating says it was created in the thirteenth century CE. Some religious scholars use two or three vague references in ancient texts in an attempt to make the Jesus myth historical. Flavius Josephus, Tacitus, and Suetonius supposedly wrote about Jesus, but references to him were fraudulently placed in copies made several centuries after the alleged crucifixion of Jesus. After the success of the supporters of Jesus was assured, they solidified the construction of Jesus. In reality, Jesus' conceptual existence is to be denied.

This construction named Jesus has caused more death, destruction, and division on earth than anything else. Paul of Tarsus called himself a "bishop of foreign affairs" and was known as the thirteenth apostle. He, emperor Constantine, and other Christians in authority incited Christians to despoil and torture unbelievers. Constantine's successors: Justinian, Theodosius, and Valentinian slaughtered unbelievers and burned pagan libraries full of real knowledge.

The fear established in early Christian history thrives today in billions of minds formatted by the fear of hell. The unbelievable gospel story is improbable. Religionists are afraid to question it because they believe they'll go to hell for doubting god's salvation plan. By their fruits shall ye know them. The Church used political violence to dispel contradictions to the 'word of god.' The existing documents used to support the gospel myth are skillfully executed forgeries. The burned libraries, Christian vandalism, and persecution of real spiritual teachers prove that God didn't create organized religion.

Copyists sectarian religionists for Jesus Christ chose which documents to be saved and those to be destroyed while creating the official Bible. Some monks tried to replace what was missing and established gospel editions by ancient authors. The hundreds of gospels in circulation added up to a philosophical nightmare because almost everyone was writing their own version of the gospel narrative. Most of the gospels were eliminated or destroyed. Nothing of what remains can be trusted. The gospel of Jesus is a man-made creation based on previous mythology, and no God wrote or inspired it. Freedom is discovering that all the religions of the book are frauds. Religion serves false gods.

The Christian archives are man-made, and the entire Bible is an ideological fabrication. Christian zealots use the writings of Suetonius, Flavius Josephus, and Tacitus to prove that Jesus was historical. They claim that Suetonius, Josephus, and Tacitus mentioned Christ and his followers in the first era, but the rules of intellectual forgery prove these writings to be a fraud. The original writings were okay, but Christian scribes corrupted them by inserting Christ references to make him appear historical. Jesus is a myth. The threat of hell causes most to believe in him.

Jesus has no history, so Christians in authority created a history for him. Since there's no evidence supporting a historical Jesus, the inventors of the Gospels inserted him in history. An anonymous monk, collaborating with Roman power, recopied the Antiquities of Josephus to add Jesus in. The Jewish historian Josephus never heard of nor mentioned Jesus in his original writings. A monk read Suetonius' Lives of Twelve Caesars and the Annals of Tacitus and was surprised that there was no mention of Jesus. Therefore, he added a passage in his own hand to insert Jesus in secular history.

This anonymous monk committed a forgery without a second thought, to support the story he believed in.

In the days of the establishment of Christianity, people didn't approach books with a concern for truth. The Christian hierarchy burned libraries and destroyed the writings of those with real knowledge, proving that the religious community isn't concerned with truth. This is why the writings of Flavius Josephus, Tacitus, and Suetonius were altered so easily. The religious world is not respectful of the authenticity of the text or the original author's rights. What's read today from the writers of antiquity are manuscripts copied centuries after they were written. Christian copyists recopied the contents of original writings to add Jesus in so that his story would flow with real history. The period in which Jesus supposedly appeared recorded nothing about him. This is why ultra-rationalists like Raoul Vaneigem and Prosper Alfaric rightly denied the historical existence of Jesus.

The Jesus story is not original, but is the most popular version of the savior god theme. In the year 45, the sons of Judas the Galilean, Jacob and Simon, started an uprising that caused them to be crucified by the Romans. Their father led his own rebellion in the year 6, and the rebel was crucified. A family of freedom fighters produced Menahem, a grandson following the footsteps of his ancestors. He started the Jewish War in 66 that ended with the destruction of Jerusalem in 70. These stories are some of the real history behind the artificially-created stories in the Bible.

The tales in the Gospel aren't original. The Jesus story isn't original. Nothing in the Old or New Testament is original; NOTHING! The story of Jesus is actually the same story thousands of times repeated. Prophets, savior gods, and messiahs abounded in the first century. There were thousands of bearers of good tidings who were no different than the Gospel Jesus. The historical holy men before Jesus invited their believers to follow them into the desert to pray, be taught, and witness manifestations of divinity. One holy man from Egypt with forty thousand followers took over the Garden of Olives. They were dispersed by the Roman soldiery. This spiritual leader claimed that his voice alone could shatter the walls of Jerusalem and give his men victory over the city. The Jesus narrative was based on some true stories and people who really existed.

The historical people and events associated with Jewish determination to overthrow Roman power are similar to what's found in the Gospels. This was a common theme at the time, which is why real historical events occurred in areas associated with Jesus. The Jesus story was based on the themes, feelings, and events of the time. Multitudes of stories record Jews using mystical and prophetic discourse to unseat Roman power. Jewish determination announced what was predicted in the Old Testament through religious and millenarian visionaries. Jews, armed only with their belief in god, believed that God could miraculously free them from the colonial yoke of Roman occupation. This historical common theme found its way into the Gospels, and the Jesus myth was built around it.

Historically speaking, occupying armies forced their laws, religion, language, religious beliefs, and customs on the conquered. Sometimes the religion of the conquerers remains with the conquered thousands of years later, as is the case with blacks. Jesus is a myth. The Gospel of Jesus is non-historical. Jesus never existed. Jesus represents too many things to discuss in this book and is only good for his symbolic and mystical qualities. My book 'The Gospel According to Jawara King' explains Jesus in detail. Jesus can be many things, and in the Gospel story, he embodied the period's hysteria. Jews believed that in the name of religion, they could conquer and triumph the Roman army of occupation. The Roman legions were the world's most battle-tested troops, so the false god of the Jews was outmatched. Abandon religion!

Jesus was created based on what was going on in the day, then inserted into history hundreds of years later. The history of the first century knew nothing of a Jesus of Nazareth. Hundreds of years later, the Jesus inserted in history represented Jewish rejection of Roman authorities. The Jesus figure represents the messianic aspirations of the period. The name of Jesus is symbolic; it's up to you to decide what it points to. Only mystical Christianity makes sense.

The Great Awakening

Abandoning all the religions of the book will cause a great awakening. Religion is a great source of darkness and negativity on this planet. As long as people continue to believe that God wrote or inspired the Bible, they will remain in darkness. The Apostle Paul wrote most of the New Testament, and he was not inspired or led by God. He had a hatred of self and a hatred for all the concerns of the world. Paul's masochism is revealed through his writings because he rejoiced in problems, saw his life through difficulties, and used what he suffered to preach to crowds. He was not speaking for God, but promoting a hatred for desire, life, love, body, sensations, independence, flesh, and freedom in the name of God.

The history of Paul shows him in some humiliating situations where those who knew the real God recognized his religious foolishness. He tried to convert Epicurean and Stoic philosophers in Athens on the Agora by talking about the resurrection of the body, but failed. Paul's Christianity was sheer nonsense for Hellenes and enlightened philosophers. Epicurus and the disciples of Zeno rejected Paul's teaching and laughed at his doctrine.

The Apostle Paul had contempt for his body and used his writings to discredit the flesh and bodies of all people. Paul says in I Corinthians 9:27, "I pummel my body and I subdue it." As a mentally ill religionist, he demands that each religious fundamentalist live as he lived. "Pummel your body and subdue it. Do as I do ..." Paul said. There is no Jesus in all this religious madness, just Paul's praise of chastity, celibacy, and abstinence.

Following the religions of the book make a single man unable to have women. Paul was not speaking for God when he wrote against sexual freedom, but recycling the misogyny of Jewish monotheism. Christianity and Islam pretend to be from God and promote religious madness in 'his' name. All the religions of the book are against women, yet women fall for religion because they think God is behind it. The texts woman believe to be inspired by God condemn womankind. Women have fallen for a male god with a male son who had all male disciples! Patriarchal men created a male god with no wife, and made him have a male son, therefore giving rulership over to two men! Christians must believe in their male god and his male son in order to be saved from hell. Out of fear of eternal torment, women accepted the man-made male god and his male son, denying the feminine principle. The majority of the fallen are women, ignorant to the fact that God is neither male or female, is genderless and formless, and has no children. Human reproduction is a human phenomenon, so the fallen should ask themselves, "how could God have a son? Why not a daughter? If God is a male who has a son, why isn't the feminine principle in the picture?" Wake up women, even the Bible says that God is Love and God is a Spirit. The real God is not a male god with a male son!

The first verses of the Bible reveal a woman's place in the male world. Women fell for these religious lies because they believe God wrote or inspired the book of Genesis. Genesis condemns woman, making her the first sinner. Paul embraced disastrous ideas of his own against woman kind, and he wrote most of the New Testament! The Holy Bible has made the woman the source of all the world's evil. Pauline epistles, writings, and acts are filled with prohibitions against women. According to Paul, women are to obey men in submission and silence. Women's destiny is to refrain from trying to control the stronger sex and hold their husbands in awe, according to religion.

The religious system's power over the world has convinced religious men of the inability to enjoy women outside of the man-made structure of marriage. Paul the masochist promoted his personal ideas as revelations from God and convinced billions of religious slaves into following false religious teachings. Paul delighted in obedience, submission, intellectual passivity, and total subservience to government authority. Paul's false doctrine of 'all power comes from God' was designed to keep individuals obedient to evil officials, magistrates, and the emperor. The 'all power proceeded from God' doctrine benefited the police, monarchs, senators, dignitaries, and ministers. Submission to order and authority keeps people from revolting against those in power. Paul's writings brainwash the fallen into believing that disobeying the powerful is rebelling against God. The love of one's tormentors is promoted in the New Testament. Paul demonstrates the church's partnership with the state, designed to protect the autocrats, dictators, and religious tyrants.

The religions of the book are at war with intelligence. Organized religion is about hatred of freedom, women, self, and the pleasures of the world. Paul of Tarsus promoted all this along with an intensified hatred of intelligence. Genesis is the origin of religion's loathing of knowledge when it claims that original sin came from tasting the fruit of the Tree of Knowledge. Just because a woman ate from the Tree of Knowledge, sin is automatically transmitted from generation to generation. Now humanity needs a saviour, god's son, as if God has children. This male god's word declares it a mortal sin to rival God in knowledge (according to Genesis). The imbecility of the obedient (religious believers) are to prefer blind faith over intelligence and education.

Even the lifestyle of many Bible characters is against intelligence and knowledge. Paul's education was nonexistent. He was a maker and seller of tents for nomads who believed with certainty that God spoke through the Old Testament. Some traditions claim that the Apostle Paul could not write. The philosopher Philo of Alexandria, Paul's contemporary, was the opposite of Paul: a great writer of intelligence. Paul of Tarsus conducted himself like an uneducated man, which is why he was openly laughed at in the public square of Athens by the intellectual Epicureans and Stoics. The first Christians weren't very intelligent, which is why the philosophers and intellectuals of the day scoffed at them.

Paul was against real spiritual knowledge, which is why he advised Timothy and the Corinthians to reject "the addled and foolish questionings" and "hollow frauds" of philosophy. The correspondence between Paul and Seneca is another religious forgery because Paul wasn't a learned man. He addressed his peers, not philosophers, because the philosophers didn't accept his religious foolishness. As Paul wandered around the Mediterranean, he only spoke to those who weren't very intelligent. Ancient manuscripts declare that Paul's religious meetings never included philosophers, intellectuals, freethinkers, or men of letters. Celsus wrote Alethes logos in the second century as a polemic against Christianity. Alethes logos means 'The True Word' or 'True Discourse.' Celsus' book characterized the early Christians as carpenters, tanners, cleaners, craftsmen and such. Celsus' Alethes logos 'The True Word,' also validates the Apostle Paul's hatred of intelligence.

The totalitarian Christian state began in 312, when Constantine advanced on Rome. The Christian emperor Constantine was against magic, astrology, philosophical ideas, and paganism. He forced his ideas upon everyone and killed all who were against the rigid religious belief structure of Christianity. On October 28, 312, Maxentius was drowned beneath the Milvius bridge. The fatal heritage of Constantine's coup d'état is still alive today, which is why modern religionists have on uncomplaining acceptance of the Bible. Christians are still obedient to Paul's call for submission to religious and political authorities. The obedience to the officials and magistrates of the empire, as taught by Paul, kept the leaders free of rebellion, revolts, or revolutions.

Christian martyrdom has been grossly exaggerated because in reality, the early Christians endured relatively rare persecutions. Constantine was the one who executed the real persecutions against intellectuals free of the mental illness of Christianity. He created policies to satisfy the Christians and help make Christianity what it is today. Under Constantine, new articles were written into Roman law, harsh laws were enacted against unfettered sexuality, and the practices of pagan cults were forbidden.

Christians in positions of authority are VERY dangerous people, whether politicians, bosses, or law enforcement officials because they will all use their positions to fight for their religious faith. The Christian Emperor Constantine used his authority to force everyone into following Christianity's religious dogma, and his work is still in place today. Constantine enacted religiously-influenced laws and made divorce more difficult. He made prostitution illegal, forbade men from having concubines, condemned sexual dissipation, abrogated the law forbidding the celibate to inherit, banned magic, and refused to outlaw slavery. Constantine made the Christian Kingdom of this world by ordering the building of basilicas, including Saint Peter's. The Christian Kingdom is indeed of this world, designed to support religious leaders, promote fear and division, and control humanity.

There is no undeniable proof that the Bible is the Word of God. 95% of those who believe that the Holy Bible is the Word of God fear hell, after being threatened by religious leaders. Ask any believer why they believe, and in less than 5 minutes they will mention hell. Religionists are afraid of eternal punishment and fiery flames of hell. They only submit to religious dogma because they've been convinced to believe that God will judge them based on what's written in their holy book. If they discovered that God didn't write the Holy Bible or any other religious holy book, they would IMMEDIATELY leave institutionalized religion. God, as promoted by organized religion, is a fraud, and Jesus is nothing but a few billion dollars a year empire.

The man who wrote 3/4 of the New Testament wasn't inspired or led by God. Paul read no Gospel during the purported lifetime of its author. He never met or knew Jesus. Even 'if' Mark wrote the first Gospel, it was written after Paul's death. Paul of Tarsus did nothing but propagate a myth and tell deceptive fables to whoever would listen. During the second half of the first century, Paul visited multitudes in dozens of countries, contaminating the whole body of the empire with his false gospel. Paul's religious disease still remains today, infecting billions of humans afraid of death and hell. Even though Paul contaminated people everywhere, there were Wise Ones who rejected his religious foolishness. He still tried to convert them by visiting Asia Minor, Athens, Italy of the Epicureans, Philo's City Alexandria, Cyrene (the city of hedonism), the Stoics of Rome, and Sicily of Empedocles. We are still experiencing the effects of his work today, unfortunately.

The most Christian emperor Constantine didn't even live up to New Testament teachings and was evil in character. Constantine's second wife Fausta told him that her stepson tried to have sex with her. Without any proof, Constantine sent servants to torture, then behead his own son! His nephew was also implicated in the lie and suffered the same fate at the hands of cutthroats. Constantine eventually discovered that Fausta deceived him and boiled her in water. The church was silent about the Christian emperor's uxoricide, infanticide, and homicide. In return, Constantine released a host of gifts on the church THAT ARE STILL IN PLACE TODAY: generous subsidies, tax exemptions for the church, and the creation of new churches looking to be enriched by gratuities. Constantine did everything in his power to keep churches and their leaders afloat in gifts.

The Council of Nicaea in 325 conferred full powers upon Constantine. His mother Helena was creative and helped him create false sites for the specific purpose of promoting the Gospels. Helena, a devout Christian, discovered (put together) three wooden crosses in Palestine with one being Christ's. The temple of Aphrodite was destroyed and the site of Calvary was buried under it. Helena was given unlimited funds by her son Constantine to build many 'discovered' sites supporting the Jesus story, including the Holy Sepulchre, the Nativity, and the Garden of Olives. She put the relics she made on display in the three churches she built with the considerable sums given her by her son. These false historical sites were built without topographical evidence or historical justification. Emperor Constantine and his mother falsely created all the major assets of Christianity, which is why church clergy made Helena a heroine of its mythology. Helena was the first Roman empress of the thanatophilic Christian pantheon and was canonized by church clergy. Constantine died on May 22, 337.

The Council of Nicaea condemned all real spiritual truth as heresy to protect the questionable Bible. Constantine's successors continued constructing the Christian state through the use of torture, vandalism, constraint, ubiquitous propaganda, and extermination of opponents. The totalitarianism of the Christian Empire destroyed libraries and symbolic sites. Christian leaders with absolute power remolded the government's ideological lines to make the whole of society follow Judeo-Christian principles. The religious monopoly over all means of communication controlled private life and the public sphere to destroy pluralism and control bureaucratic organization.

Christian history is a bunch of lies and exaggeration. Christian scholars claim that early Christians suffered persecution, but the Vulgate exaggerated. The Christians were not victims but victimizers, and any persecution they experienced wasn't as severe as Christian apologetics claim. Historians working conscientiously have disputed the figures of early Christians devoured by lions in the arena. Eusebius of Caesarea wrote about tens of thousands of dead Christians murdered for the Gospel. Eusebius was Constantine's domestic intellectual, recruited to use his writing skills to lie for the Gospel. Modern estimates say that no more than 3,000 Christians were martyrs of the Gospel, which is nothing compared to the 10,000 gladiators who fought to the death in celebration of the end of the war in 107 against the Dacians. The information written by Eusebius of Caesarea is all a fraud because he was paid by Constantine to write Christian promotional propaganda.

Real Christian history is hidden under heavily promoted lies. In 380, emperor Theodosius I declared Catholicism as the state religion. The Council of Nicaea set the tone to eliminate all other forms of spirituality. In 392, emperor Theodosius I banned pagan worship to force Christianity upon everyone. In 449, Valentinian III and Theodosius II ordered the destruction of everything that might contradict the Bible or expose it as a lie put together by men.

Real Christian history isn't taught in churches or theological seminaries. You have to search for the truth because the truth is always hidden. Constantine fellowshipped with Sopatros, Nicagoras of Athens, Hermogenes, and other pagan intellectuals, then severed all contact with them in 330. He had to get away from the enlightened ones in order to protect his religious belief structure. Those who didn't fall for the Gospel tale were the Wise Ones. Enlightened individuals had to be eliminated by religious authorities in order to protect the man-made Bible. Sopatros was executed in 335 for witchcraft. The Neoplatonist philosopher Porphyry died in 305, and his writings were burned in 335. Anything that didn't agree with the Holy Bible was made to be evil, and real spiritual power was viewed as demonic manifestations of the Kingdom of darkness.

Emperor Theodosius severely dealt with Arians, Montanists, Eumonians, and other heretics. Those in tune with the real God who refused to believe that the Bible was the Word of God were labeled as heretics. Those operating in true spiritual power independent of religious dogma were called heretics and killed to protect the fake powerless Gospel. During the reign of Theodosius II in 435, the writings of the patriarch of Constantinople, Nestorius, were burned. The Eastern and Western Empire were searched to ensure that all his writings were destroyed. Any spiritual or philosophical writings that weren't in total agreement with the holy Bible were consigned to flames, and the wisest intellectuals were brutally murdered to protect the Gospel tale. Christianity isn't true spirituality.

The history of the religions of the book is about the repression of rational thought and the promotion of irrational religion. The church not only was against anything contrary to the Bible, but intellectualism. From Genesis to Revelation, religion is against humanity eating from the tree of the knowledge of good and evil. Knowledge is forbidden unless it supports the Bible. Those in church history who ate from the tree of knowledge were put to death by the church. Hypatia of Alexandria was the first female mathematician in history. This Hellenized Egyptian was a teacher, mathematician, Neoplatonist, and astronomer. Religious slaves and those of the day knew that Hypatia of Alexandria was one of the foremost intellects of her time. A Christian mob killed her during an anti-pagan riot in 425. The Christians pulled her from her carriage and dragged her through the streets in the name of the Gospel. Christian zealots stripped her naked at a church, then used sharp oyster shells and broken tiles to scrape the flesh from her bones in the name of Jesus. Religious believers tore her body to pieces, dishonoring the Christian belief in love of one's neighbor. The Christian mob then burned her mutilated remains in the name of God. Religion is mental insanity!

The Theodosian Code was set up to justify all manner of crimes, assassinations, persecutions, and misdeeds. To legitimize religious oppression, lawmakers devised legal formulas to protect Christians by condemning non-Christians. The law was set up to support the ruling caste's domination over the general population. In United States history, laws were enacted after the Civil War in the former Confederate states to assure the continuance of white supremacy. These black codes were laws set up to keep whites in control on a legal level. It may look like all races are equal, but there still remains laws created by and for the white man to support his religious beliefs and maintain white supremacy. During the Second World War, the Vichy government passed anti-Semitic laws. The lawmakers define the label of justice and use the force of law to maintain domination.

The law in the year 380 condemned non-Christians and rescinded their civil rights. Christians wanted to make their lives difficult, so Christians in authority forbade unbelievers from teaching or participating in the law. The law was set against all who rejected the holy Bible, so those who wanted to participate in the life of the city had to convert. Christians wrote the law, so they decreed the death sentence for all who were a threat to the word of god, ministers of the Gospel, or Christian places of worship. The religions of the book are ALL evil.

In the name of the law, all who opposed the Gospel could be killed. Legal formulas were devised to persecute nonbelievers while the Christians were running around destroying pagan shrines and everything contrary to their man-made Gospel. Covered by the law for all manner of crimes and persecutions, Christians legally looted, confiscated, and ravaged temples and stole their furnishings. With the blessings of Christian authorities, protected by the legal texts put together by Christians in power, Christians freely destroyed pagan shrines. The holy Bible was used to define what conformed to imperial decrees. The law banned pagan practices, authorized the confiscation of non-Christian goods, and fought against heresies. The law is always influenced by the religion of the lawmaker, which is why religionists in power are dangerous.

Paul of Tarsus helped establish this path of destroying anything against the word of god. In the Acts of the Apostles (19:19), Paul attended a burning of magical books. There's a 99% chance that the books being burned contained more spiritual truth than the holy Bible. The early Christians were ruthless, burning Gnostic shrines and synagogues. Statues representing other forms of spirituality were destroyed by religionists. The fragments of the priceless statutes were recycled into Christian buildings. Places of worship where good people practiced alternative forms of spirituality were utterly ravaged in the name of god by the Christians. Religious believers used all the debris from their destruction to repave roads and build bridges. What was sacred to non-Christians was destroyed, and the rubble used to repair highways and such. Sacred trees in Constantinople were uprooted. The temple of Aphrodite was destroyed, and the land it was built on was used as a parking space for horse-drawn vehicles. The early Christians did nothing but cause widespread damage!

Before Constantine converted to Christianity, the Roman Empire persecuted Christians. Emperor Diocletian consulted an oracle in 303 AD because he felt that his soothsayers' methods were ineffective. Diocletian also told the oracle that the gods didn't answer him when he sought advice. The oracle told Diocletian that the Christian god was preventing the Roman gods from communicating, so he persecuted the Christians on behalf of the Roman Empire. When Constantine the Great converted to Christianity, he blamed the oracle for the persecution of his Christian brethren and retaliated in the name of Jesus. He shut down the temple of Apollo, along with all other spiritual centers, and executed ALL the priests. Christians in power are always dangerous.

All subsequent emperors followed in the footsteps of Constantine by forcing the Gospel upon everyone. According to the text dated February 19 of the year 356, anyone convicted of worshipping idols or participating in sacrifices to any god other than the Judeo-Christian god was sentenced to death. Christians in Antioch captured a wise prophet of Apollo and tortured him along with other unbiblical spiritual leaders. Domitius Modestus went after intellectual leaders of Alexandria and Antioch at Scythopolis in Palestine. Domitius Modestus conducted interrogations for the purpose of leaving no educated man alive; for these intellectuals could challenge the Gospel. Many Neoplationist philosophers perished at the hands of Bible-thumping Christians. The ferocious repression by Christian Bible-bangers almost destroyed all that represented the true God. The God of the Bible has nothing to do with the real God, and religious dogma is nothing but man-made shit.

Christians attacked the Mithraeum (temple of Mithras) and the Serapeum (temple of Serapis) at Alexandria in 389 and put many philosophers to death. Around 401, Christians destroyed a statue of Hercules at Suffectum, which is now Sufes in Sbiba, Tunisia. John Chrysostom encouraged the Christians to destroy all that represented the kingdom of darkness, motivating Christian monks to ransack all the shrines on the Phoenician mountains. All of the violence executed by the early Christians against non-believers and their various forms of spirituality was the result of the writings of Paul of Tarsus. Paul used his writings to despise knowledge, culture, intelligence, and other spiritual books. Paul's religious madness was the root of vandalism by the early Christians and their culture of death.

Through the writings of the religious freak, the Apostle Paul, Christians were convinced that academic learning and anything contrary to the Bible hindered access to and a relationship with God. Through the false message Paul promoted, all books by spiritual writers and authors accused of heresy were burned. Any book not in 100% agreement with the word of god was at risk of being burned. Great spiritual authors of enlightenment, such as Mani, Arius, and Nestorius were accused of heresy. Neoplatonist works were all burned or destroyed as a result of being labeled as books of divination and magic. All freethinkers who possessed libraries were in danger. So much fear was going around that in 370, the citizens of Antioch burned all their books in the public square. They were terrified of persecution from the Christian zealots for Christ. Christianity is about fear and terror, then and now. Christians are only Christians because they fear hell, after being convinced of hell's existence by the Christian Empire. With no hell, there would be no Christians.

The Neoplatonic school in Athens was shut down by Christians in authority in 591. All the holdings of the Neoplatonic school in Athens were confiscated by the Christians in the name of god. The Christians were triumphant finally, after Paul's shakey start at proselytization. In the beginning, Paul was laughed at by Epicureans and Stoics, and rejected in the home of philosophy. Through his writings, the Apostle Paul manifested a posthumous victory as a result of promoting hatred, intolerance, and contempt.

The early Christians were about nothing but death and destruction. Christians arrested Hellenes at Constantinople in 562 and paraded them through the streets in the name of god. Bonfires were lit all over, and anything representing the gods of non-Christians was cast into the flames. Christians lit a huge bonfire on Kenogion Square and tossed all the books of the great philosophers into the fire. The Great Library of Alexandria was burned down by Christians trying to protect the false information in the Bible. A library that was housed in a temple dedicated to Serapis the god, in the Serapeum, was demolished in 391 by order of the bishop of Alexandria. The Bible is not the word of god!

<u>Run to the Light!</u>

The construction of Jesus was based on previous historical and religious figures. The whole Bible is a forgery. Jesus symbolizes the Jewish hope in the miraculous. His story was created using the universal savior god theme. Jesus and previous savior gods were all born of a virgin, performed miracles, and attracted followers through their charisma. The Jesus figure isn't original.

The Jesus character is based on the commonplaces scattered throughout the literature of antiquity. Only fools consider the Gospels to be sacred texts inspired or written by God. Comparative study would set purported sacred texts in context as not being the Word of God. The miraculous in the New Testament doesn't agree with logic, but is in full agreement with what was miraculous in antiquity. Jesus was composed of borrowed biographies of previous god-men. Jesus is a fake. Serious students of antiquity can find the Jesus tale described in the lives of previous characters. Jesus is similar to Homer's Ulysses. Paul of Tarsus characterized Jesus, revealing similarities with a protagonist in Petronius' Satyricon, Encolpius. The biography of Apollonius of Tyana, written by Philostratus, appears to be about a rival to Jesus Christ. Jesus has been made an epic hero based on the histories of earlier epic heroes. Either way, 'the greatest story ever told' is a forgery! Get saved from religious madness.

The evangelist Mark is supposedly one of the authors of the adventures of Jesus. Traditional Christian history claims that Mark wrote his text around the year 70. There is no proof or any verifiable information indicating that Mark knew Jesus in person.

Mark wrote a fiction, yet attested to its authenticity in good faith. Mark supposedly wrote his Gospel, but Mark didn't write any Gospel. Even if Mark wrote the Gospel According to Mark, a thorough examination reveals his Gospel to be a hoax, fraud, and register of propaganda. It was created from people who were indifferent to Jesus' message or needed convincing. The purpose of Mark's Gospel is to persuade, please, convince, seduce, attract, and captivate for the purpose of conversion. Mark's recourse to the miraculous is designed to interest his readers into a recycled story based on the commonplace literature of pagan antiquity.

The New Testament should be compared to other works, like Diogenes Laërtius' 'Lives, Teachings, and Sayings of Eminent Philosophers.' As you give all texts equal literary status, the historical writings composed by men prove that no religious texts were inspired by the Holy Spirit. Readers of ancient texts know that Jesus is no more divine than the authorial literary devices of Pythagoras, Socrates, Plato, and others who wrote for their readers' edification. The book of Mark is written to make Jesus loved. Diogenes Laërtius used the same principles to solicit love for his philosophers of the ancient tradition. The evangelist Mark used his Gospel to recount a life full of supernatural events for Jesus. Christians are victims of DECEPTION.

Earlier biographers, way before the Gospel of Mark was written, overcrowded their 'original' texts with extraordinary and astonishing adventures of exceptional men. The Gospels aren't original. Everything written about Jesus was based on previous writings about supernatural men who didn't live, think, speak, nor were born or die like ordinary mortals. Mary, the mother Jesus, conceived in virginity through divine impregnation. Plato was also born of a young mother with an intact hymen. The story of Plato says that the archangel Gabriel announced to the carpenter's wife (Plato's mother) that she would give birth by God, independent of her husband's assistance. How could Joseph (a carpenter) and Plato's father (a carpenter) agree to the idea that God impregnated their wives without any objections? These stories are fairytales, which is why there's nothing extraordinary in the Gospels that wasn't written before.

God said of Jesus that 'this is my beloved Son in whom I am well pleased.' Plato was also gratified when Apollo called him in person. The same stories in the Gospels are found in previous mythology because Christian scribes borrowed from them to create Jesus' story. Joseph's son is supposedly the Son of God, borrowed from the story of Pythagoras. Pythagoras had disciples who saw him as Apollo in person, coming from among the Hyperboreans. Jesus performed miracles, brought the dead back to life, and restored sight to the blind. Empedocles, who came before Jesus, also brought a corpse to life. Jesus was made to excel in prophecies. Big deal, he wasn't the first. Anaxagoras accurately predicted meteor showers and excelled in prophecies way before Jesus. Jesus is a non-historical artificially created religious superhero based on previous characters of antiquity.

In the Jesus story, Christian scribes have him teaching his disciples, converting others with his religious rhetoric, and dying on the cross. This is the common theme of all the philosophers of antiquity. Cynics and Epicureans deployed the same talent as Jesus, only earlier. John was Jesus' favorite disciple, similar to the bond linking Epicurus and Metrodorus. Jesus of Nazareth spoke metaphorically; a characteristic of Pythagoras. Jesus never wrote except for when he traced characters in the sand with a stick. He immediately erased them. The same thing happened with Socrates and the Buddha. Long before Jesus, there were philosophers of healing speech and the spoken word. Socrates died for his ideas. Later Christian scribes created Jesus to do the same. Jesus the Messiah went through a tough night at Gethsemane. While serving in the Athenian army, Socrates had out-of-body experiences in Thrace on the battlefield of Potidea. Many others had raptures before Jesus on the Mount of Transfiguration. Mary found out that she was going to be a virgin mother through a dream. Socrates met Plato a day after he dreamt of a swan. The New Testament is a forgery!

Plato believed in the immortal soul, life after death, and the existence of the immaterial. Jesus was created to believe the same, modeling Plato's character. After Jesus' crucifixion, the Son of God from Galilee rose from the dead and returned among men. Before him, Pythagoras had the same experience. Jesus returned after 3 days, while the linen-shrouded philosopher Pythagoras waited 207 years before returning to Greece. All of these stories about Greek philosophers are fables. Myth writers were trying to convince readers of the exceptional nature of their invented character and convince people of the miraculous described.

The Gospels are not the Word of God, and to believe so is to renounce the critical spirit. The Enlightened person who really knows God reads the Bible with the same approach as the classical prose of antiquity. Just as one surrenders to literary effect while reading Homeric poems, one must do so to properly understand the esoteric meaning of scripture. The Gospels are unreliable, but people only believe in them due to the threat of eternal hell-fire. The Gospel genre declares that something is true, then expects its declaration of truth to create its truth. The testamental stories are indifferent to what's probable and real, yet religionists are required to believe them just because the Bible says to, at the threat of eternal torment.

Institutionalized religion uses the power of language to convince religionists that what a holy book affirms creates what it declares. Just because a holy book declares that it's the word of God doesn't mean that it is so. A holy book is not inspired or written by God just because a scripture or verse says so. What's written doesn't create what it declares. If what's declared manifests, it's because of the power of your own mind, not God. Whatever you believe will begin to manifest in your life. People believe a scripture with all their hearts, then believe that their holy book god came through for them when it was really the Law of Belief. The Law of Belief declares that you will see what you believe.

Matthew, Mark, Luke, and John didn't write their gospels. Most Christians are unknowingly deceived, and it's not certain whether or not their leaders are knowingly deceiving the fallen. If the Apostle Paul was historical he was deceived. Paul and others believed that the Jesus story was true and that their own words about him were true. Paul and billions of Christians after him never encountered Jesus physically and only believed based on what they've heard.

Christians miss the mark because they credit this Jesus fiction with a real existence. The only way to positively benefit from religious texts is to see them as metaphorical and symbolic. A literal interpretation of scripture causes ontological blindness, serious mental illness, and division. Crediting religious fiction with reality is the cause of all religious madness on planet Earth. Believing in religious fables and studying a religious holy book as if God wrote it makes one suffer from religious self-intoxication.

Christians credit a fiction with reality and believe in fables told by religious leaders. Christian political leaders infused the Gospel tale with more and more substance by building historical locations for tourists to visit. The probable nonexistence of Jesus is covered up by several centuries of details added into history by Christian rulers. The Jesus myth has evolved to the point where empires, nations, and billions of people on planet Earth subscribe to this artificially created truth. The fictions of the Bible were forced upon humanity through Paul's militant ardor, Constantine's coup d'etat, and other Christians who forced their false god upon others. Christian history, like the repressions of the Theodosian and Valentinian dynasties, established Christianity as a major religion (through fear and force). That fear is still in place today through the threat of hell for not believing. People only receive this false religious mythology because they've been convinced that they'll spend eternity burning in hell if they don't. There is no hell.

What billions believe to be the Word of God is not God's word, but a man-made bundle of contradictions. Jesus is a myth, whose construction took place over several centuries after his purported existence. Diverse and multiple writers put the Bible together using previous holy texts from earlier spiritual groups. The Bible is not the Word of God, even though religious scribes created it to appear as if God wrote or inspired it. Multiple biblical writers and Christian scribes recopied one another until there was an abundance of contradictory religious texts attributed to the authorship of God. If the religious system can't convince you that God wrote the Bible, it will try to make you believe that God inspired it. Anything to separate their holy book from all other spiritual or religious texts about God. The Bible was put together to appear that God is behind it, which is why so much stuff was added, subtracted, or omitted. For the construction of the myth, stories, laws, and events were borrowed from earlier religious texts. The Bible is a fraud having nothing to do with God.

The Church Hierarchy took thousands of contradictory texts written by diverse writers and decided which texts were reliable and which ones obtruded upon the credibility of the project. Some texts were received, while others were set aside, hence the Apocrypha and synoptic Gospels. Even metaphysical extraterritoriality intertestamental writings abounded. There were thousands of pages of apocryphal Christian writings full of other Jesus stories before religious authority decided on the canon.

Toward the end of the fourth century, church councils and their synods left writings out that compromised the goal of the unequivocal narrative. The body of the text of the synoptic Gospel was decided by Christians in positions of authority. With the thousands of Gospel texts in circulation before they decided on the canon, they made some errors that prove to humanity that God didn't write or inspire the Bible. The church and its councils failed to remove all of the improbabilities and contradictions from the synoptic Gospels.

The Bible has an incalculable amount of errors and mistakes, exposing itself to be a man-made creation. The four Gospels all contradict each other. The Gospel of John says that the wooden tablet with the reasons for Jesus' sentence set down by the judges was nailed above Christ's head to the wood of the cross. The Gospel of Luke says that the titulus (wooden tablet with written charges) hung around the neck of the condemned. The Gospel of Mark says almost nothing and leaves no deciding opinion. The writing on the titulus says four different things after comparing Matthew, Mark, Luke, and John. The contradictions in the Gospels themselves are endless; the fault of the official church who tried to manufacture an unequivocal myth to pass as God's infallible word.

John's Gospel says that Jesus bore his cross alone on the road to Golgotha. The other Gospels say that Simon of Cyrene helped him. Each Gospel you consult will tell you something different about the same so-called 'historical' story. One Gospel says that Jesus appeared to a single person, while another Gospel says he appeared to a handful of people. Yet, another Gospel says that he appeared to a group. To add to the tissue of contradictions, the conflicting appearances in the four Gospels occur at different locations! The contradictions in the body of the Gospels themselves prove that no god wrote or inspired the 'holy' scriptures.

Even those who try to look past biblical contradictions must deal with the improbabilities of 'God's Word.' The Gospels tell us that their was a verbal exchange between the condemned Jesus and Pontius Pilate, the Roman governor. Historically, cases of interrogation were undertaken by the underlings of the Roman governor, NOT the governor himself. There is no way a historical scholar could envisage Jesus conversing with Pontius Pilate, especially since he wasn't a planetary star yet. Christians with influence over history inserted Jesus into history and made him the Christ and savior of the world. At the time, Jesus would've been nothing more than a common-law defendant, no different than thousands of other Messiahs occupying power's jails. From a historical perspective, there is no way an exalted official would talk to a local average jailbird. Based on historical records, Pontius Pilate would've spoke Latin and Jesus Aramaic, so they wouldn't have been able to converse as John's Gospel declares. In reality, Jesus and Pontius Pilate wouldn't have been able to communicate back and forth without an intermediary, interpreter, or translator.

The thousands of improbabilities found in biblical texts prove that they're sheer myth. Leave institutionalized religion and run to the Light!

The authors of religious texts were attempting to fulfill their intent, not God's. Biblical writers pretending to be inspired by god made the Jews God's chosen people and exalted the Roman occupiers. The authors of the biblical texts did nothing for God, and only created a collection of improbabilities. The most questionable aspects of the Gospel of Jesus Christ are required to be believed in order to be saved from hell. If you don't believe in the virgin birth, death, burial, and resurrection of Jesus, you can't be saved. According to the Christian religious system, those who don't believe that God raised Jesus from the dead will be condemned to eternal hell. By making the questionable aspects of the Gospel story a requirement for salvation, religionists and those afraid of death, out of a fear of hell, will violently refuse to question the improbabilities of the gospel tale.

I know the Christian Empire demands that you must believe in the Crucifixion in order to be saved, but the crucifixion is nothing but another improbability. Real history, not the fake history created by the Church, bears witness that Jews at that time were stoned to death, not crucified. Therefore, if Jesus was historical and really killed, he would've been stoned to death according to the customs of the time. Jesus was accused of calling himself 'King of the Jews,' when historically, Rome wasn't concerned with messiahs and prophecy. Only those who challenged imperial power were crucified, and Jesus of Nazareth never explicitly posed this challenge. There was no such place as a city called Nazareth at that time anyway! Even if Jesus of Nazareth was crucified, his remains would've been thrown into a common grave. Bodies being laid to rest in tombs is a Gospel fabrication. God had nothing to do with the sheer invention of the Gospels. Leave organized religion and run to the light!

Jesus is an invented concept, and his whole reality is mythological. Jesus is not a historical figure. In the minds of religionists over a hundred years AFTER his purported existence, certainly he existed. They killed for him, burned libraries and spiritual books for him, and did everything they could to convert the world to him. Jesus only existed in their minds as a mental phenomenon. Even now, Jesus is only a religious superhero that exists in the minds of the fallen. The Gospel is just a story that religionists believe in to escape hell. The requirements for salvation keep religious slaves from questioning whether Jesus is historical or not. Paul never knew or met Jesus, yet took it upon himself to spread the gospel. Christians are doing the same today, having no proof that Jesus existed. Jesus never existed historically. Jesus is a myth who exists in the minds of men as a mental concept that they believe in. The religious community fails to examine the contradictions and improbabilities of the scriptures, which is why most will die as religious slaves.

Jesus represents a crystallization of the aspirations of his era. The authors of antiquity all used a reverence for the miraculous, so the Gospels aren't unique. The Jesus myth was created by men in power, and then the fallen allowed themselves to be created by it. Believers invented their creation and used fear to keep it alive in the minds of humans thousands of years later. Fear-based religions aren't from Almighty God, but men. 98% of Christians only submit to religious belief structures because they're afraid of hell, have been threatened with hell, or have been convinced that Almighty God is behind the religious dogma presented to them. Jesus is the object of a cult, and accepting him as your savior to avoid hell is the very essence of willing self-deception. Those afraid of hell and death will reject the common sense, critical thinking skills, and intellectualism needed to discover that the Bible is a fraud.

The Pauline contamination destroyed the sane mind of the religious fundamentalist. The early Jesus, whom Paul never met, rarely spoke out against the customs of everyday life, meaning that he wasn't a religious fundamentalist. Mark 7:15 and 10:7 have Jesus unopposed to marriage, but overall, he was a man of faith (believing before seeing). The rigid demands concerning sensuality, the body, and sexuality given by Paul aren't found in the Jesus character. Paul of Tarsus answers all the questions that Jesus was silent about with religious madness that has nothing to do with God. The Apostle Paul promotes a hatred of real living, the body, and life. Paul, not Jesus, is the root cause of Christianity's radical antihedonism. Even today, the fallen are following his religious foolishness because they think God wrote or inspired it. No gods wrote any of these holy books. Leave the mental illness of trying to live up to religious dogma and RUN to the light!

Paul, a fundamentalist Jew, claims that he persecuted and brutally threatened Christians. His story says that he was converted on the road to Damascus in 34 after falling to the ground and hearing the voice of Jesus. Paul was blinded by a bright light and remained sightless for three days until God sent Ananias the Christian to lay hands on him to recover his sight. The whole story is pure hysterical pathology, neuroses, and religious hysteria. Paul claimed that Jesus spoke to him, exposing his mythomania. Paul convinced others that he was the elect of God and that the imaginary character Jesus chose him to transform the world. He then wrote 3/4 of the New Testament and created the world in his own image. No God had anything to do with it.

Christians believe that the Apostle Paul was inspired by God while writing his writings. Paul is the cause of the majority of religious insanity displayed by Christians! What Paul wrote is not the Word of God, nor inspired by God, and didn't come from God. The religious world is a reflection of a man controlled by the death instinct: Paul of Tarsus. The writings of Paul are the reason for the intellectual intolerance and ideological brutality of the Christian world. Paul promoted contempt for women, hatred of the vital body, and unnecessary pain through his distain for worldly pleasure. Paul writes with a hatred and contempt for the things of the body. He praised chastity and abstinence while loathing sexuality. Paul had a passion for celibacy and used his writings to get other people to conduct themselves like him (expressed in I Corinthians 7:8).

Paul expressed symptoms of hysteria through his reluctant consent to marriage. He views it as the best of bad choices, preferring the renunciation of all things corporeal. Paul practiced celibacy even though it wasn't imposed upon him and militated for a world resembling his idea. He declared all forms of sexuality for himself void and demanded that the rest of the world emulate him. Paul's writings are determined to make all humankind bow to his limiting rules, and billions yield because they believe God inspired his religious foolishness.

The Madness of Our Civilization

The same fable explaining the origins of evil in the world is found in Mosaic law, Loranic doctrine, and Christian tales. A woman is blamed for negativity in the world for committing an act which spread evil all over the world. The story is in the Torah and the Old Testament of the Christian Bible in Genesis 3:6. The Koran has the same story of Adam and Eve in paradise in (2:29). In the story, god forbids Adam and Eve to approach the Tree of Knowledge while an evil presence (snake, demon, Satan) urges disobedience. This monotheistic version isn't an original story, but an interpolation of the Greek Pandora fable, where a woman commits an irreparable act.

Humans have allowed religious holy books to instruct them on what's permitted and forbidden. Falling for organized religion is the madness of our civilization. Religious laws/instructions are found in the Talmud, Torah, and the Muslim Hadith. The three monotheisms are all serious mental illnesses which hold the physical world in low esteem. Muslims and Jews share the same concepts and both have a fixation on purity. Religion is about inflexible laws and strict rules attributed to God, though men created these laws NOT God. Religion is based in fear, which is why eternal salvation or damnation is dependent on the observance of religious dogma. The Muslim Hadith gives detailed instructions on everything from A to Z. It gives religious rules for anal cleansing, preparation before prayer, and sexual relations. It forbids anal penetration, urination in the direction of Mecca, and sex during one's partner's menstruation.

The three monotheisms are all part of the same 3-headed demon. The Muslim and Jewish taboos are similar to each other because the three heads of organized religion are connected to the same body. The monotheisms associate the body with impurity and claim that it's unclean, dirty, and must be subdued. These so-called holy books are bonfires of intelligence and must be done away with. What's found in religious holy books wasn't written by God, and following what's in them doesn't make one holy. Organized religion being allowed to dominate our planet is the madness of our civilization and the fall of humanity.

Religion is the hatred of knowledge and intelligence. Church helps religious slaves to obey false religious laws rather than think. Submission and obedience is codified in religious holy books, conditioning religionists not to think for themselves. The three monotheisms are the religions of the book. These three books are mutually supportive of the same religious enslavement, even though on the surface they seem different. The brethren of the Abrahamic religions are all victims of mental illness. Pentateuch believers believe the Koran and the New Testament to be frauds. The Muslims have low esteem for the Gospels and the Talmud, while the Paulines care little for the Torah. Either way, all the so-called holy books lead to intellectual darkness.

The belief that false religious texts were inspired and dictated by God is the fall of humanity. Religious ideologies should be examined from a philological, allegorical, philosophical, or symbolic perspective. Every intellectual qualifier proves that religious texts are all symbolic and allegorical from an historical standpoint. None of these texts are a work of revelation, and God didn't do any revealing! The pages of the Bible didn't descend from heaven, and nothing written therein was dictated by God.

Texts believed to be inspired by God are no more divine than the writings of the Icelandic sagas and Persian fables.

Moses and other religious characters are improbable. None of the evangelists knew Jesus personally. The Apostle Paul never met him, yet wrote most of the New Testament. Christians believe that Moses wrote down what Yahweh said, but the Hebrew script didn't exist during Moses' time. Moses could've only written Yahweh's words if he wrote hieroglyphics. The story of Moses and other religious characters is a hoax because the Bible is nothing more than the repackaging of ecclesiastical dogma and ancient fables. Making phony religious texts the Word of God is the reason for the madness of our civilization.

The testamental canon arose from political decisions, not God. In the first half of the fourth century, Emperor Constantine mandated Eusebius of Caesarea to assemble a canon from the 27 versions of the New Testament. The New Testament proper is grossly outnumbered by the more numerous apocryphal writings. The Bible as we know it is an artificial creation designed to be the infallible Word of God. This is why Paul of Tarsus ordered the burning of dangerous books in Acts 19:19. Dangerous books are all books contrary to the testamental canon. Christian emperor Constantine imprisoned, persecuted, or killed many polytheist priests, philosophers, and social outcasts against biblical teachings.

The impoverishment of civilization began with the hatred of non-Christian books, as promoted by Paul of Tarsus in Acts 19:19. Christian emperors are responsible for the establishment of the Inquisition and the eradication of spiritual teaching deviating from the official sanctioned doctrine. In the 16th century, the Index of Forbidden Books was created as part of the campaign to eradicate all non-Christian books. The Bible claims to contain everything, therefore everything it did not contain was banned. The very active presence of political Christians in power in the shadows of the Judeo-Christian god over the centuries has produced devastating results. Come out of the darkness into the Light by studying for yourself and discovering the true God within.

Muslims believe that they have the most reliable holy book. The three gods of the religions of the book are all counterfeits, and their followers don't possess the Word of God. Religious fundamentalists are not seekers of Truth or else they would know all the information in this book. The Wise Ones discover that the three monotheisms are frauds and abandon religious fundamentalism. Monotheism rejects the rational work of scientists, but the scientific works of the nonreligious are more reliable than all holy books. The wisdom found in secular, pagan, and heretical books is more profound than what's found in religious texts. Wisdom can be found anywhere without the use of myths and fables, therefore, humanity would be better off without dogmatic religious texts.

Muhammad didn't write the Koran; a book that didn't exist until 25 years after his death. The Hadith is the second source for Muslim authority, and it didn't come into play until the ninth century. The Hadith didn't appear until two centuries after the Prophet Muhammad's death. The authority of the definitive version of the Koran was established by the political authorities, not God. Marwan, governor of Medina, collected and burned all other existing versions of the Koran. To avoid historical confrontation, Marwan destroyed all existing texts to defend the definitive Koran. No matter what, God didn't write it.

Marwan was just one of many political/religious authorities who used book burnings to protect a holy book. Each of the three holy books claims to be the one true holy book. Each of the three main religions believes that its religious ideology contains the whole of what humanity needs to learn and know. Ancient encyclopedia-like compilers created the 3 books claiming to be the Word of God by attempting to gather the essentials. To make other books unnecessary, religious scribes stole wisdom already found in secular and pagan texts and attributed it to Divine revelation. Any real knowledge found in the religions of the book was borrowed from earlier 'heretical' texts. Holy books contain nothing original and were designed to appear as if God created them. Religious scribes used knowledge from thousands of previous sources in an attempt to make a profound holy book, which is why you can find some real knowledge in the religions of the book.

Muslim authors who thought and wrote freely were attacked, even though they didn't discredit the Koran's teachings. Muslim leaders exiled, persecuted, prosecuted, or assassinated any writer who wrote with the slightest deviation from the Koran. Some of the Muslim leaders who administered these heavy punishments were Mahmoud Mohammed Taha, Mohammed Iqbal, Mohammed Khalafallah, Ali Abderrazia, Taha Hussein, Fazlur Rahman, and Nasr Abu Zayd.

Monotheism rejects the work of scientists and hates anything that goes against the religions of the book. If a religion accepts scientific works, it's only for its own selfish purposes. The Koran honors many things for its own end. Islam embraces optics, algebra, geometry, astronomy, and mathematics for religious reasons only. They are used to decree prayer hours, create religious calendars, and use the stars to calculate the direction of Mecca. Islam embraces geography for the convergence on the Kaaba, to assist pilgrims flocking to Mecca. Islam values medicine, but only to avoid what Allah considers impurity. Grammar, law, and philosophy are prized by Islam only to help understand commentary on the Hadith and the Koran.

The religious instrumentalization of science only uses reason for theocratic purposes. Science is pursued in Islamic lands only to improve religious practice. Muslim culture produced groundbreaking research, inventions, and discoveries in astronomy, algebra, and secular science. One hadith recommends and promotes the quest for scientific knowledge, but not for the ideal of social progress. Organized religion only allows scientific and other knowledge to be pursued in the logic of its instrumentalization via religion. Religion is of the Kingdom of Darkness.

Christianity believes that the Bible contains all knowledge necessary for the effective functioning of society. Christian rulers in power have inhibited all research and writings questioning biblical contents. Even now, Christian believers are taught to stay away from anything that scrutinizes or contradicts the claims of scripture. One of the lessons of Genesis is that knowledge is not desirable. The Church has caused incalculable damage with its idea that science distances us from God. Millions of 'real' holy books were burned in the church's prolonged crusade against science.

Christianity's inception began in the second century of the common era WITHOUT God. Men in authority, not God, condemned paganism in all its aspects. True knowledge that wasn't accepted by the church was rejected and dismissed as error. Real spiritual books were tied to false gods, Polytheism, magic, and all their aspects were rejected by the religious establishment. Non-Christian books full of knowledge were burned, and other writings not Christian enough were destroyed. The holy Bible was not the real spiritual/intellectual knowledge of the earlier centuries, but Euclidean mathematics, Herophilus' anatomy, Aristarchus' astronomy, Eratosthenes' geography, Hippocrates' medicine, Ptolemy's map, Aristotle's natural sciences, Aristarchus' heliocentrism, and the discoveries of Greek geniuses. All of the accomplishments of these great men were achieved independently of religious systems and the gods of religious holy books.

The monotheist religions are a refusal of enlightenment. Religionists must be kept in mental darkness in order for religious leaders to continue nurturing holy fables. The history of science's relationship with Christianity reveals that science is more from God than religion. The church has always been wrong about everything in science. Organized religion can't deal with epistemological truth, so it persecutes the discoverer in the name of god. The church condemned genetic laws and rejected the heliocentric hypothesis of antiquity.

Throughout history, the church missed God and condemned that which is true. God was moving in 'the heathen,' but the church didn't realize it because it's against anything not in agreement with god's 'purported' word. The genius of Democritus and Leucippus led them through their intuition to discover the atom in the 5th century BCE without material means. They didn't have any enlarging instruments, microscope, or a lens, yet were able to extrapolate from the motes of dust in a ray of light the presence of invisible particles to the eye. They concluded that the existence of atoms makes up all matter and everything in the world itself.

The atomist tradition continued through 8 centuries of Greek and Roman antiquity through Leucippus, Diogenes of Oenanda, Epicurus, Lucretius, and Philodemus of Gadara. A complete account of Epicurean physics was explained in Lucretius' De Rerum Natura (On the Nature of Things). His work explained everything necessary to decode the world, from atomic constitution, generation and decomposition, form, weight, the theory of declivity, to nature. Ancient physics revealed that everything is made up of matter, soul, and spirit, therefore the real God and mankind share the same makeup. You and God are one.

Religion is nothing but fictions and fables. God leads people through intuition, which is why Democritean intuition was validated, and Leucippus and Democritus' intuition was confirmed. Philosophical ideas given to men by the real God have received the stamp of authenticity from the scientific and nuclear world, though rejected by the Christian caste. The church used all its power to discredit atomist physics and coherent philosophies explaining all reality.

Anything or anyone not in agreement with the Christian religious texts was dangerous in the eyes of the Christian caste. Giordano Bruno was burned at the stake by Christians in 1660 on the Campo dei Fiori. Giordano Bruno didn't even deny God's existence, he just taught the coexistence of the material world and God. In his work, he didn't offer insults to the god of the Bible, nor blasphemed religious doctrine. Bruno understood the physical level of atoms. He didn't deny the existence of the spirit and understood particles to be centers of life where spirit manifests itself as God. Divinity exists in all matter, and all things are composed of atoms.

The church only believes in God's incarnation in the form of the Son, Jesus, born of a virgin and the 'holy' Ghost.

The church didn't believe in atoms, where in which true Divinity exists. Galileo represented the church's hatred for science and information from God revealed to humans outside of religious holy books. Religionists are the scum of the earth, which explains the conflict between faith and reason. Galileo was more in tune with God than any of the leaders or followers of the religious system. The pope and the Inquisition condemned Galileo and his book 'A Dialogue Concerning the Two Chief World Systems' (1632). The religious community has very little real knowledge and doesn't serve the real God. Galileo knew the real God, which opened his spirit to receive and teach that earth is a satellite of a sun located at the center of the universe.

The intangible god manufactured by Judeo-Christianity is not the true God. The real God didn't write any holy books and doesn't need them to deal with mankind. God has nothing to do with the religious rituals of organized religion. The gods that the religions of the book serve are man-made creations that have nothing to do with true spirituality. Religious believers of the three monotheisms suffer from mental dysfunction/illness. The church (full of lost souls) believes in transubstantiation. The words of Jesus at the Last Supper say, 'This is my body, this is my blood' (Matthew 26:26-28). The fiction of transubstantiation has Christians obsessed with Christ's body and blood. The church plays tricks with bakery products by pretending that the real presence of Christ's body and blood are in the bread and wine of 'holy' communion.

The Bible is against knowledge. Paul told the Corinthians that 'as for knowledge, it will pass away' (1 Corinthians 13:8). The early church was against all forms of scientific research. The disciples of Democritus had their lives discredited by the church, and their ascetic ethos were labeled as immorality. Nicolas d' Autrecourt, in 1340, created an atomist theory of light, believing in light's corpuscular nature. The church burned all his writings

331

and made him recant or die. All scientific research associated with atomism was persecuted and banned by the Jesuits as of 1632. The prohibition of real knowledge was maintained for centuries and is still on the prohibited list of the institutionalized church (Articles 285 and 2124 of the Catechism).

The church missed the boat because it placed biblical knowledge over science. For 10 centuries, the church lost out on all the major discoveries of science. The Apostolic, Catholic, and Roman authorities tried to contain and halt intelligence because they didn't want any intellectuals to scientifically prove that the Bible is not the infallible Word of God. Those who didn't turn to religious scripture for all their knowledge were labeled as rebellious individuals. Scientists who were students of determined research believed in the truths of reason and wisely rejected organized religion's fables of faith.

Aristotle was the Vatican's cherished philosopher. The church rejected atomism in favor of Aristotelianism. Truth seekers only believe in experimental methodology and claims verifiable from observation. Genesis says that God created the world in a week from nothing, so anything that contradicted the biblical texts was eliminated by the Vatican. The church opposed any teaching that excluded the internationality of its creator god. Those who really know God only believe in that which is scientifically demonstrable.

The church rejected the teachings of Aristarchus. Eventually, scientists confirmed Aristarchus' idea of the sun sitting at the center of our world through meticubus and precise calculations. Lamarck proposed an idea that species change, while Darwin claimed that species evolve according to the laws of natural selection. Lamarck and Darwin published their discoveries, and they had a right to formulate their own ideas. Scientists advanced the idea of polygenesis and were able to prove the simultaneous existence of humans at multiple geographical locations. This truth contradicted the church and its teaching that Adam and Eve were the first man and woman. According to official church doctrine, no one existed before the primordial couple, who supposedly brought original sin into the world. The Pre-Adamites existed before sin, which is a false concept explained in my book 'the Gospel According to Jawara King.'

The biblical logic of guilt, error, and redemption is the cause of mental anguish, division, and holy insanity. The Bible is false; what's verifiable is real. Geologists have come up with scientific dating of the world from poring over fossils and brushing dirt from stones. Immanent chronology is scientifically verified from seashells found on strata, mountaintops, and layers. Scientific dating DOES NOT correspond with the false god's sacred numerology in 'his' word, the Bible. Christian philosophy claims that the world is 4,000 years old, yet scientists led by the real God have proven the existence of a world before Adam and Eve's world. The Bible is full of lies and deception.

The church condemned Sigmund Freud. Freud wrote 'The Future of an Illusion,' enlightening humanity as to how institutionalized religion works. With the real God's help, Sigmund Freud taught that all religion proceeds from an "obsessional neurosis" related to "hallucinatory psychosis." Christians have never met Jesus personally and only believe in him based on what they were told. Jesus is simply a character in their imagination who helps them psychologically. Jesus has been confused with the spiritual energy of the universe, and the real God has been confused with the gods of religious holy books. Religious believers who continue in this deception have an unshakable determination to deceive themselves. Those looking for God in any of the religions of the book are rejecting the truth. The Bible can help guide one to the truth, but is not the truth. A Buddhist saying says, "The finger pointing to the moon is not the moon." Another saying is, "the word water is not wet." God and the Bible are not one and the same, so all Christians have made a book a false idol. Religion isn't needed and should be abolished from the Earth. Albert Einstein said, "Everything is energy and that's all there is to it. Match the frequency of the reality you want and you cannot help but get that reality. It can be no other way. This is not philosophy. This is physics."

Religion still doesn't want you to eat the fruit of the Tree of Knowledge. Paul of Tarsus called for knowledge to pass away. The church is not from God, which is why church history is full of persecution of the wise, imprisonments, burnings at the stake, and the Inquisition. It was forbidden to read the Bible without priestly mediation in the early Christian centuries. Church leaders wanted to make sure that people didn't approach the Bible with analysis, reason, and criticism. If religionists would read the Bible with the mind of a geologist, historian, or scientist, analysis and reason would prove the Bible as a fraud. Bessnet and the Catholic church violently attacked Richard Simon and other Wise Ones who knew that God didn't write the holy Bible. Richard Simon was one of the first critical thinkers to publish a critical analysis of the entire Bible.

Religious dogma is the opposite of the real. The monotheisms are against knowledge, intelligence, and science. The three religions of the book distain man's basic drives and natural instincts. Religious services are a celebration of ignorance. Religion uses the weight of original sin to beat those who fear hell into submission. By aiming for the heavenly city, they lose sight of earth. There's no need to turn to organized religion, for you are the Eternal One.

Jawara King Publishing Group
1220 L. Street NW, Suite 100-262
Washington, DC 20005-4018
    1 (202) 492-3290
Email: jawaraking@yahoo.com
Website: www.JawaraKing.com
All photography by Jesus Torres of Torres Photo • Digital • Art

Available Now:

Available Now:

TRANSFORM YOUR WORLD THROUGH THE POWERS OF YOUR MIND

A Guide to Planetary Transformation and Spiritual Enlightenment

DR. JAWARA D. KING

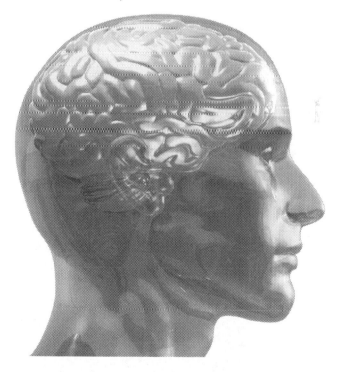

Available Now:

DR. JAWARA D. KING

THE
AWAKENING
OF GLOBAL CONSCIOUSNESS
A Guide to Self-Realization and Spirituality

Available Now:

B. I. B. L. E.

The Gospel According to Jawara King

JAWARA D. KING, D.D.
AUTHOR OF *The Awakening of Global Consciousness*
A Guide to Self-Realization and Spirituality